Investigating the Social World 2

Edited by Deborah H. Drake, Andy Morris, Alan Shipman and Katy Wheeler

Contents

Block 3
Analysing common resources

Chapter 1
Introducing common resources and rights

by Andy Morris and Alan Shipman

Contents

Introduction

The first part of this book investigates a range of contemporary, global **common resources**. Such resources include forests, oceans and the atmosphere, all of which are being consumed or exploited at a rate that threatens their stability, as well as that of the wider environment. The impact of human beings on the environment and the relationship between human populations and common resources is a contested and often fraught area. There is disagreement between scientists, environmentalists, politicians and social scientists. Hence, the following chapters investigate how the relationship between human populations and common resources is understood, debated, politicised and 'managed'.

Three important and related issues underpin this investigation of common resources. The first is the question of how boundaries become established between what is called 'the natural', a term often associated with the resources just described, and 'the social', commonly used to evoke a separate and distinct consideration of humans and human activity, such as the consumption of these resources. The idea of a clear division between 'nature' and 'society' is one that is increasingly called into question by social scientists.

Second, it is important to consider some other observations and **theories** generated by social scientists in thinking about the long-standing challenges and debates over the use of common resources – in particular, the 'tragedy of the commons'. This term is most commonly associated with the work of the US environmental scientist Garrett Hardin (1968), which highlights the tendency for commonly available resources to be overused and depleted. The key principle is that one person's gain in overusing a resource imposes losses that are shared out among many others. Once this overuse becomes common practice, it becomes increasingly difficult to offset. This is illustrated by Hardin through the example of farmers grazing increasing numbers of privately owned cows on common pasture.

Third, the theme of rights is explored in the context of the distinct but related disciplines of environmental studies, politics and international relations, economics, and geography. Drawing on these different disciplines highlights that rights are not only claimed and contested, but that they emerge in various and often overlapping forms, including

Common resources
Resource areas that are not privately owned and where it is not possible to exclude people from using them, leading to problems of overexploitation and potential environmental damage.

Theories
An interconnected set of ideas and concepts that forms an argument about how things function and relate to each other. To take a famous example, Charles Darwin's 'theory of evolution' argues that species have evolved in relation to their environment through selective adaptations.

property rights, environmental rights, human rights, rights for nature or the rights of the non-human world.

This introductory chapter will:

- consider the distinction made between understandings of 'the natural' and 'the social', and how it can be helpful to think about the limitations of this distinction
- introduce the relationship between common resources and population growth
- introduce the idea of rights, some of the key historical and political foundations for our understanding of rights, and the contestations that have arisen from them.

---

1   The natural and the social

Making a distinction between the natural environment and the social environment affects how they are studied. The natural environment has largely been interpreted by 'natural scientists', the first of whom tended to range across all the disciplines that are now separate specialisms (biology, chemistry, physics and geology, for example). The social world has, similarly, become a focus for many different approaches to social science, such as economics, politics and sociology, which develop different ways of thinking and talking about the 'social' environment.

These different approaches can be complementary, but they can also come into conflict. Policymakers, in government or at the top of large organisations, must often extract a common plan from competing ideas about the options that are available and their implications.

However, these two environments can be thought of as inter-related rather than separate. The social environment arises from the presence and actions of people, but also shapes what people think and do. Humans emerged from, and have adapted to, the natural environment, but it is increasingly being reshaped by human activity. Both environments, natural and social, affect what each person can do – constraining some activities and enabling others. Awareness of these environments requires each individual to consider how they and their actions relate to those around them.

Understanding and, where necessary, combining these two worlds requires different viewpoints that can lead to different explanations and evaluations. Some social scientists go further and take a radical view about the relationship between the natural and social worlds. For the sociologist and philosopher Bruno Latour (Figure 1.1), the distinction between 'natural' and 'social' is unhelpful and, he argues, fundamentally misguided. He points to the following example:

> On page four of my daily newspaper, I learn that the measurements taken above the Antarctic are not good this year: the hole in the ozone layer is growing ominously larger. A few paragraphs later, I come across heads of state of major industrialized countries who are getting involved with chemistry, refrigerators, aerosols and inert gases. But at the end of the article, I discover that the meterologists don't agree with the

Commensurable
Two or more items or concepts are commensurable if they can be meaningfully compared by stating them in the same language or giving them the same unit of measurement.

chemists. Towards the bottom of the page, Third world countries and ecologists add their grain of salt and talk about international treaties, moratoriums, the rights of future generations, and the right to development [...] none of these is **commensurable**, yet there they are, caught up in the same story.

(Latour, 1993, p. 1)

A central concern for Latour is that imposing boundaries when thinking about the world, including the environment, can lead to a rather disjointed view. Latour's remark illustrates this by considering how the newspaper is organised into different sections, such as 'national', 'international', 'science' or 'business', for example. He shows how the story of ozone depletion does not fit well into such neatly bounded interests. Latour argues that boundaries are often falsely constructed to distinguish between nature and society. The relationship between human populations and natural resources is not as straightforward as it might seem. It is not just a question of humans that consume on the one hand, and common resources that are consumed on the other.

Figure 1.1   Bruno Latour argues that boundaries are often falsely constructed to distinguish between nature and society

Activity 1 uses the example of forests to help illustrate this viewpoint.

Activity 1

What is the first thing that comes to mind when you think about a forest? Make a note of your thoughts.

Discussion

The first word you wrote down may well have been 'trees'. Possibly you also thought about a quiet, atmospheric place and an absence of humans.

Figure 1.2   A forest settlement in Padang, Sumatra

However, while a forest might commonly be thought of as an isolated, atmospheric and unpopulated place, there are many examples where forests have been used as places to live and subsist (Figure 1.2). In the Global North, forests are also places of leisure to walk, climb or cycle, for example (Figure 1.3). The Black Forest in Germany or the New Forest in England are examples you may be familiar with. This range of uses – forests as places to live, work and participate in leisure – disrupts the idea that a forest is an entirely natural thing. Instead, it suggests that the natural is also woven into the livelihoods and practices of humans.

Figure 1.3   Salcey Forest, a Forestry Commission site in Northamptonshire, UK

The human influence in forests is also apparent in the work of organisations such as the Forestry Commission, which is responsible for managing and maintaining large areas of Scottish and English forestry plantation, harvesting more than four million tonnes of wood each year (Forestry Commission, 2014). These forests are perhaps more comparable with agricultural fields. They are clearly sites of managed human production, and the organised planting and felling of these forests creates visual patterns and structures distinct from what a 'natural' forest might be expected to look like.

What is perhaps less familiar is the notion of a forest without any trees at all. However, as the environmental historian Oliver Rackham points out:

> A Forest [spelt with a capital F] is land on which the king (or some other magnate) has the right to keep deer. To the medievals a forest was a place of deer, not a place of trees. If a Forest happened to be wooded it formed part of the wood-pasture tradition; but there were many woodless forests.
>
> (Rackham, 1997, p. 65)

Figure 1.4   A managed forest being harvested

While a forest can provide a clear example of a common resource, thinking about its different uses helps to highlight the idea that such resources are bound up not just in debates about the environment, but in political and economic decisions, power struggles between different groups, competing markets and disputed boundaries. One example is the continuing concern about, and campaigns to prevent, the depletion of the Amazon rainforest in South America.

Natural resources do not sit outside the human world but are bound up within it. Not only is the natural element of this story difficult to untangle from the human element, but the struggles between humans about the use of common resources and the environment make it clear that humans are a far from unified group. So the contentions over common resources are as much about the problematic relationship between different humans as they are about the relationship between humans and the common resources they exploit.

Over a number of centuries, a persistent theme has influenced the tensions between different groups over the use of these resources. That theme is the negative impact of an increasing human population, and Section 2 will use Hardin's theory of the 'tragedy of the commons' to explore the resulting pressure on common resources.

Summary

- 'The social' and 'the natural' are often difficult to separate, and their distinction can be problematic.

- A more complex and entangled view of the social and the natural helps to inform a better understanding of the contentions and challenges that arise over common resources.

2   The tragedy of the commons

The relationship between a growing human population and the use of resources that everyone can freely access presents a fairly clear story of increasing pressure of demand. To think about this relationship in a little more detail, it might be useful to consider a specific, tangible example of a common resource which most of us experience on a day-to-day basis.

2.1   Roads

Public roads, like any common resource, are freely available to use, but their continued and sustained use is not without consequences. The example of roads can help to highlight two enduring issues that have been identified in respect of all common resources: their use and their management.

Activity 2

Look at the picture in Figure 1.5 of the M1 motorway in the UK taken during the 1960s. Is there anything about this picture that surprises you?

Discussion

In any contemporary picture of the same motorway (or any motorway), it would be almost impossible to capture – in daylight – such an empty road. Indeed, people even complained when the UK government authorised the building of the first motorways, saying that they were scars across the countryside that only a few would ever use. You might also have noticed that there is no crash barrier in the central reservation, something which led to instances of early motorway users carrying out U-turns if they missed their intended exit junction.

Figure 1.5   The first motorways were seen by some as scars across the countryside

Motorways exclude some groups, such as walkers, cyclists and certain slow-moving vehicles. However, most people can make use of them – and everyone can use other types of public road. As car ownership increased, available road space became scarcer and journey times went up. By the 1990s, some city planners were becoming concerned about gridlock. So many cars and trucks were joining the same roads simultaneously that nothing could move, with even emergency vehicles getting stuck for hours.

Roads have joined a growing number of common resources that once seemed to have sufficient capacity for everyone, but now suffer congestion and degradation because of unrestricted use and a rising number of vehicles and journeys.

This issue or problem is an instance of what Hardin (1968) called the 'tragedy of the commons'. This refers to a situation where increasing use of a resource starts to deplete it so that the arrival of the next user leaves a little less for every existing user. The 'tragedy' arises when a resource is *non-excludable* (accessible and available to everyone) and *exhaustible* (limited in supply, so what one person takes becomes unavailable to others). This idea is explored further in Chapter 4. Because instances of the tragedy have become more frequent (affecting, among other things, the world's forests, energy and water supplies, marine resources, farmland and even the atmosphere), preventing and resolving it has become a major policy concern.

Activity 3

Returning to the example of roads, can you think of ways in which governments (and other organisations) have tried to reduce the problem of non-excludability (i.e. where it is not possible to exclude people from using them)?

Discussion

The motorists' 'tragedy of the commons' is that roads are not as open as they once were. Some classes of vehicle are excluded from larger roads, or confined to one lane. Tolls or congestion charges have been imposed on some roads to deter vehicles from using them. Parking has been restricted or banned in many places, or is charged for where it used to be free. Residents of some streets get traffic calming installed to deter traffic from entering, or at least to slow it down. In each case, the accessibility and availability of the resource is restricted in some way.

2.2   Background to the tragedy: resourcing a growing population

Increasing usage of resources is often related to population growth. Figure 1.6 tracks the growth in the population of the UK from the 9th century to the beginning of the 21st century. At the beginning of this period, the UK population was approximately the same as that of present-day Greater Manchester – 2.7 million (ONS, 2014) – and it now stands at over 20 times this figure (65 million in 2014). This significant population increase over the centuries is a trend replicated in many other parts of the world. (Global population was estimated at 7000 million (7 billion) in 2014, up from around 2.5 billion in 1950 and 6 billion in 2000. (Worldometers, n.d. a)) Whether such a population increase can be sustained by the earth's resources is a contentious question. Some people believe that there is an ultimate limit on the number of human lives that can be resourced by the earth. Other people argue that technological developments leading to increased agricultural yields and improved energy efficiency, along with adaptations in human consumption patterns, make the former argument outdated and inaccurate. These can be called pessimistic and optimistic viewpoints respectively.

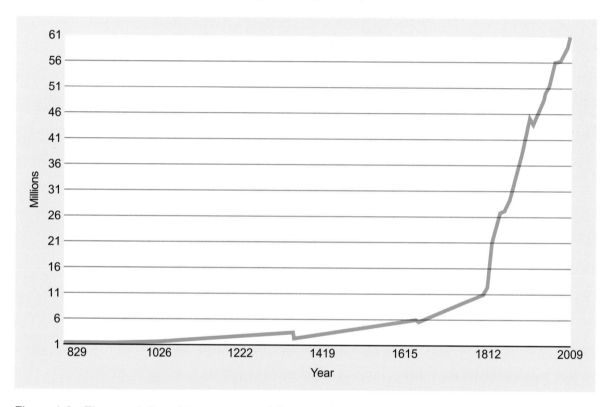

Figure 1.6   The population of the area now defined as the UK, 800 AD to 2009 (Source: adapted from ChartsBin, 2009)

2.3 Population growth and food

The pessimistic view of population growth and its danger for all humankind is not new. It was famously expressed in Thomas Malthus's *Essay on the Principles of Population* (1798). Malthus not only identified the importance of population growth, but drew some very clear conclusions about its causes and effects. He wrote:

> I say, that the power of population is indefinitely greater than the power in the earth to produce subsistence for man. Population, when unchecked, increases in a geometrical ratio. Subsistence increases only in an arithmetical ratio. A slight acquaintance with

numbers will shew [show] the immensity of the first power in comparison of the second.

(Malthus, 2008 [1798], p. 4)

Figure 1.7   Thomas Malthus

Malthus foresaw impending disaster because of the relationship between geometrical progression (1, 2, 4, 8...), which he associates with population growth, and arithmetical progression (1, 2, 3, 4...), which he associates with food production growth. If humanity survived at all, it would only be because periodic pestilence and war would cut the population back down to the level that could be supported by a slow-growing food supply. This view of dangerous, inexorable population growth and the fear that it will inevitably outstrip food supply is often described as 'Malthusian'.

In spite of that pessimism, food production has tended to grow more rapidly than Malthus predicted. For example, the introduction of high-yield varieties in the 1960s allowed India to become self-sufficient in grain, even as its population was growing rapidly. Despite frequently voiced concerns that intensive farming will eventually deplete and erode the soil so that production drops, or that 'monocultures' of high-yield food plants will be suddenly wiped out by disease, most countries' food production has continued to grow in most years. India's grain production in 2014 was 35 per cent higher than in 2000 (Reserve Bank of India, 2014). Amartya Sen, a prominent Indian social scientist, has assembled evidence that past famines occurred because food was inadequately distributed, not because there was not enough to go around (Sen, 1990).

Population growth has also slowed in many countries, even levelling off or declining in some. For example, India's population grew by 20 per cent in the period 1985–94, 16 per cent in 1995–2004 and 12 per cent in 2005–14 (Worldometers, n.d. b). This slowdown was achieved in part by controversial sterilisation campaigns, which coerced women to 'volunteer' by offering financial incentives (Burke, 2014). China, the only other country whose population exceeds one billion, attempted to restrict family sizes by law, introducing its 'one child only' policy in the 1980s. Such campaigns and policies raise the issue of the relationship between rights and responsibilities – a relationship that is explored further in Section 3.

Summary

- Hardin's model of the tragedy of the commons illustrates the way common resources can become depleted through overuse, a process influenced by the lure of private gain.

- The rapid population growth of recent centuries has had a bearing on the use and management of common resources.

- In the late 18th century Thomas Malthus put forward the argument that population would outstrip food production. This view has since been challenged.

3   Rights and responsibilities

A useful place to start considering the concept of rights is *Rights of Man*, written by the radical political thinker Thomas Paine (1737–1809) over two volumes in 1791 and 1792. Paine was a strong defender of the rural poor, who had continued to be marginalised in an increasingly industrialised agricultural environment. He was also a keen supporter of the French Revolution (1789–1799) and the American War of Independence (1775–1783), and later settled in the United States as a citizen. The political activity in France and America influenced a great deal of radical writing at the time, much of which centred on the rights of the socially marginalised. Another key text at the time was *A Vindication of the Rights of Woman* written by Mary Wollstonecraft (1759–1797) and published in 1792, a work that is commonly regarded as the foundational feminist text.

Figure 1.8   Thomas Paine and Mary Wollstonecraft

Paine outlines his positon in the following statement:

> If any generation of men ever possessed the right of dictating the mode by which the world should be governed for ever, it was the first generation that existed; and if that generation did not, no succeeding generation can shew any authority for doing it, nor can set any up. The illuminating and divine principle of the equal

rights of man, (for it has its origins from the maker of man) relates, not only to the living individuals, but to generations of men succeeding each other. Every generation is equal in rights to the generations which preceded it, by the same rule that every individual is born equal in rights with his contemporary.

(Paine, 1998 [1791], p. 117)

Activity 4

The wording of Paine's quote is a little archaic and you may need to read it more than once. What do you think are the key ideas in it?

Discussion

A central concern for Paine is the rights of what are now often referred to as 'future generations', a common preoccupation for contemporary social and environmental scientists in considering the sustainable management of common resources. Paine is concerned that the 'mode by which the world should be governed' is not something for any single generation to decide upon, but that each generation and each individual is 'born equal in rights'. A simpler and more familiar expression of this view is to say that each person is only a temporary 'steward' of the planet, and has a responsibility to maintain it for future generations. The other key aspect of Paine's view is the 'equal rights of man' and that each person can make an equal claim to be heard. This is the foundation for an important way of understanding rights – as something to be asserted, claimed or even fought for.

A little earlier than Paine, the 18th-century French philosopher Jean-Jacques Rousseau (1712–78) asserted that society could only function on the basis of what he called 'the social contract'. The basis of this idea was that individuals and societies were codependent and that the rights of the individual could only be claimed once the individual submitted to the ideal of the society, or as Rousseau put it: 'alienation to the whole community of each with all his rights … since each gives himself up entirely, the conditions are equal for all' (Rousseau, 1998 [1763], p. 15). The idea of the social contract has also had great currency in contemporary British politics and was popularly evoked in New Labour's 1997 election manifesto, where it was stated that 'rights and responsibilities must go hand in hand' (The Labour Party, 1997).

In other words, rights must be earned, and earned through taking a responsible place in society for the benefit of all within it.

Figure 1.9   Jean-Jacques Rousseau (left) and Tony Blair, leader of New Labour in 1997 (right)

3.1   Human rights and property rights

Among the rights that Paine, Wollstonecraft and Rousseau addressed, 'property rights' have been especially contentious and central to debates about inequality. Almost everyone (though there are dissenters) accepts the concept of 'self-ownership': people's entitlement to their own body, including the right to exercise any special physical or mental talent that it might bring them. Few cultures have any issue with the idea of people 'owning' small numbers of personal items. However, when it comes to owning large tracts of land, or sums of money, societies (and social scientists) differ widely over what is appropriate.

Ideas about property rights often exhibit the distinction (and tension) between the natural and social worlds, introduced in Section 1. In many societies, it is viewed as reasonable (and important for social order) that people who have bought a house, a car or a phone should have rights over it, and be able to exclude others from using it. Yet many would question whether someone who owns a forest, or a large tract of land, should have the same exclusive rights, and some would question whether these should be privately owned at all. This issue was famously highlighted in 1932 when a group of ramblers conducted a mass trespass of Kinder Scout in the Peak District, an act which is regarded as highly significant in leading to improved access to rights of way in the British countryside.

Property can be categorised as 'private' (belonging to one person or family), 'common' (belonging to a whole community) or 'public' (assigned to the government or state). Public property is managed on the public's behalf, but the state can impose the same exclusions as a private owner. You can walk freely on a common, but not on all government-owned land.

'Private', 'common' and 'public' are not mutually exclusive categories. Many types of property fit into more than one, or move between them in different circumstances. A shopping centre might look like a common resource, but it is usually owned by a private company that can restrict access to it. Privately owned property may be subject to compulsory purchase if needed for a public purpose, such as building a new airport or railway. Property rights are also rarely absolute, in the sense of owners being able to do anything they please with their property. Their use is circumscribed by a wide range of laws and rules that restrict the owner's rights, and usually also impose some obligations.

While some social scientists argue that private property rights are universal, and should even be recognised among basic human rights, others view them as much more culturally and historically specific. Not everyone is comfortable with (and some try to prevent) large private accumulations of land, buildings and other material wealth. Concepts of private property change over time within societies. For example, Western countries abandoned slavery in the 19th century, but until then, even people could be regarded as private property, and slave owners were compensated for their loss of slaves when slavery was abolished.

As these examples highlight, property rights and human rights are not neatly and easily defined, but complicated by different social, cultural and historical influences, and this has led to them being deeply contested. Just as Thomas Paine suggested that future generations are central to our understanding and preservation of rights, it is the plight of those future generations that also guides ideas and debates about the use and stewardship of common resources. The rights of 'man' and the rights of the environment are connected through debates about access, equality and responsibility, whether these are seen as the concern of individuals, communities, governments, industries or international organisations.

Summary

- A contemporary understanding of stewardship is informed by Thomas Paine's 18th-century views on rights, where each person has a responsibility to maintain the environment for future generations. This highlights the connection between rights and responsibilities, and the relationship between the individual and society.

- Specific rights are often hard to define and can come into conflict with one other, as illustrated in the relationship between human rights and property rights.

4 Overview of Chapters 2 to 5

Chapter 1 has covered three main areas:

1   conventional understandings of 'the natural' and 'the social', which view these as separate and bounded categories, and ways in which this distinction can be useful in examining the relationship between human populations and common resources

2   the issue of population growth and its relationship to arguments about common resource management

3   the historical origins of ideas about rights associated with 18th-century revolutions in France and America, and how thoughts about the relationship between rights, responsibility and ownership have developed within contemporary international debates.

This introductory chapter has raised some of the challenges and tensions that characterise debates about common resources: the responsibilities of their management, the right to their use and how the idea of their 'ownership' may be negotiated and contested. The chapters ahead will explore these issues in more detail and, in doing so, will draw on a range of environmental, political and economic ideas.

In Chapter 2, Joe Smith considers the evolution of our understanding and valuing of environmental concerns during the latter part of the 20th century and beyond. He charts the historical development of a global 'environmental imagination' and the way a growing public consciousness of threats to common resources affects demands for environmental rights. He also considers the politics of managing environmental change.

In Chapter 3, Dan Conway and Eddie Wastnidge consider the ways that international political boundaries have created patterns of cooperation and conflict in seeking to manage and protect rights of access to common resources, such as water.

In Chapter 4, Alan Shipman examines the economic argument that private ownership of common resources might lead to their being managed more efficiently and sustainably, but that this poses challenges to the long-held idea that common resources are a public right.

In Chapter 5, Shonil Bhagwat, Nikoleta Jones and Giles Mohan explore the contested land rights of indigenous peoples in the face of commercial exploitation of resources in India as an example of how property rights and human rights are drawn into a debate about common resources.

References

Burke, J. (2014) 'India's population policies, including female sterilisation, beset by problems', *The Guardian*, 13 November 2014 [Online]. Available at www.theguardian.com/world/2014/nov/13/india-population-growth-policy-problems-sterilisation-incentives-coercion (Accessed 3 June 2015).

ChartsBin Statistics Collector Team (2009) *Historical Population of United Kingdom, 43 AD to Present* [Online]. Available at http://chartsbin.com/view/28k (Accessed 21 January 2015).

Forestry Commission (2014) *What We Do – How We Work* [Online]. Available at www.forestry.gov.uk/forestry/infd-9ccc78 (Accessed 9 February 2015).

Hardin, G. (1968) 'The tragedy of the commons', *Science*, vol. 162, no. 3859, pp. 1243–8.

The Labour Party (1997) 'New Labour because Britain deserves better' [Online]. Available at www.politicsresources.net/area/uk/man/lab97.htm (Accessed 22 May 2015).

Latour, B. (1993) *We Have Never Been Modern*, Hemel Hempstead, Harvester Wheatsheaf.

Malthus, T. (2008 [1798]) *Essay on the Principles of Population*, Oxford, Oxford World Classics.

Office for National Statistics (ONS) (2014) 'Subnational population projections, 2012-based projections, Table 2', 29 May [Online]. Available at www.ons.gov.uk/ons/publications/re-reference-tables.html?edition=tcm%3A77-335242 (Accessed 9 February 2015).

Paine, T. (1998 [1791]) 'The rights of man', in Philip, M. (ed.) *Thomas Paine: Rights of Man, Common Sense and Other Political Writings*, Oxford, Oxford University Press.

Rackham, O. (1997) *The History of the Countryside*, London, Phoenix Publishers.

Reserve Bank of India (2014) 'Table 17: Agricultural production – foodgrains', in *Handbook of Statistics on Indian Economy* [Online]. Available at www.rbi.org.in/scripts/PublicationsView.aspx?id=15807 (Accessed 3 June 2015).

Rousseau, J-J. (1998 [1763]) *The Social Contract*, Ware, Wordsworth Editions.

Sen, A. (1990) *Poverty and Famines*, Oxford, Oxford University Press.

Worldometers (n.d. a) *Population: World population* [Online]. Available at www.worldometers.info/world-population (Accessed 4 June 2015).

Worldometers (n.d. b) *Population by country: India* [Online]. Available at http://www.worldometers.info/world-population/india-population/ (Accessed 4 June 2015).

Wollstonecraft, M. (2004 [1792]) *A Vindication of the Rights of Woman*, 3rd edn, Penguin, London.

Chapter 2

The politics of environment

by Joe Smith

Contents

Introduction

The natural and social environments continually interact. People and their societies are shaped by the landscapes, climatic conditions and natural resources around them and these in turn are reshaped by human activity, as discussed in Chapter 1. This chapter continues this theme and shows how environmental issues have developed over time. It examines how the environmental movement developed, and how, later, scientific research emerged that promoted a more global imagination about these issues. It explores big questions such as:

- What motivates environmental concern?

- What are the issues that environmentalists care about, or that environmental organisations campaign on?

- At what scale of issue do they typically work?

The chapter includes discussion of conflicting rights, and the relationships between humans and the non-human world, in the present day and in the future.

This chapter will explore:

- the deep historical and cultural roots of contemporary environmentalism

- the influence of new research in shaping a global environmental imagination over the last few decades

- the distinctions between environmentalism as a social movement and the broader policy and political responses to global environmental change research

- the value of concepts to social scientists, including the concept of interdependence in relation to environmental change.

Section 1, 'Environmentalism: a new way of looking at the world' presents a short history of ideas about the Western world's changing relationship with its environment from the 17th century onwards.

Interdependence
The term has been put to many uses, but in the early 21st century has been used to indicate the dense interconnections between social, economic and ecological systems. The term helps to indicate that in many cases, these are not simply interconnections but also relations of dependence, where connected systems are threatened if another element is absent or breaks down.

Section 2, 'The emergence of a global environmental imagination' explores the role of research and policy in understanding the significance of environmental problems.

Section 3, 'Living in an interdependent world: new ethics – new politics' explores the concept of **interdependence**.

1   Environmentalism: a new way of looking at the world

'Environmental issues', 'environmentalism' and 'the environment' are all terms that are widely used. Activity 1 asks you to pause to think a bit harder about what these words mean.

Activity 1

Take a few minutes to note down some environmental issues that particularly concern you. Think about what scale they relate to. In other words, are they more about local, regional, national or global concerns? Or is this the wrong way of thinking about them? You may want to look back at some of the materials that engaged with ideas about scale in Block 2.

Discussion

Everyone will have a unique perspective on these issues. Here is one response given to this question:

> When I'm walking to my allotment I might be annoyed by the fumes from a line of cars at the junction, or enchanted by a rare sighting of a kingfisher along the brook. Both of these are very local environmental concerns. They leave me wanting to see less dependence on cars in cities, but also glad that at least some wild places have been protected from development, even in cities. But when I watch or read the news I'm reminded about global environmental issues, particularly climate change and losses of biodiversity.

Environmental groups campaign on a wide range of issues, on scales ranging from very local to global. They have campaigned to protect specific habitats, such as particular wetlands or forests, and particular species, such as orangutans, whales or endangered birds. An international body might campaign to protect the Amazon, while a local wildlife group might try to preserve a meadow or wood from development. Such campaigns have existed for decades, in some cases for more than a century. In more recent years, environmental groups have worked on broader issues, including climate change and resource depletion. These are global concerns and their implications stretch into the future as well as across the planet.

1.1   Environmentalism and industrialisation

Ideas about environmental hazard go back much further than contemporary concerns about hazardous waste or climate change. Environmental historians who have studied the late Middle Ages point to measures introduced to manage air quality in London or the water quality of the Thames, for example. By the mid- to late 17th century, the writer John Evelyn was drawing attention to air pollution in London in his book on the city's chronic air problems, published in 1651 (Figure 2.1) and the hazards of deforestation 'in his Majesty's dominions' (Figure 2.2). Evelyn's book, *Silva, or a Discourse of Forest Trees, and the Propagation of Timber in His Majesty's Dominions*, published in 1662, was a response to fears among naval leaders that deforestation threatened their access to timber for ships, and hence the nation's security. Evelyn's writings show that pollution and resource depletion were raised as issues several centuries ago.

Romantic Movement
The Romantics or Romantic Movement started as an artistic movement in the 1700s and persisted through the 19th century in art, writing (particularly poetry) and design. It celebrated nature and has been an influence on conservationist and environmentalist movements.

However, it was the explosive growth of cities, consumption of resources and large-scale movements of people and goods associated with the Industrial Revolution from the late 18th century onwards that gave impetus to new ways of thinking about humanity's relationship with its environment. The effects of these changes could be seen, smelt and heard. Industrialisation was dirty and noisy, and dramatically transformed landscapes. The **Romantic Movement** in the arts and literature can be understood as a direct reaction to these changes. For Romantic poets such as Coleridge and Wordsworth, nature was a resource of beauty, spiritual renewal and fulfilment. It held the potential to transform human experience.

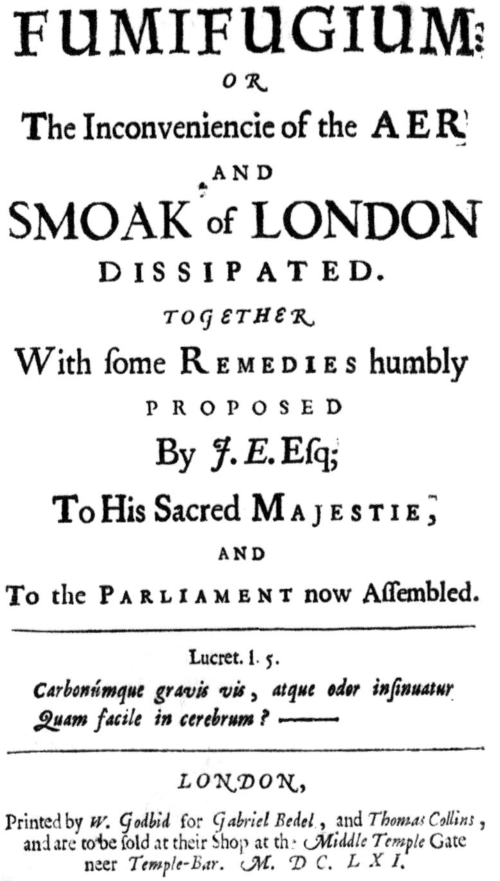

FUMIFUGIUM:

OR

The Inconveniencie of the **AER**

AND

SMOAK of LONDON

DISSIPATED.

TOGETHER

With fome REMEDIES humbly

PROPOSED

By *J. E.* Efq;

To His Sacred MAJESTIE,

AND

To the PARLIAMENT now Affembled.

Lucret. 1. 5.

Carbonúmque gravis vis , atque odor infinuatur
Quam facile in cerebrum ? ———

LONDON,

Printed by *W. Godbid* for *Gabriel Bedel ,* and *Thomas Collins ,*
and are to be fold at their Shop at the *Middle Temple* Gate
neer *Temple-Bar. M. D C. L X I.*

Figure 2.1   The title-page from John Evelyn's book on London's chronic air pollution problems

These same influences generated new ideas in politics, most clearly in William Morris's (1834–1896) distinct brand of socialism. Morris is best known today as a designer, whose work expresses his belief that 'the pleasure that resides in art is identical with that which dwells in nature' (quoted in Smith, 2006, p. 6). He was developing these ideas in the context of his workshops in London, the world's first large-scale city, which he described as a 'sordid and loathsome place'. Morris felt that the 'poison of riches' was leaching beauty out of the land and warned that '[g]reen and beautiful places are still left in the countryside of England but the hand of decay is on them' (Henderson, 1978, p. 61).

Figure 2.2   The Cawthorpe Oak in winter, from John Evelyn's 1662 book

Conservation
The conservation movement and its associated institutions emerged in the mid- to late 19th century in response to the rapid industrialisation and urbanisation of the period. Conservation bodies varied in their focus and origins around the world, sometimes concerned with human health, sometimes with conserving 'heritage' (from buildings to whole regions) or natural beauty.

Initially Morris supported the work of what are today called **conservation** bodies, such as the Commons Preservation Society, which was created to preserve beautiful open spaces for everyone's enjoyment. It is interesting to note that this society, as with other early conservation, heritage and environmental protection organisations, drew on a combination of legal and publicity tools to try to advance its cause. Modern environmentalists use much the same mix. This was shown in 2014 in the UK when the government sought to introduce legislation allowing the selling off of nationally owned forests. Campaigners employed both lawyers and media specialists, as well as public relations techniques, to maximise impact. They were successful in halting the proposed legislation.

However, William Morris's contemporary, Robert Somervell, noted that the Commons Preservation Society's scattered efforts, resulting in 'occasional and hurried glimpses of strange beauty', were wholly inadequate (Somervell, 1877, pp. 22–3). One of Morris's responses was that all art should be based in nature. He also argued that the future of art would have to rest with the working classes. These two ideas together explain his intense commitment to hand-crafted objects. Morris gave the impulses behind the Romantic Movement a political edge by proposing that the working classes could only be the future guardians of art if the conditions and purposes of labour were transformed.

Figure 2.3 Morris's *News from Nowhere*

In his book *News from Nowhere* (Figure 2.3), Morris offers a vision of a utopian society of contented craftworkers who have been set free from industrial capitalism – and its oppressive social structures – and money. The book combines ethics, aesthetics, ideas about nature and socialism, and a catalogue of the evils of capitalism. By contrast with workers under capitalism, Morris's central character, Old Hammond, is 'free, happy and energetic'. Morris is uncompromising:

> Apart from the desire to produce beautiful things, the leading passion of my life has been and is hatred of modern civilisation… Think of it. Was it all to end in a counting house on top of a cinder heap, with … a Whig committee dealing out champagne to the rich and margarine to the poor in such convenient proportions as would make all men contented together, though the pleasure of the eyes was gone from the world.

> (Morris, 1992 [1890], pp. 279–80)

A key element of Morris's thinking that is prominent in environmentalism today is the way he considered future generations and felt that their interests should be represented in the present. One example of this thinking is offered in a speech he made arguing for the preservation of old buildings, in which he suggested that: 'We are only the trustees for those who come after us' (Morris, 1889).

Less radical contemporaries of Morris pursued more practical steps to protect places and species from the consequences of economic development. In the UK the National Trust and the Royal Society for the Protection of Birds were set up. The purchase of land offered these bodies a direct means of protecting nature and heritage sites. In the USA the Sierra Club, a conservation organisation, was founded, and campaigns were initiated to create protected areas all over the developed world. These goals were pursued by gathering influential support, including from the newly wealthy who had benefited greatly from precisely the economic development that was putting so much pressure on nature. The outcomes varied widely. In the United States the national parks are publicly owned and tightly protected areas. In the UK the same term, 'national parks', describes more loosely regulated areas containing much private property, but with restrictions on how it can be used. Your earlier study of the Cairngorms National Park (Book 1, Chapter 4) highlighted the ways in which these protected areas in the UK can serve as places of residence, work and leisure simultaneously.

1.2   Conflicts between conservation, access and resource use

The historian Mark Spence argues that 'national parks serve as a microcosm for the history of conflict and misunderstanding that has long characterized the unequal relations between the United States and native peoples' (1999, p. 8).

The early North American conservationists were particularly concerned to protect what they understood as pristine 'empty' wilderness. The first national park in the United States, Yellowstone, came about in 1872. This saw it designated as public land. However, that was only possible by ignoring the long history of use of the land by Native Americans. These peoples, who had often been driven off lands such as Yellowstone, did not think of them as wild at all, but as landscapes they had managed to provide food and other resources.

However, it is important to note that the relationship between land, law and people is dynamic. The meaning that the public parks of North America hold for people, and the uses they might be put to, were not set in stone in the late 19th century. Debates continue today about the unjust nature of the designation of these parks when they were created. Native Americans (who also use the term First Nations to describe themselves, particularly in the context of campaigning and negotiations about treaties) have used their leading role in these debates to gain increased influence over the use of some of these protected areas. Since the late 20th century, the First Nations peoples and their representatives have won more influence over a number of key issues. This has resulted in 'access to sacred sites, renewal of relationships to ancestral homelands, and revitalization of subsistence-based knowledge and practices (not to mention the historical significance of reclaiming stolen lands)' (Carroll, 2014, p. 32).

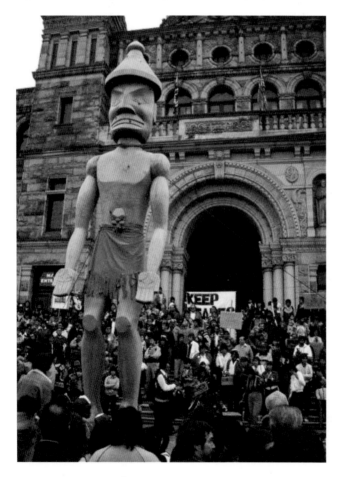

Figure 2.4 The Nuu Chah Nulth First Nations protest

As well as contesting the use and sovereignty arrangements of national parks, First Nations have often been very active in challenging destructive land uses outside parks, and in establishing their own parks. In 1984, the Nuu Chah Nulth First Nations people mounted a huge protest on the steps of the British Columbia Legislature, calling for the preservation of Meares Island from logging (Figure 2.4). The First Nations won a British Columbia Supreme Court case that ordered that the island should not be logged. Meares was made a tribal park by its owners, the Tla-o-qui-aht and Ahousat First Nations. A member of the First Nation that set up the tribal park made a sign that stands at the entrance (Figure 2.5). He said at its unveiling: 'This is a sign that's going to be affecting people for a long time: helping people understand that Tla-o-qui-aht are here, helping people that don't want to respect our homelands and our waters, helping people know that this belongs to people that are handing it over to our grandchildren.'

Campaigns such as this show that the way people think about the non-human natural environment is often shaped by – and shapes – the way they think about their identity, history, sovereignty, rights and the future of their communities. However, the extraction of natural resources from First Nation lands can also generate debate and conflict within these communities, given the opportunities for revenue and jobs they represent.

Figure 2.5   The entrance sign to the tribal park formed on Meares Island

Carroll argues that substantial issues remain to be resolved about the nature of the past enclosure of spaces to create 'public' parks. The cases explored by Carroll raise interesting and important questions about who the 'public' is that is served by the parks, who is 'sovereign' within them (in other words, who has control and ultimate authority over the land) and how very long-term environmental interests are best served. In his article about the relationship between indigenous peoples in North America, the US and Canadian governments and the way land is organised and used, Carroll points to the potential that tribal parks such as the one created on Meares Island might hold for positive compromises. He finds that:

> In the hands of Indigenous communities, land trusts and cultural conservation easements have provided practical ways to reassert rights to traditional territories and in the process create meaningful and productive relationships with non-Indigenous landowners and conservation organizations.
>
> (Carroll, 2014, p. 31)

1.3   US conservationism

A leading American conservationist, Ralph Waldo Emerson, had travelled in Europe and met the Romantic poets. His 1836 book *Nature* argued for the unity of nature, science and spirituality. It summarised a philosophy or religion that he termed Transcendentalism, wherein nature offered proof of the presence of the divine in all things. A follower of Emerson, Henry David Thoreau sought to live out these ideas and 'simplify, simplify' by living off nature for two years in the wilds. Figure 2.6 shows a replica on the site of the hut he lived in during this period. The resulting account of his time living next to Walden Pond in Maine opens thus:

> When I wrote the following pages I lived alone, in the woods, a mile from any neighbour, in a house which I had built myself... and earned my living by the labor of my own hands only.
>
> (Thoreau, 1960 [1854], p. 7)

Figure 2.6   A replica of Thoreau's hut at Walden Pond

Thoreau's concerns are very selectively remembered today: he promoted civil disobedience and critiqued industrialised labour. To this extent he shared much in common with Morris. However, his championing of individualism, self-sufficiency and hard work, alongside his conviction in the spiritual benefits of preserving natural wilderness, have been better remembered in the US context and speak to a distinctively US ideology. The spiritual strands of his thinking fed into the movement for national parks, which their proponents saw not just as a good in themselves, but as vital to the public health of urban populations.

During the 1930s and 1940s, Ansel Adams, one of the most popular photographers of the 20th century, gave visual expression to the idea that the United States' (apparent) wilderness offered a resource of awe and wonder. Adams' photos have shaped the way many US citizens think about, and have represented, ideas of US wilderness ever since. However, the creation of heavily protected parks was aimed at more than 'preserving' something from the past. Many in the national parks movement were concerned to offer the current and future inhabitants of the country's fast-growing cities access to clean, fresh, inspiring outdoor spaces. Figure 2.7 offers just one of many thousands of examples of images by amateur photographers that pay direct homage to Adams, and hint at the value the parks hold for contemporary (mostly urban) US citizens a century after they were created.

Figure 2.7   Snake River: an amateur photographer's work that pays homage to Ansel Adams' photography

US conservationists, and the artists and writers who all formed and promoted their ideas, such as Thoreau and Adams, did much to influence the thinking of environmentalism around the world. Indeed it is much easier to trace their influence than the socialism of Morris, with his concern for the everyday experiences of the urban working class. Adams' images of a pristine nature and Thoreau's writings from his solitary cabin confirm that the 20th-century environmental movement was as much about protecting the environment *from* people as it was protecting it *for* people. This environmentalism viewed cities and everyday human life not as part of the environment, but as an ever-present threat to a 'fragile' nature. As in Evelyn's time, increasing numbers of people gathered in city settlements, creating pollution and resource pressures that threatened the environment. Yet 20th-century environmental groups tended to view cities and society as the source of threats to a separate nature rather than as themselves the subject of analysis or campaigning.

Activity 2

Are the individuals that have shaped environmentalism more concerned with the past, present or future? You might want to refer to some of the people referenced in Section 1, such as Morris, Thoreau and Adams.

Discussion

This is a difficult question to answer even if you have a great deal more information to hand than is presented in this chapter. It is possible to say that Morris drew heavily on an idealised notion of the past to picture a utopian future in his novel *News from Nowhere*. Thoreau is drawing on notions of an idyllic past when he seeks to simplify his life and rely on his own wits when living for two years at Walden Pond, although he clearly wants to influence ideas about how society should live in future. Adams' photographs can suggest that his ideas about national parks are simply about conserving them in a particular pristine state. In fact, the US national parks movement was also influenced by a desire to give the populations of the United States' fast-growing cities access to fresh clean air in the wilderness.

Summary

- This short history of ideas about the Western world's relationship with its environment has shown that concerns about environmental degradation stretch back to the 17th century.

- Concern increased with industrialisation and expanding urbanisation in the 19th and early 20th centuries.

- The section has introduced ideas about conflicts over land uses and the emergence of new forms of legal protection of the natural world, including the creation of national parks.

2   The emergence of a global environmental imagination

Through the course of the 20th century, the Global North saw fast-paced economic development, in step with great advances in technology and science, and steady increases in both human numbers and rates of consumption, above all in cities and towns.

These changes meant that new forms of environmental pollution were being generated, but also that science researchers were capable of better understanding the issues at stake. Both the experience of environmental and social costs associated with environmental degradation, and the newly emerging environmental sciences, contributed to new ways of thinking about environmental change, and humanity's role in it.

2.1   The widening resonance of 'local' incidents

Twentieth-century economic development brought security and leisure to many more people, but the pollution it brought with it also started to take some of the fun out of life. Evidence of pollution took several forms: some could only be traced in the wake of careful research. However, city dwellers did not need scientists to tell them they were under threat: they could taste it in the air. Particular weather conditions would leave them choked by air pollution. The combination of the use of solid fuel (especially coal) in homes and for electricity generation, together with the rapid growth in road transport, created 'smogs' (a term to describe a combination of smoke and fog). Dense smogs were experienced in all large cities, and had been notorious since the late 19th century. In 1952, the combination of weather conditions and increased use of coal led to what had long been nicknamed 'pea souper' fogs. There was a sharp increase in death rates that public health researchers directly associated with the air pollution. It was not possible for public health researchers to establish precisely the number of deaths above the normal rate, and many of those who died were already suffering from respiratory problems; but the spike in numbers dying was very clear once all available data had been gathered. This marked increase in death rates – supported by clear evidence of cause and effect, combined with media pressure and widespread direct experience of the smogs – drove the government to legislate for measures that would improve air quality.

Figure 2.8   Arsenal goalkeeper Jack Kelsey peers into the 1952 London 'smog' – it was so thick the game was eventually stopped

Activity 3

Figures 2.8, 2.9 and 2.10 offer three different kinds of evidence about the London smogs of 1952: a photo, a newspaper article and a graph. How do they each help to tell the story of this significant event, and in what ways do they differ?

Discussion

The photograph of a football goalkeeper peering into the smog instantly tells a story about the direct physical experience of the smogs. It is also a 'human interest' story with a central character engaged in a popular sport that readers can identify with. The newspaper report relies on a very different kind of storytelling, rooted in comparison with past experiences and other factual evidence gathered by the reporter. The headline, however, has been carefully composed to attract attention in a paper full of stories. The graph that plots death rates against the levels of smoke in the air through the relevant period in December 1952 offers an even more analytical form of evidence, rooted in careful research. Such graphs can lend impact to a newspaper story, but are also influential in convincing politicians, policymakers and medical professionals of the need to act.

WORSE THAN 1866 CHOLERA

Deaths After Fog

The rise in deaths in the week after London's great fog early in December was greater than that in the worst week of the cholera epidemic in 1866. This is disclosed in a report of the health committee of London County Council, which will be considered by the council on Tuesday.

The committee reports that the figures recorded by the council's observation station at the County Hall for smoke and sulphur dioxide pollution of the atmosphere on December 7-8 are the highest which can be traced in records, which date back to 1932. In addition, for the six-day period from December 5, when the atmospheric condition was particularly bad, the temperature remained considerably below normal.

Deaths registered in London rose from 945 for the week ended December 6, to 2,484 for the following week. The general death-rate in this latter week was slightly greater than that associated with the severe fog of 1873, and was comparable with rates experienced at the peak mortality of major epidemics.

The excess of deaths over normal per million inhabitants for the week ended December 20, 1873 (peak of fog) was 243; the excess for the week ended August 4, 1866 (peak of the last great chlolera epidemic) was 426, and the excess for the week ended December 13, 1952, was 445. The corresponding figure for the worst week of the influenza pandemic of 1918 was 785.

No Particular Age

The sudden increase in deaths in the week ended December 13, 1952, although more pronounced among babies and the elderly, was not confined to persons of any particular age. The increase was associated almost entirely with disorders of the circulatory or respiratory systems. Compared with the average of the previous three weeks, deaths from bronchitis increased ten times, from influenza seven times, from pneumonia nearly five times, from pulmonary tuberculosis four and a half times, from other respiratory diseases six times, and from heart and circulatory disorders nearly three times.

The attention of the Minister of Health is being drawn to the statistics in connection with investigations which Government departments concerned may be making.

The report describes the cause of the fog as: "Almost complete absence of air movement and low surface temperature, which produced what is technically described as an 'inversion', whereby the normal upward air circulation by convection currents was arrested, with the result that smoke, sulphur oxides and other air contaminants increased.

Figure 2.9   Newspapers added to the pressure for government action on air pollution in the wake of the worst 'smogs' in many years (Stoddard, 2012)

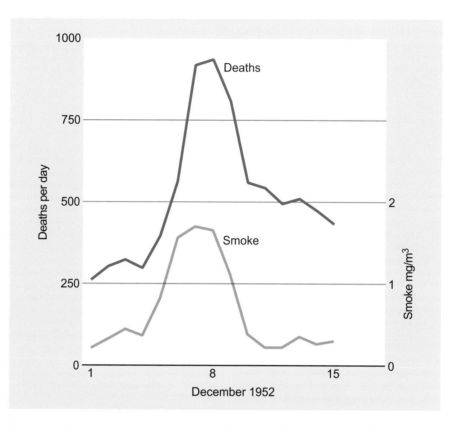

Figure 2.10   Smogs were present in all major cities, but it was the London smog disaster of 1952 that focused the attention of (London-based) politicians (Source: Met Office, n.d.)

A very different kind of risk to human health created by modern life was much more difficult to identify. In 1956 the Japanese fishing port of Minamata gave its name to a neurological disease that eventually killed at least 3000 people in two regions of the country. Research identified that an industrial process that had resulted in the leaking of mercury compounds into the bay was responsible. From here, the mercury made its way into human diets by travelling along the food chain in a community where fish and seafood formed a very important part of the diet and local economy. The toxic metal had gradually built up in the bodies of shellfish and fish that were then consumed by humans. It took nearly two decades to win any compensation for victims. Minamata was a company town, where the Chisso Corporation had huge economic and political influence. The Chisso Corporation opposed campaigns for compensation, their defence centring on the uncertainties about cause and effect. However, it was proven through careful medical and environmental research that industrial pollution, originating in Chisso's plants, had resulted in mercury getting into the food chain. An American photographer, married to a Japanese woman, spent two years during 1972 and 1973 in the area cataloguing daily life. He created moving portraits of the victims. One of the most affecting images was of a mother bathing her severely disabled child. The image travelled around the world, both putting pressure on the company and lending further momentum to the environmental movement. Such an image gave a human face to this environmental problem. In 1973, a lawsuit was won on behalf of the victims with this decisive verdict:

> The defendant's factory was a leading chemical plant with the most advanced technology and ... should have assured the safety of its wastewater. The defendant could have prevented the occurrence of Minamata disease or at least have kept it at a minimum. We cannot find that the defendant took any of the precautionary measures called for in this situation whatsoever. The presumption that the defendant had been negligent from beginning to end in discharging wastewater from its acetaldehyde plant is amply supported. The defendant cannot escape liability for negligence.
>
> (bigross86, 2011)

In the same period, former US government biologist Rachel Carson demonstrated that good research and a populist approach to publicity could progress environmental concerns. She had been gathering evidence that might explain declining bird populations and other changes in nature. She identified the pesticide dichlorodiphenyltrichloroethane (DDT) as a likely culprit. This was difficult news. The chemical had played a central role in humanity's struggle to treat typhus and malaria due to its effectiveness against mosquitoes. Yet Carson persuasively argued that its widespread and indiscriminate use was changing natural systems. Evidence alone might not have been sufficient. She was an engaging writer and phrasemaker, and the well-chosen title of her 1962 book, *Silent Spring*, helped to lodge it in the bestseller lists. Specifically, she focused on the threat that DDT posed to songbirds, hence the title, and made clear that it was not just the birds, but the people who love to hear them, who would be victims of this industrial chemical. Carson also showed how environmental science was tracing the way persistent chemicals travelled. She showed how they were released by US industry and then made their way into the body tissue of Antarctic penguins thousands of miles away. Carson's book set in train campaigns that led to the banning of DDT and much tighter controls on a range of persistent chemicals in the 15 years that followed its publication.

Activity 4

What characteristics do the events surrounding the UK urban smogs, Minimata disease and Carson's revelations about DDT have in common, and what differences are there? What combinations of scientific evidence and more emotional appeals can be identified in each case?

Discussion

Although they all relate to different places, they all occurred in industrial societies that had seen rapid economic growth in the preceding decades. Each of the pollution problems identified was directly related to industrialisation and growth. However, in the case of the UK urban smogs, there was very wide and direct public experience of the problem and the evidence of increased death rates was quite quickly gathered. Individual households were also part of the problem, through their burning of coal to heat homes. The intense media response, which included evocative images and language as well as factual evidence, led to a quick policy response. Legislation could deliver air quality improvements.

In the case of Minamata, the link between cause and effect took much longer. This was in part because the problem was rooted in chemical pollution entering the food chain in ways that were not immediately visible. It was also because a powerful interest – the company that dominated the town and wider region – fought to protect its own interests.

Rachel Carson's revelations about DDT also combined emotive language and images alongside carefully gathered factual evidence, but it represented a critique of a whole sector of the industrial system rather than focusing on a specific pollution incident.

2.2   Science and the global imagination

The success of *Silent Spring* is a story about one author catching the public imagination. Minamata and Britain's city smogs are instances of hard campaigning or media-driven events, but it is very unlikely that the cases just described would have been sufficient on their own to nurture the kind of global environmental imagination that is evident today. It is important to set those events within a wider scientific context.

The broader environmental science context of the 1950s and early 1960s was not at the time one of crisis but rather of celebration at collaboration in pursuit of new insights. The expanded scope and capabilities of natural science research after the Second World War nourished accounts of a more interdependent physical world, even as the Cold War was entrenching economic and political differences in the global system. International initiatives in the 1950s and 1960s supported novel perspectives on the earth as a single integrated system with global-scaled dynamics. The emerging prominence of this science was both marked and nourished by the first International Geophysical Year (IGY) of 1957/1958. The IGY was the source of much media attention, including a television special introduced by the Duke of Edinburgh. This was a scientific collaboration involving over 5000 researchers from 61 countries (Dodds, 2008). The work was met with a celebratory tone in the media, perhaps on account of the stark contrast that such collaboration presented with the perilous state of international politics and, above all, the nuclear arms race.

Exploration of the ocean floor under the auspices of IGY paved the way for the theory of plate tectonics – earth sciences' first fully global theory. Ambitious integrated studies of land, sea, air and ice started to generate understandings of the dynamics of the global climate and prompted the earliest concerns about human-caused global climate change. The IGY also catalysed the scientific exploration of space, resulting in the first photographic images of the 'whole earth'. The USSR launched Sputnik, the first artificial satellite, in 1957, a move that started the 'space race' and prompted the US government to create its space agency, the National Aeronautics and Space Administration (NASA). Sputnik's launch was a propaganda coup for the Soviet government, but also supplied valuable scientific information about the earth's atmosphere to the global scientific community.

From the late 1960s through to the mid-1980s, several branches of what have often come to be called the environmental sciences began to produce findings that all pointed in one direction: that human societies were having far-reaching negative impacts upon the non-human natural world.

Biodiversity
A contraction of 'biological diversity'. In general, it describes the variety of life on earth and, specifically, the total sum of the genes, species, habitats and ecosystems in a given environment.

Conservation was emerging as a concern within disciplines such as zoology and botany. It was becoming increasingly obvious to researchers that the animals and plants they were studying were disappearing with their habitats as human populations and cities grew and agriculture expanded. The biologist E.O. Wilson coined the term **'biodiversity'**. This term helped to sharpen media and policy interest in the researchers' work, with threats to biodiversity, including species loss, gaining attention, particularly in the developed world. While these concerns spanned the globe, they were focused on precisely located processes where particular species were threatened.

It is important to note that the international politics of conservation and biodiversity has always been tense. For leaders of countries in the Global South (such as Brazil, host to the Amazon rainforest, or African countries with their charismatic wild species), conservation policies were often perceived as a return to developed world colonialism. The failure to integrate the needs of communities and economies in the Global South with the needs of wildlife led to an impasse in policy and action. It also drew attention to the fact that the natural sciences were not sufficient in themselves to understand the dynamics of environmental change: social sciences would also be required.

Quite separate research in atmospheric chemistry spurred the next major development in the emergence of a truly global environmental imagination. A team of researchers working in Antarctica identified a thinning of 50 per cent of the ozone layer above the pole (see Figure 2.11). This was dubbed the 'ozone hole'. It was demonstrated that industrially produced chemicals, **chlorofluorocarbons** (CFCs), were responsible. CFCs were very widely used in the post-war period in cleaning and personal care products, refrigerants and packaging. One of the prime hazards of the thinning ozone layer was that it increased levels of ultraviolet radiation on earth. The threat of increased skin cancers was not confined to one social class, country or profession: it was understood as a universal threat generated by almost universally used products.

Chlorofluorocarbons
A family of compounds containing carbon, fluorine and chlorine atoms. CFCs are chemically inert and stable and were formerly used as refrigerants, propellants and in foams. Following the discovery that they affect the ozone layer, their production and use were banned.

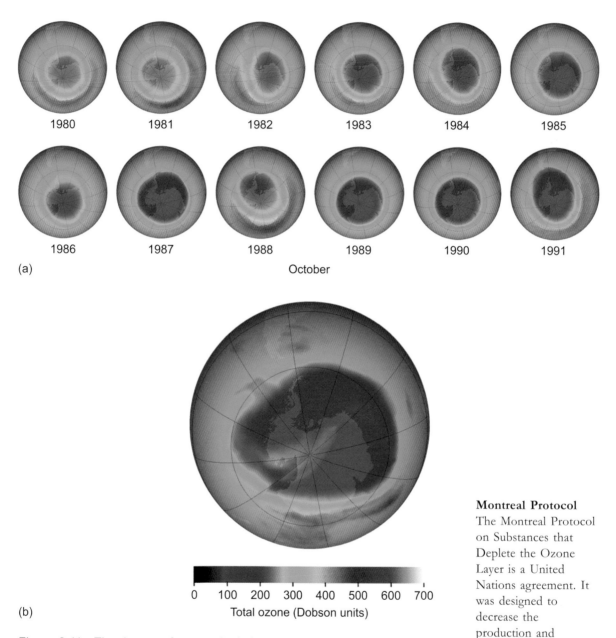

(a)   October

(b)

Figure 2.11   The degree of ozone depletion across time

Environmental groups and the media amplified the research findings, and the combined pressure resulted, within just two years of the publication of the key scientific paper on ozone depletion, in the **Montreal Protocol**. The Protocol was a binding treaty that delivered a phase-out of CFCs and other ozone-depleting chemicals. In the case of the 'ozone hole' the science was clear, as was the policy required:

Montreal Protocol
The Montreal Protocol on Substances that Deplete the Ozone Layer is a United Nations agreement. It was designed to decrease the production and consumption of ozone-depleting substances to reduce their abundance in the atmosphere and thereby protect the earth's fragile ozone layer. It was agreed in 1987 and came into force in 1989.

Carbon dioxide
A naturally occurring chemical compound consisting of carbon and oxygen. A molecule of carbon dioxide consists of one atom of carbon and two atoms of oxygen with the chemical formula CO_2. Carbon dioxide is produced in respiration and from the burning of carbon-intensive fossil fuels, and is consumed in photosynthesis.

Intergovernmental Panel on Climate Change (IPCC)
Established in 1988 by the World Meteorological Organization (WMO) and the United Nations Environment Programme (UNEP). Its purpose is to provide scientific and technical advice to the United Nations Framework Convention on Climate Change (UNFCC) and assess current information on climate change, its impacts and how to mitigate (reduce) the effects and/or to adapt to it. It produces authoritative reports on these matters approximately every five years.

elimination of the responsible chemicals as fast as possible. It was also a clear and simple story with vivid pictures and a memorable direct name ('the ozone hole') that communicated the problem, and a near-term, fearful and universal consequence, namely skin cancer. Political agreement was also made easier by the availability of alternative chemicals available that could substitute CFCs.

Imagery has often been influential in shaping action on environmental issues. This is particularly true of ozone depletion. Images such as those shown in Figure 2.11 helped to visualise the problem and motivate rapid government action. Image (a) portrays the increase of ozone depletion over time between 1980 and 1991. It communicates complex chemistry and difficult data gathering into a simple message. Evidence during 2013/14 presented in image (b) points to gradual recovery in the ozone layer, demonstrating the success of the Montreal Protocol of 1987. It also shows that recovery from global environmental change problems can be very gradual.

The next major discovery about the global environment, climate change, threatened far greater consequences, but was much more challenging for campaigners, the media and mainstream politics to respond to. Theories about how the earth was surrounded by a 'blanket' of **carbon dioxide** (CO_2) were initially offered in the first half of the 19th century. The IGY of 1957 created the possibility of gathering and sharing data about earth systems on a global scale, and by the late 1970s it was possible to start to thoroughly test the late 19th-century hypothesis that the vast amounts of CO_2 that had been emitted since the beginning of the Industrial Revolution might be capable of warming the planet. The seriousness of this possibility, combined with the scale of the scientific challenge, saw the international community (through the United Nations) create the **Intergovernmental Panel on Climate Change (IPCC)** in 1988.

Figure 2.12 shows the IPCC's opening meeting. It was the first global scientific review process on any topic on this scale, and its international membership helped to form a solid basis for policy debate. In an ongoing review process, the IPCC gathers together all of the relevant research across a very wide range of science and social science disciplines and seeks to summarise the current state of knowledge in ways that are usable by policymakers, politicians, the media and publics.

Figure 2.12   The Intergovernmental Panel on Climate Change was set up in 1988 to gather and summarise the science relating to climate change

The IPCC's First Assessment Report was published in 1990, and the Fifth Assessment Report was published in several parts during 2013 and 2014. Figure 2.13 shows a 2013 meeting, by which time the IPCC had become a much bigger process. By then, this enormous scientific peer review process had led to the involvement of hundreds of scientists from around the world working to summarise the work of up to 2000 of their colleagues. The political consequences of climate change had become very clear, and hence the IPCC process had become the subject of intense scrutiny and, in some spheres, critique.

Figure 2.13   Delegates during the 26th Session of the IPCC, Stockholm, Sweden, 2013

Figure 2.14   Drilling ice cores in the Antarctic; hard-won scientific insights lie at the heart of the development of a global environmental imagination, and are all subject to the IPCC's review process

The work that is reviewed ranges from drilling and analysing ice cores in the polar regions to understand past climates (see Figure 2.14), to social research into household energy use. As well as reviewing past data, the IPPC generates scenarios of future emissions and determines the band of most-likely temperature rises associated with each. The scenarios range from 'business as usual', where no action is taken to reduce emissions, to projections of vigorous action to reduce (or mitigate) emissions.

The international political process concerning climate change is structured by the UN Framework Convention on Climate Change (UNFCCC), which has held regular Conventions of the Parties since it came into being at the ambitious UN Conference on Environment and Development in 1992. Nearly all countries are signatories to the Convention, helping to forge a global response to a global problem. However, progress on firm agreements has been very slow. This is reflected in the fact that emissions of CO_2, the main **greenhouse gas**, have in fact risen substantially since the UNFCCC was set up.

Greenhouse gas
Gases, including carbon dioxide, water vapour, methane and nitrous oxide, interact with infrared radiation and, when present in the atmosphere, have the effect of warming the global climate. Without naturally occurring greenhouse gases, the earth's temperature would be several tens of degrees Celsius colder than it is now (and life would not have evolved in its current form).

Figure 2.15 Making carbon dioxide emissions visible (from *Can We Save Planet Earth?*, a 2006 BBC TV special).

Campaigners, the media and policy communities have struggled to find ways of making people more conscious of the carbon pollution in everyday business, institutional and home life that contributes to climate change. Figure 2.15 shows one attempt by designers working on a documentary that allowed viewers to see a 'cloud' of black blocks of carbon build up over a typical US house as they went about their daily lives. This appeared on a 2006 BBC TV special on climate change, *Can We Save Planet Earth?*, fronted by David Attenborough, and sought to make the main (invisible) greenhouse gas, carbon dioxide, easier for people to understand. The programme makers took care to show viewers how some simple, often positive, changes to everyday life could dramatically reduce the digitally created 'cloud' of black blocks above the house.

Activity 5

1   Look at Figure 2.15 and consider whether you think this is a successful attempt to 'make carbon visible'.

2   Consider reasons why carbon emissions reductions are difficult to achieve for contemporary political systems. Figure 2.15 might give you a good starting point for this question.

Discussion

1   Figure 2.15 helps to communicate how gases generated by everyday activities accumulate in the atmosphere. The graphic device is simple and effective, and references in its colour some of the fossil fuels that give off carbon dioxide when burnt, such as oil and coal.

2   The photo shows a house, a car and a neighbourhood. All of the daily activities undertaken there are carbon intensive, and the global threat of climate change derives from many millions of decisions each day. Also, the consequences are not felt immediately, and they are not generally felt locally in the most polluting and richest parts of the world. All of these factors represent huge challenges for political systems that have developed in response to very localised issues (regional or national) in the 'here and now'.

By the early years of the 21st century, global environmental change research had established understandings of complex interacting human and environmental systems. It had become difficult to avoid the idea that individual actions can lead to global environmental consequences. This marks a dramatic shift in how humanity thinks about its place in the world.

The political task of responding to climate change is one of the most demanding challenges facing contemporary societies. Despite regular and widespread social protests about climate change, for example in the New York leg of the People's Climate March shown in Figure 2.16, and despite significant advances in important areas of business and policy world responses to the topic, emissions continue to rise dramatically. The following section expands on the politics of climate change and explores the concept of interdependence. It considers the ways in which this concept can make a contribution to understanding 'where human beings are in the world now', and that may also make some contribution to a more purposeful response to global environmental change issues.

Figure 2.16   The People's Climate March, New York, 21 September 2014; campaigners still argue that political action is 'too little, too late'

Summary

- This section has presented a concise account of how research and policy gradually began to understand the significance of environmental problems, and has highlighted the growing understanding of global, as well as locally specific, concerns.

- It has summarised the evidence of chemical pollution, and environmental and health problems, caused by industrial societies.

- It has plotted the emergence of global environmental science, including research into ozone depletion and climate change.

3   Living in an interdependent world: new ethics – new politics

Politicians, journalists and publics are all faced with the need to make sense of, and respond to, emerging awareness of complex interactions between the earth's atmosphere (air), hydrosphere (water), lithosphere (rock), cryosphere (ice) and biosphere (life). Section 2 showed how global environmental science has demonstrated that these physical interactions are also in dynamic relationships with political, economic and cultural processes that are increasingly global.

Interdependence is a potentially powerful way of recognising the scale, but also subtlety, of interactions among and between global and local processes of economic, social and environmental change. To acknowledge that we live in an interdependent world doesn't tell anyone how to behave, but it can make them much more sensitive to the wide range of relationships that they are influenced by and in turn can influence. The concept of interdependence has been put to many and varied uses over the last century – academic, political and cultural – and must be placed in context if it is going to do useful work in the present. This summary focuses on the environment-related uses of the term (though it has parallel and related uses by, for example, the civil rights movement in the United States).

Concepts are sometimes called the basic building blocks of research. Once a researcher knows broadly what question they want to study and why, using or creating concepts ('conceptualisation') helps to give shape to an inquiry. Concepts help to place the researcher's work within a much wider landscape of investigation, and help them to both identify and make the most of previous related research. They also help future researchers to connect and enter into dialogue with their arguments.

In the early 20th century, the scientific–ecological strands in this thinking were inseparable from certain philosophical and sociological ideas. Donald Worster's history of ecological thought points to mathematician and philosopher Alfred North Whitehead's contribution to 'organicism' and 'holism'. Whitehead argued that 'the various parts of nature are so closely interdependent, so densely woven into a single web of being, that none may be abstracted without altering its own identity and that of the whole' (Worster, 1977, p. 317). This insight asked questions of science practice, but Whitehead also sought to indicate a direction for society. The urban historian and planning theorist Lewis Mumford drew on these ideas, and those of ecological botany that had inspired his teacher Patrick Geddes, in shaping his 'organic ideology' of the 1920s. Mumford was looking for a grounding for his goal of restoring communal values to the United States. The US naturalist Walter Taylor offered support for this line of thinking with his observation that 'there is little rugged individualism in nature' (quoted in Worster, 1977, p. 320).

To describe the world as interdependent does not provide a simple guide to action, nor does it suggest there is any less conflict or dispute in human affairs, but it does help to focus attention on ideas about responsibility and vulnerability. Human geographers in particular have tried to show how 'interconnected geographies (and histories) ... create vulnerability for certain peoples and places rather than others' (Philo, 2005, p. 442).

Interdependence isn't so much a guide to action as a ground condition – a description of humanity's state of being in the world. It is being confronted with clear evidence of the extensive state of economic, social or ecological inter-relations. Some of the 'problem solving' approaches of the 20th century, such as the identification of problems and solutions and of technical or market fixes, seem too inflexible to cope with the evidence that humans inhabit a dynamic and often unpredictable world. Without forgetting the technical, economic and other analytical tools (and the rather varied experiences of getting them to work), an interdependent world calls for much more careful attention to inter-relations and their consequences. Looking and listening out for others; being responsive and creative; anticipating change; sharing learning; behaving as if there are limits – even if we are aware that they are impossible to quantify: these are some of the features that may help people to thrive in an interdependent world.

Summary

- This section has introduced the concept of interdependence and the potential of this term as a means of better understanding the current condition of human societies and their relationships with the non-human natural world.

- It has outlined the value of using concepts in the social sciences more generally, using 'interdependence' as an example.

Conclusion

This chapter summarised the origins and development of environmental ideas over several centuries. It focused in particular on the last 150 years, including a summary of the emergence of modern environmentalism in the late 19th century. The discussion of Morris's and Thoreau's ideas showed that these were often reactions to industrialisation, but also that this was quite a broad movement from the start. Discussion of national parks in the United States indicated that questions of conservation and protection can raise controversial issues about sovereignty and rights (in particular with the case of First Nations).

The chapter went on to describe how developments in environmental science added new impetus to environmentalism, shaping a movement that enjoyed far-reaching influence from the late 20th century onwards. This science developed to reveal global problems generated by human actions. The last section of the chapter explored the concept of interdependence, and included a more general discussion of the value of concepts in the social sciences.

This chapter has:

- explored the deep historical and cultural roots of contemporary environmentalism

- introduced the way new environmental science research undertaken since the late 1950s has helped to shape a global environmental imagination

- engaged with the distinctions between environmentalism as a social movement and the broader policy and political responses to global environmental change research

- investigated the value of concepts to social scientists, including the concept of interdependence in relation to environmental change.

References

bigross86 (2011) 'Photos do lie', forum message to *World Affairs Board*, 26 January (Accessed 21 January 2015).

Carroll, C. (2014) 'Native enclosures: tribal national parks and the progressive politics of environmental stewardship in Indian Country', *Geoforum*, vol. 53, pp. 31–40.

Dodds, K. (2008) 'The ice: unstable geographies of Antarctica', in Clark, N., Massey, D. and Sarre, P. (eds) *Material Geographies: A World in the Making*, Milton Keynes, The Open University.

Henderson, P. (1978) *The Letters of William Morris to His Family and Friends*, New York, AMS Press.

Met Office (n.d.) *The Great Smog of 1952* [Online]. Available at www.grida.no/geo/GEO/Geo-3-010.htm (Accessed 4 June 2015).

Morris, W. (1889) *Address at the Twelfth Annual Meeting – SPAB* [Online]. Available at www.marxists.org/archive/morris/works/1889/spab16.htm (Accessed 19 January 2015).

Morris, W. (1992 [1890]) 'News from nowhere; or, An epoch of unrest: being some chapters from a utopian romance', in *The Collected Works of William Morris*, vol. XVI, London, Longmans Green.

Philo, C. (2005) 'The geographies that wound', *Population, Space and Place*, vol. 11, pp. 441–54.

Smith, J. (2006) *What do Greens Believe?*, London, Granta.

Somervell, R. (1877) *A Protest Against the Extension of Railways in the Lake District*, Windermere, J. Garnett.

Spence, M.D. (1999) *Dispossessing the Wilderness: Indian Removal and the Making of the National Parks*, New York, Oxford University Press.

Stoddard, K. (2012) 'How the Guardian reported on London's Great Smog of 1952', *Guardian*, 5 December [Online]. Available at www.theguardian.com/theguardian/from-the-archive-blog/2012/dec/05/great-smog-london-1952-archive (Accessed 4 June 2015).

Thoreau, H.D. (1960 [1854]) *Walden; or, Life in the Woods*, New York, Signet.

Worster, D. (1977) *Nature's Economy*, Cambridge, Cambridge University Press.

Chapter 3
Governing common resources

by Daniel Conway and Edward Wastnidge

Contents

Introduction

In this chapter, you will consider how international political boundaries have created patterns of cooperation and conflict in seeking to manage, exploit and protect shared or common resources, such as water. These common resources can also be the focus for political disputes between states over rights of ownership, regulation and access, and ultimately a source of diplomatic and military conflict.

The chapter will explore how common resources have come to play a major role in contemporary global politics and how disputes over them relate to wider power struggles.

This chapter will explore:

- global common resources and **resource domains**

- governance regimes as an international means of defining, organising and regulating global common resources

- sovereignty as a key principle in international relations and how this principle has changed and is being challenged in contemporary international affairs.

Resource domain
An area of land or sea containing commercially important natural resources.

Section 1, 'Oceans and seas as a common resource', provides an overview of the concept of common resources from an international relations perspective, particularly in relation to the concept of **sovereignty**.

Section 2, 'Governance and regimes', looks at the formation of regimes to govern shared resources.

Section 3, 'Common resources and state sovereignty', outlines the concept of sovereignty, briefly explores how it came into being and considers whether the duty to protect the commons undermines it.

Sovereignty
The exercise of comprehensive, supreme, unqualified and exclusive control over a designated territorial domain.

Section 4, 'Case study 1: Hydropolitics in Central Asia', explores water resources in that area.

Section 5, 'Case study 2: South and East China Seas', looks at the contested territory of the sea in East Asia, where China has sought to lay claim to territory.

1   Oceans and seas as a common resource

Since the 17th century, the basic principle of the modern international system has been the sovereign ownership of territory, coastal waters and, more recently, airspace by states. As Chapter 1 explained, global common resources refers to a type of resource that lies outside the political reach of any one **nation state** and therefore could be accessed by any nation state. The picture is further complicated by changing and shifting political circumstances, which mean that the boundary between the nation state and particular resource domains is not a fixed one. In practice, common resources can be international and shared by several nations. The Mediterranean Sea is an example of this: the states surrounding the Mediterranean Sea are all legally entitled to claim sovereignty over the sea surrounding their borders.

An example of the tensions that can arise over maritime access, one that fortunately has not resulted in armed conflict, is the dispute between the United Kingdom and Spain over control and access to Gibraltar and its surrounding waters. On a number of occasions, the UK Foreign Office has taken the serious diplomatic step of 'summoning' the Spanish ambassador to protest and warn against the redirection of Spanish naval ships across what the British government considers to be its territorial waters surrounding Gibraltar, at the tip of the Iberian Peninsula. On one such occasion in 2014, the Spanish government quickly responded by summoning the British ambassador in Madrid and expressed its 'deep unease' at the 'unacceptable interference by the United Kingdom in the routine activities of the Spanish Navy in Spanish waters' (Merco Press, 2014). Spain disputes Britain's sovereignty over Gibraltar and considers the waters surrounding it to be Spanish territory. This may seem like a curious series of events to have taken place in the 21st century between two allies and members of the European Union, but it was characteristic of this diplomatic dispute between the UK and Spain. That the dispute focuses on the sea reflects a much broader trend in international politics: disputes over access, ownership and the regulation of common resources in the world, including the high seas, have increasingly come to the fore in recent decades.

When the UK was ceded the territory of Gibraltar in the Treaty of Utrecht in 1713, ownership of the surrounding waters was not considered relevant. However, by the latter half of the 20th century the international community had defined, via the United Nations, how access to, and ownership of, the seas should be regulated. However, this hasn't removed the possibility of conflict between states over common resources, particularly if there are broader economic, political or environmental concerns at play. In recent years, the UK has sought to restrict Spanish fishing rights, citing the need to protect scarce fish resources, and Spanish fisherman have protested in response (see Figure 3.1), claiming it is their right to fish in what they consider to be their territory. Specific disputes have also focused on the right of Gibraltar to sink an artificial reef to protect wildlife without Spanish permission, and on the ownership of 'sunken treasure' on ships wrecked in the waters surrounding Gibraltar. Those involved have used traditional state 'sabre-rattling' techniques, ranging from formal diplomatic complaints to sending naval vessels. Both sides have also involved international bodies to help resolve these disputes, including the European Union, the United Nations, the European Court of Justice and courts in the United States.

Figure 3.1   Spanish fishermen stage a protest in disputed waters near artificial reef, Gibraltar, August 2013

In this area of the Mediterranean, two states claim sovereignty and try to restrict each other from gaining access. While common resources can be beyond sovereign state jurisdiction, throughout the 20th century states have increasingly sought to claim sovereignty over areas of global common resources as the demand for resources has grown and new technologies have enabled their exploitation. Global common resources include resources such as the oceans, the atmosphere, forests and rivers, which have historically been guided by the principle of belonging to the common heritage of humankind.

Global common resources became more of a challenge for the international community (including states and international organisations) in the 20th century. This is because technological developments now allowed states to reach both new resources – such as deep-sea drilling to access oil and gas – and new areas, such as the air and outer space. At the same time, advances in scientific understanding have increased international concern about the environment and potential consequences should the use of these resources not be managed appropriately, as discussed in Chapter 2.

Activity 1

Consider the examples of global common resources discussed so far. Can you think of common resources in your local area? Who has access to these commons and who regulates them? Are there any controversies or debates about them?

Discussion

You may have thought of places such as parks, communal land, lakes or rivers. Or perhaps you thought of community resources that are shared, such as leisure centres, car parks or allotments. Unlike global common resources, these are likely to be areas that are easier to access and may automatically fall under the authority of the state. Even so, there may be debates about who should have the right of access and how best to regulate these areas. These debates could be focused on environmental concerns, property rights, economic efficiency and social justice. For example, property developers may wish to build on parkland and greenfield sites. Global common resources face many of the same pressures and debates, with the added complication of either lying outside state control, or being subject to contestation between different states over the rights of access and ownership.

Figure 3.2   A cannon in St Kitts, West Indies: three miles offshore was considered to be state territory because it was the average distance a cannon could fire

The oldest recognised commons were the oceans, or more correctly, the high seas. For centuries they were defined as being outside the three-mile limit of the territorial sea, which came under state jurisdiction (Vogler, 2000, p. 7). The reason for this is that three miles was the range of a cannon shot. Beyond this limit it was accepted that the high seas were open to all for the purposes of navigation, fishing and more recently the laying of cables and aviation. However, once offshore oil exploration and factory fishing became technically feasible, the status of the high seas as a common resource started to be challenged. Nation states began to press for sovereign economic rights over coastal fisheries and continental shelves. The mining of the seabed also became a technical and economic possibility.

In a landmark speech delivered to the UN General Assembly in 1967, Arvid Pardo, the foreign minister of Malta, suggested that the deep seabed should not be treated as beyond the remit of ownership, but should come under communal international management, or governance, as the 'common heritage of mankind' (Vogler, 2000, p. 6). The sea's resources should be shared among the international community on an equitable basis. This call, along with the pressure from other countries to enclose and define the substantial areas of the high seas, led to a long-running attempt to reform the status of the oceans' common resources: the Third United Nations Conference on the Law of the Seas (UNCLOS), which occurred between 1973 and 1982. In the late 20th and early 21st centuries, there have been negotiations and agreements focusing on specific resources in the oceans, such as whales, fish stocks and the exploitation of minerals. Many of the conflicts and disputes about how these resources should be regulated focus on the rights of states to access resources.

There is great concern that global common resources are approaching (or are in) crisis. The influential metaphor of the 'tragedy of the commons' (Hardin, 1968) highlights humanity's relentless desire to exploit the world's resources which, if left unchecked, could lead to their complete exhaustion and global crisis (Vogler, 2000). However, there has been concern throughout history about the consequences of overexploitation and ultimate exhaustion of the world's finite resources. According to Hardin, common resources should not be considered as freely available to all, but regulated and certain activities restricted to prevent catastrophe.

Summary

- 'Global common resources' refers to resources that lie outside the political reach of any one nation state and are open to access by a number of nation states.

- Conflict can occur between nation states over ownership of common resources, such as between Spain and the UK over the waters surrounding Gibraltar.

- The 'tragedy of the commons' refers to the view that, left unregulated, common resources will quickly become exhausted.

- The late 20th century saw increasing regulation of global commons by international organisations.

2 Governance and regimes

There is an ongoing debate about the extent to which common resources are in crisis (Buck, 1998, pp. 111–29; Young, 1997). If you accept that there is a crisis, the solution to the 'tragedy of the commons' is potentially provided by the state and the international community of states acting in cooperation. For example, when problems of pollution or land use are essentially local, they can be dealt with by the state under whose jurisdiction they fall. Governments can (in principle) take control and act in the common interest. They can enforce taxes on emissions, for example, or prohibit damaging environmental activities and penalise those who transgress environmental rules. However, common resources do not fall under the jurisdiction of any one state; and there isn't a world government to effectively manage resources in the way a nation state can. However, although there is not a world *government*, it is possible for there to be an international **governance regime**.

The 1982 United Nations Convention on the Law of the Sea (UNCLOS) is an example of how the international community, albeit not all states, agreed to a governance regime for the oceans. UNCLOS provides an international legal framework that defines and regulates state territorial waters as well as states' access to resources in the seas. As you can see from Figure 3.3, UNCLOS defines different zones where states have sovereignty and the point at which the sea becomes a commons with no sovereignty rights. These regulations include both the sea as an expanse of water and the seabed beneath it. UNCLOS does allow for states to request extensions of sovereignty beyond the standard 200 miles from the coastline, should there be reason (such as the discovery of large oil or other mineral resources, for example). There is a formal process by which states can apply and obtain approval for this via the UN and there is a Permanent Court of Arbitration based at The Hague to deal with disputes between states.

Regulations designed to clarify the governance of airspace are also in use and in this context 'international treaties define a state's sovereign airspace as 60,000 feet above its geographic boundaries and above 12 miles of sea from its coastline' (Murphy, 2010, p. 30).

Governance regime
A set of rules and regulations that have been negotiated and agreed between international partners and that are enforceable via an institution or a clearly defined decision-making procedure.

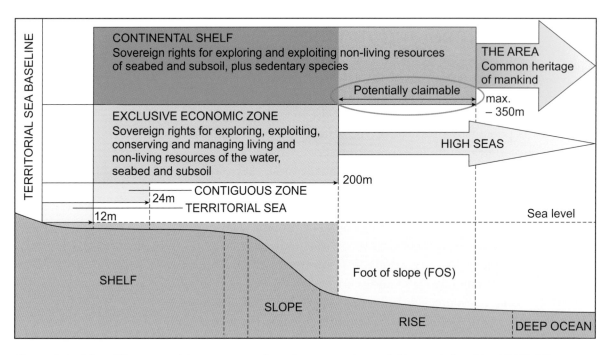

Figure 3.3   The different maritime zones and marine sovereignty rights as defined by UNCLOS

The processes that governments follow in making national policy about regulating resources are complex, and adding an international dimension complicates the process further. The formation of international governance regimes for common resources can be affected by national (and therefore internal) concerns. For example, scientific information, such as the environmental impacts of regulating or not regulating resources, influences government and non-governmental organisations at both national and international levels. Business, trade and environmental groups often compete for influence over government policy. Treaty ratification via parliaments, and effective compliance following ratification, add further complexity that can damage the effectiveness of international governance. Also, although states may sign a treaty obligating them to follow environmental regulations, the treaty may need to be passed into domestic law by a national parliament, and its effectiveness depends on states' willingness to prosecute individuals or organisations who break the terms of the treaty.

Nations can have many concerns affecting international regime formation. For example, one US motive to participate in forming an Antarctic governance regime, which divided up the Antarctic territory between states, was to have a location for United States military training in the extreme cold and one that was far away from the rival Soviet presence in the Northern Polar regions. The United States therefore sought to claim sovereignty over an area of the Antarctic for security and strategic reasons. Nations must also reconcile domestic interests as well as international ones. For example, the United States refused to sign UNCLOS, in part to protect domestic business interests in deep seabed mining. It eventually signed the treaty in 1994 and recognises it as an aspect of international law, but the US Congress has not yet ratified the treaty. There is still political disagreement in Congress over the effects the treaty would have on US sovereignty, security and business interests.

Figure 3.4   A US Airforce aircraft participating in Operation Deepfreeze in the Antarctic

National interests relating to common resources can also reflect political, economic and security concerns at national level. Restricting or disrupting access to the sea or airspace can quickly become a political and security threat for states and regions. For example, from the 1960s until the 1990s, many African states banned apartheid South Africa from the use of airspace across Africa. This had immediate security and economic threats to South Africa, heavily reliant as it was on European and North American trade. The South African government negotiated with its US allies to adapt Boeing 747 aircraft to fly the long distance around Africa and over the Atlantic (see

Figure 3.5). South African Airways was also given permission from Portugal to build a runway and terminal on the Portuguese colony of Ilha Do Sal in the Atlantic to enable refuelling stops on the route to Europe and the United States.

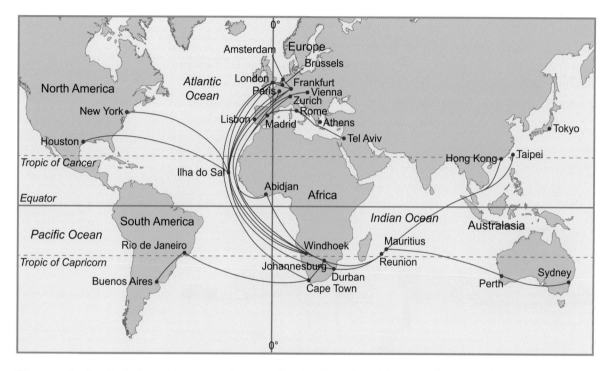

Figure 3.5   South African Airways route map showing how the airline was forced to fly around Africa

A more recent example of a security threat is the existence of piracy off the Somalian coast. The ocean surrounding the Horn of Africa contains major commercial shipping routes serving the Middle East, Asia, and Europe (via the Suez Canal). In the context of the Somalian civil war, which began in 1991, criminal gangs have attacked, robbed and hijacked shipping off the Somalian coast. This security threat has led to the international community responding to protect shipping and police the sea off the Horn of Africa. This response first came from a coalition of 25 nations' naval forces creating 'Coalition 150' based in Bahrain and then from a UN mandate, which deployed European Union naval vessels in Operation Atlanta.

Summary

- Managing common resources has been done primarily through the negotiation and framing of international governance regimes.

- These governance regimes are a set of rules and regulations that are negotiated multilaterally between international partners and are enforceable via an institution or a clearly defined decision-making procedure.

- The United Nations Convention on the Law of the Seas (UNCLOS) is an example of a governance regime.

- Competing state interests, both domestically and internationally, can lead to controversy and disagreement about the rights of access and exploitation of common resources.

- The denial of access to common resources can quickly become security threats to states in economic, diplomatic and military terms.

3   Common resources and state sovereignty

The notion of common resources in the contemporary world poses challenges for the idea that states are sovereign, and that the international community can also act like a sovereign nation state. So, where did the notion of sovereignty originate, and how has it changed in light of the need to form global governance regimes? In everyday language, the word 'sovereign' means an individual or body that has supremacy, rank or authority over others. In political terms, sovereignty originally developed in Europe to justify the attempt by monarchs to consolidate control over their kingdoms where authority had originally been shared by a feudal aristocracy and the Catholic Church. The concept of sovereignty contributed to the formation of European states, particularly after the signing of the Peace of Westphalia in 1648, following the Thirty Years War. The Westphalia negotiations established the principle of autonomous and sovereign states in Europe that would not interfere with one another's domestic affairs.

What became known as the Westphalian system developed into the dominant international governance system over the following centuries, promoting the principles of statehood and government at state level. As European empires declined across the 20th century, the establishment of the UN in 1945 recognised newly independent sovereign nation states and provided an international framework by which states could formulate, monitor and implement international rules. As part of this, the UN enabled the negotiation of the right to sovereignty, access and exploitation of the sea between states (see Smith et al., 2009).

National sovereignty, therefore, may be thought of as a special case of property rights. By entering into international agreements on trade, access to resources, regulating pollution and so forth, nations accept constraints on their absolute freedom of action. Signatory states agree in the 1967 Outer Space Treaty, for example, to forgo the traditional right of territorial acquisition by discovery and occupation in exchange for peaceful access to the domain of outer space. Some international agreements impose restrictions on the activities that have traditionally been the rights of national governments, such as the right to use any weapons in wartime (the international ban on the use of landmines, for example). Some impose restrictions on the activities of people and corporations that are under their national jurisdiction, such as the ban on the manufacture and use of chlorofluorocarbons (CFCs).

The emergence of international resource domains, and of pollution, reveals how the traditional concept of state sovereignty may no longer apply in tackling contemporary global challenges. Global pollution (of air and water) relates to a plethora of processes and problems, and can only be addressed if there is international cooperation and agreement. The depletion of fish stocks and the use of ozone-destroying chemicals in industrialised states have serious consequences for public health and economic prosperity worldwide. Nation states have chosen to cooperate in the formation of new international governance regimes, which modify states' sovereign control over the affected resources and economic processes.

Activity 2

Do you think the international community has a duty to collectively regulate and restrict damaging environmental activities as well as the right of access to global common resources, even if it undermines the concept of state sovereignty? Or do you think that, as states such as China and India have sometimes argued, states do have the right to develop their economies and have access to resources in their region as they see fit?

Discussion

There is no right or wrong answer to this debate.

As you have read, there has been a strong argument that international regulation is essential to protect the environmental integrity of common resources, such as the high seas, and global common resources have increasingly come under regulation during the 20th and 21st centuries (such as in the case of the atmosphere). These governance regimes inevitably reduce nation states' sovereignty over certain areas.

However, one could argue that Western and Northern states (such as those in Europe and North America) have had centuries to exploit common resources and create regulations to their own benefit. In this line of argument, newly developing states – such as India and China – should also have the right to access resources in their region for their economic benefit.

Summary

- Sovereignty means to have ultimate authority and control.

- The European nation state system, established at the Treaty of Westphalia, is premised on sovereign nation states.

- The international regulation of global common resources challenges, or at least adapts, the traditional notion of state sovereignty, requiring states to defer to international regulations about common resources and change certain behaviours, such as those relating to environmental damage.

4   Case study 1: Hydropolitics in Central Asia

So far you have seen that, in broad terms, 'common resources' refers to those resources that lie beyond the political reach of any one state, and how regulating these common resources poses challenges to the notion of state sovereignty. But now you will consider a specific example where resources are shared between the territories of particular nation states across particular national borders. The following section explores the contested politics over such resources through the example of water as a transboundary resource in Central Asia.

4.1   The politics of water

Following the end of the Cold War, concerns about security threats beyond the traditional superpower rivalry of the United States and the then Soviet Union began to gain currency. As noted earlier, one of the key areas that started to concern academics and governments alike was the need for collective action to prevent incidences of the 'tragedy of the commons'. This was not only important in terms of avoiding environmental catastrophe, but also had a potentially powerful impact on relations between states. Water can often be considered as a regional or global common resource. It is a shared resource that crosses national boundaries and whose use is contested. Water is particularly important because access to it is considered a basic human right. Consequently, water is a resource that has the potential for both cooperation and conflict – perhaps the two key features of the international domain in which states interact.

The interactions between states over water can range from disputes over contested maritime boundaries and access to transboundary water resources (such as rivers flowing from one state to another), to cooperation between states on managing water courses and preventing environmental problems. The term **'hydropolitics'** is used in politics and international studies to describe this dynamic. As you will see in the following case study, changes in domestic and international politics can also have a major effect on the politics of water, for example, when new states come into being and are faced with competing claims and the desire to assert themselves as sovereign entities.

Hydropolitics
The dynamics of conflict and/or cooperation over water resources that cross national boundaries.

The management of water resources has become a concern for governments across the world, particularly in areas where scarcity of water is becoming an issue. In the early 1990s, scholars argued that water was likely to become a source of conflict in the coming years (Gleick, 1993; Homer-Dixon, 1994). Others, however, rejected the notion of 'water wars' as something of a myth. For example, Wolf (1998) observed that, with the exception of a few minor skirmishes, a war has never been fought over water – as yet.

The potential for conflict does, however, become more acute when water resources cross borders. This is particularly true for rivers that are sources of energy, irrigation and drinking water for a state or states. These competing uses create a dynamic of dependence between the 'upstream' and 'downstream' states in terms of control over the resource. If the upstream state controls the headwaters of a particular river that a neighbouring, downstream state requires, then it potentially holds a considerable amount of power over them. Situations such as this are often referred to as 'zero-sum games': 'one party's gain is balanced by another party's loss. If you subtract total losses from total gains, they sum to zero' (Allen, 2014, p.158). Put simply, one state's gain is achieved through the other state losing out, and the potential for conflict is clear. However, this view is contested by some who highlight the historical cooperation between states on such issues (Daoudy, 2007; Wolf, 1998). As noted earlier, there have been no major conflicts over water thus far, and international organisations have been set up to promote cooperation over water resources through the United Nations' Convention on the Protection and Use of Transboundary Watercourses and International Lakes.

In the case of Central Asia, water politics have become an increasingly pressing issue since the states of the region gained independence following the break up of the Soviet Union in 1991. You will see how the spectre of conflict and potential for cooperation loom large over the international relations of the region in relation to water, and you will also explore how this relates to the notion of sovereignty that you were introduced to earlier.

4.2   Hydropolitics in Central Asia

The Soviet Union was formally dissolved on 31 December 1991. This was one of the major events in international history, ending the Cold War and changing the nature of global politics. But it was also the beginning of a new era for the people living in its constituent republics as they became newly independent states. With this independence came a whole set of conflicting issues as the former Soviet republics grappled with the realities of becoming sovereign entities no longer controlled by Moscow. The newly independent states inherited the remnants of a centrally planned economy that had served the interests of the Soviet Union. As a result, whole swathes of these new states' infrastructures were integrated with one another, from the oil and natural gas pipelines running from the Caspian Sea to the Russian heartland, to the management of water resources and irrigation systems. These now crossed international borders rather than lying within the one, unified state.

The difficulties that the republics encountered in establishing themselves as independent, sovereign states were further complicated by simmering ethnic tensions, which had in turn been exacerbated by the arbitrary drawing of the individual republics' borders during the early years of the Soviet Union. These problems are well illustrated in Central Asia, which became home to five independent states: Kazakhstan, Kyrgyzstan, Tajikistan, Turkmenistan and Uzbekistan. Figure 3.6 shows the political borders of newly independent states that were inherited from the Soviet Union. It also highlights the main ethnic groups found in the region, so you can see the complexities at play here.

While the Soviet Union's drawing of borders in Central Asia was broadly carried out along patterns of ethnic settlement and linguistics, it failed to take into account the region's complex ethnic geography. As an example, the primarily Tajik majority cities of Bukhara and Samarkand were incorporated into the Uzbek Soviet Socialist Republic (SSR), and the predominantly Uzbek city of Osh became part of the Kyrgyz SSR. This exercise also imposed the idea of nationality among the peoples of the region, which had previously not been the main self-identifying factor in Central Asia. It arguably represents a classic case of 'divide and rule' whereby a ruling power divides a territory up in order to manage it and prevent it from uniting to challenge its rule. These boundary lines became the international borders of sovereign states after 1991.

Figure 3.6   A map shwoing major ethnic groups in Central Asia

4.3   The water problem

You may wonder what all this has to do with water. Central Asia was at the heart of the Soviet cotton-growing industry, a water-intensive industry that remains vitally important to the region today, particularly in Uzbekistan. During the Soviet era, a huge irrigation network was built to serve the cotton industry. The diversion of water from the region's two main rivers, the Amu Darya and Syr Darya, throughout the 1960s and 1970s led to one of the most significant environmental tragedies in recent times – the desiccation of the Aral Sea, which lies on the border of Uzbekistan and Kazakhstan. Once the world's fourth largest lake, by 1991 the Aral Sea had shrunk to half its surface area (Weinthal, 2002), and the shrinkage continues with most recent measurements estimating the sea to be around 10 per cent of its original size. This desiccation has caused major health problems in the area, with the now exposed seabed covered in salt and toxic chemicals that are carried into the surrounding population.

While the water usage related to the cotton **monoculture** in the region remained a domestic issue until 1991, the subsequent emergence of independent states in the region meant that each new country sought to establish sovereignty over its resources. This meant that water became an international issue, as the headwaters of the region's two main rivers were now located in separate states from the ones that relied heavily on them for their agricultural needs. Ninety per cent of the region's water resources are located in Kyrgyzstan and Tajikistan, and yet Uzbekistan uses over half (52 per cent) of the region's entire water (UNEP et al., 2005) as a result of its cotton industry.

Monoculture
Crop consisting of a single species.

Further complicating the picture, another major legacy of the Soviet era in Central Asia was the creation of 'an electricity–water nexus, whereby the generation of electricity from hydropower in upstream countries was linked to the water needs of those downstream' (Muckenhuber, 2010). Under the Soviet regime, huge reservoirs were constructed in upstream Kyrgyzstan and Tajikistan to aid cotton production downstream (primarily in Uzbekistan), with the water-flows managed centrally from Moscow. Hydropower stations were also built and incorporated into the region's energy grids, so that the power generated could be distributed across the region. Coal and gas were supplied from Uzbekistan to the upstream republics that lacked fossil fuel resources, again all centrally managed by Moscow. However, on independence, this created a major issue as the states were locked into an interdependence that clashed with their desires to protect their sovereign resources as independent states. Consequently, the upstream states of Kyrgyzstan and Tajikistan view their water, and control over it, as a commodity, but they are subject to fuel deliveries and reliant on energy from Uzbekistan owing to the Soviet-era energy infrastructure with which they were left.

These resources have become bargaining chips for the respective countries and now play a key role in relations between them. Since independence there have been regular diplomatic clashes among the states. Kyrgyzstan and Tajikistan were among the poorest of the Soviet republics but they now control the water required by Uzbekistan for its cotton and agricultural industry. They also want to develop their considerable hydropower potential, as they lack fossil fuels for power generation. If they hold back water, it has a detrimental effect on downstream Uzbekistan. If they release a large volume through their dams to generate power, then this can also cause severe flooding downstream. Both scenarios have a damaging impact on Uzbekistan's cotton industry. In retaliation, Uzbekistan has periodically ceased its gas supplies to Kyrgyzstan and Tajikistan and closed its borders. The closing of borders is especially problematic as the transport infrastructure inherited from the Soviet era cut across what are now international boundaries. Uzbekistan is also the most populous state in the region, is the main military power, and has threatened force against its neighbours if water is used as a weapon against it.

4.4   Complex borders

The potential for further exacerbation of such tensions can be seen when focusing on the area where the borders of Kyrgyzstan, Tajikistan and Uzbekistan meet – the Ferghana Valley. This has long been one of the most populous areas of Central Asia, and has traditionally served as its agricultural heartland. The drawing of borders between the then-Soviet republics during the 1920s left the valley criss-crossed by a complex web of borders including several enclaves, whereby one territory is completely surrounded by another. During Soviet times, these borders were merely administrative, with little in the way of actual demarcation (where borders are physically defined). They had little impact on daily life. Following independence they became international borders, but remained poorly demarcated, particularly in the mountains surrounding the Ferghana Valley. This complex political geography and difficult topography is illustrated in Figure 3.7, with the national borders marked in red. Note the presence of the large Toktogul and Kariakkum reservoirs in Kyrgyzstan and Tajikistan respectively, and the lower altitude of the valley in the centre of the map, largely located inside Uzbek territory and home to the region's cotton industry.

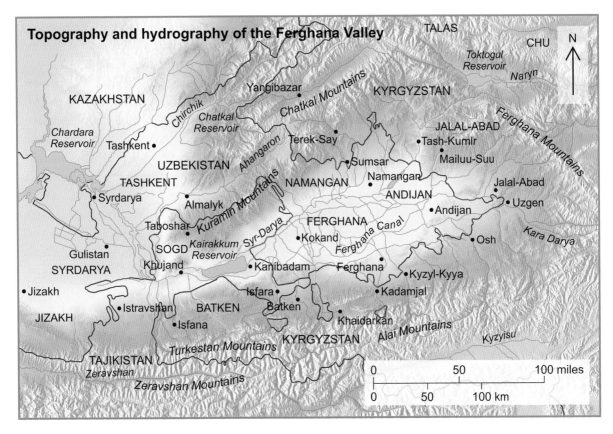

Figure 3.7 Topography and hydrography of the Ferghana Valley (Source: UNEP et al., 2005, p. 15)

Water disputes can also take on an ethic dimension in the region, with minority groups (such as the large Uzbek population in the Kyrgyz city of Osh) often living in the border areas. Disputes among local communities over water here can quickly escalate because of mobilisation among community networks rooted in ethnic solidarity. Because each state contains significant minorities that have close ties to communities in neighbouring states, such communities are often treated with suspicion. There have been campaigns for greater cultural and linguistic rights among the large Tajik minority living in Uzbekistan, and the significant Uzbek population living in the Osh region of Kyrgyzstan has also periodically risen up against perceived discrimination.

The Ferghana Valley has traditionally been a religiously conservative area, and has at times chafed against the secular governments of the region. The Valley has often been targeted because of Uzbekistan's government perceiving it as being home to the al-Qaeda-affiliated

Islamic Movement of Uzbekistan (IMU), who have fought alongside the Taliban in Afghanistan, and have carried out sporadic attacks across the region. This has particularly incurred the wrath of Islam Karimov, president of Uzbekistan since independence in 1991. Under the pretext of the US-led War on Terror, Karimov campaigned to rid the region of Islamic extremism, thus further inflaming tensions. As a result, Kyrgyzstan, Tajikistan and Uzbekistan have, in addition to their clashes over water, accused each other of harbouring terrorists or of not doing enough to tackle the problem. The wider regional picture must also be considered. The region is susceptible to instability spilling over from Afghanistan, as the actions of the IMU demonstrate. Central Asia has also seen an influx of Chinese and Western investment in the considerable oil and natural gas resources in the Caspian Basin, which forms the South-West border of Kazakhstan, as well as a more assertive Russian presence in a region it considers as its own 'near abroad'. Therefore, 'outside forces' have a further influence on the region's international relations.

4.5   Conflict or cooperation?

It is clear that the situation in Central Asia is complex and has the potential for conflict. The water issue – along with the other problems such as lack of development, over-reliance on cotton, and the spectre of terrorism – has led to the region becoming highly **securitised**. This means that such issues are held up as vital to each state's national security.

Securitised
(Of territory) given a high level of security preparation or security-service presence; (of debt) assembled into a tradeable bond or security.

Activity 3

How might such problems lead to conflict between the states of Central Asia? What are the potential triggers for conflict there? How do water issues exacerbate other existing tensions?

Discussion

There are a number of potential triggers for conflict in the region. If, for example, Tajikistan or Kyrgyzstan were to withhold water supplies to downstream Uzbekistan, then this would deprive the latter of a basic right (in having access to water), and seriously damage its economy. Uzbekistan could retaliate by withholding gas supplies to the two states, which could have a major impact on their populations during the severe winters experienced there. This could have a knock-on effect and exacerbate inter-ethnic relations within each state owing to the region's complex borders and ethnic mix. One state might feel obliged to step in and support its ethnic kin in a neighbouring state if their rights are not being fully respected.

Although this paints a rather bleak picture, cross-border problems also bring the potential for cooperation. Let's look at water again as an example. Up until now, the states of Central Asia have primarily concentrated on **bilateral** initiatives to reconcile issues in their relations. While such moves can tackle issues in the short term, they are not sustainable because the tensions between the states cannot be considered in isolation (Mosello, 2008) and in fact involve a great number of wider, complicating factors as outlined earlier.

Bilateral
Conducted between two states or governments.

Upon independence, all five of the Central Asian states signed the Almaty Agreement, which committed them to maintaining Soviet-era allocations of water. This reflected the principles of international agreements such as the Helsinki Rules of 1966, and the UN Convention on the Protection and Use of Transboundary Watercourses and International Lakes (Mosello, 1998). This was followed up by further **multilateral** initiatives among the Central Asian states such as the Interstate Coordinating Water Commission (ICWC), the Interstate Council on Problems of the Aral Sea Basin (ICAS), and the International Fund for the Aral Sea (IFAS). However, these have essentially reinforced Soviet-era management and central planning over water in the region, and the problems have continued as states have sought to pursue their own national interests. Thus while attempts have been made to find common solutions, the spectre of conflict remains when considering the role of water in affecting relations between the states of Central Asia. As states that are still relatively new in their exercise of sovereignty, they are keen to preserve their national interests, which are often at odds with those of their neighbours.

Multilateral
Conducted between a number of states or governments; can also denote a multilateral institution, such as the UN or World Bank.

In this case study, you have seen how common **transboundary resources** are a pressing issue due to water being a basic human right. In the next section, you will see how competition between states and contestations over sovereignty have led to increasing diplomatic tension between states in East Asia.

Transboundary resources
Resources shared across one or more state boundaries.

Summary

- The picture of hydropolitics in Central Asia is complex and relations between the states are complicated by:
  - artificial borders that were drawn when the region was part of the Soviet Union
  - industrial and power infrastructure put in place during Soviet times, which means that certain areas are dependent on others for resources, such as water and power
  - regional environmental problems, such as the desiccation of the Aral Sea
  - the fact that the republics of Central Asia are all relatively new as sovereign independent states.

5   Case study 2: South and East China Seas

At the start of the chapter, you read about the dispute between the UK and Spain on sovereignty over Gibraltar and its surrounding waters. Section 4 revealed how changes in geopolitics, specifically the collapse of the Soviet Union and the emergence of new states, cause tensions and conflict when resource domains cross borders.

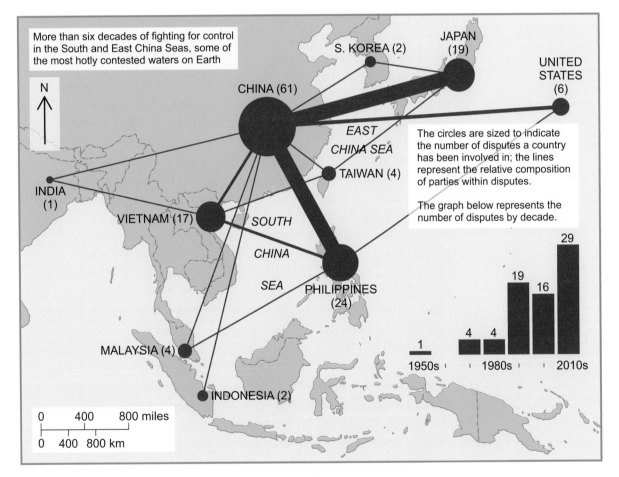

Figure 3.8   A map showing disputes in the South and East China Seas

As Figure 3.8 shows, disputes over access and ownership of areas of the sea and islands within it have grown considerably in the East Asian area, with China involved in the most disputes. These disputes could potentially have far greater international consequences than the disagreement over Gibraltar. They have escalated in recent decades because of the growing economic and political power of Asian countries and the technological ability to exploit resources in the seabed. The Asian region is increasingly powerful in the global economy but these disputes over common resources have become a growing foreign policy concern, for the United States in particular. Since the Second World War the United States has been a guarantor of security for Japan, Taiwan, the Philippines and South Korea. The region accounted for 33 per cent of the world economy in 2007 (compared to 21 per cent and 23 per cent for the United States and Western Europe, respectively) (Denmark, 2010) and the increasing political and economic power of some Asian countries ensures that they have significant influence when it comes to addressing global issues such as climate change.

The South China Sea is bordered by four nation states – Borneo, China, the Philippines and Vietnam – while the East China Sea is bordered by China and Japan. While not of explicit interest here, there is also a third body of water in the area: the Sea of Japan, which connects North and South Korea, Russia and Japan. Diplomatic relations in this area have long been strained but particularly so in recent years. For example, the reignition of Japan's disagreement with China over the Senkaku/Diaoyu Islands in 2012 symbolises Japan's concern about China's growing political and economic might (Klare, 2012). The islands are small and uninhabited but their proximity to shipping lanes, their rich fishing grounds and nearby potential oil, gas and methane reserves make them a significant asset (BBC, 2014). Both Japan and China lay claim to the islands, arguing that they have the right to control them, but the United States recognises only Japan's sovereignty. In recent years, China has been increasingly aggressive in sending vessels and aircraft into the area. Chinese and Japanese fishing vessels have also collided with one another as part of the dispute. The US government has been increasingly concerned with this dispute over sovereignty, urging both sides to negotiate and abide by international law.

Contestation over natural resources is particularly acute as the region is home to only 3 per cent of the world's proven oil reserves and 8 per cent of its natural gas reserves (Klare, 2012). This means that Asian countries have to import the majority of their energy supplies. China, for example, already imports more than half of its oil and Japan almost all of its oil and gas. As Klare has stated, 'according to the US Department of Energy, in the next 25 years, Asia's energy consumption

is expected to grow faster than anywhere else in the world'
(Klare, 2012). This makes the likelihood of tensions over the
sovereignty and rights to exploit resources in resource-rich areas like
the Senkaku/Diaoyu Islands increasingly likely.

As you read earlier in this chapter, UNCLOS allows states to claim a
200-mile extension of sovereignty from the coastline and all of the
countries involved in this region have asserted this right. Indeed, China
has gone further and requested an extension of sovereignty beyond 200
miles into an extensive area of the East China Sea (Klare, 2012). China
has indicated that it considers it to be its right to exploit the oil and
gas resources in the area and has sought to prevent other states from
undertaking deep-sea exploration of potential resources.

The United States has been increasingly drawn into these disputes and
the regional body, the Association of Southeast Asian Nations
(ASEAN), has also tried to mediate in them. Yet it remains to be seen
how equitable and lawful the claims for sovereignty and exploitation of
common mineral resources will actually be. China argues that many of
its claims predate the framing of UNCLOS in 1982, so it should not
be restrained by UNCLOS. It has also pointed out that the US
Congress has not ratified UNCLOS. China claims that there is an
element of hypocrisy in the United States' insistence in China obeying
UNCLOS when the United States has not ratified it. This has led to
concerns that China may start to ignore the treaty altogether and not
abide by the Permanent Court of Arbitration's decisions. As well as
having political ramifications, claiming sovereignty and exploiting the
seabed's mineral resources could have major environmental
consequences if not done responsibly. Disputes over sovereignty and
the common resources in the South and East China Seas are likely to
continue.

Summary

- The politics of the South and East China Seas are increasingly contentious.

- The changing geopolitics of the area – the economic and political rise of China and the comparative decline of the United States – means that countries such as China claim they have the right to access and exploit areas of common resources.

- There is increasing demand for finite resources and energy supplies.

- There is also concern that UNCLOS, as an international governance regime, will no longer be sufficient in regulating the access, ownership and exploitation of the seas in this region.

Conclusion

This chapter has explored how common resources and areas of the world that have been considered to be the common property and responsibility of humankind have come to be managed (and arguably mismanaged) in the 20th and 21st centuries. The sea and inland waters are longstanding examples of global common resources, but they can also encompass other resources such as oil and gas. Following technological developments, these resources can now be exploited. In a world hungry for additional food, minerals and energy to support growing populations, states are increasingly involved in disputes and conflicts over the right to control and exploit these resources. The concept of sovereignty, central to the development of the **nation state** system, has also started to shift and become contested. Common resources have become strategically important, making them the focus of power struggles between states. International and multilateral organisations, such as the United Nations, have played an increasingly important role in trying to define and police rights and responsibilities regarding common resources on a global scale. Yet as power relations among states and geopolitics have changed – for example, the collapse of the Soviet Union creating new states and new borders; the economic and political rise of China; and the comparative decline of the United States – contestation over common resources has become increasingly acute. The outcome of these power struggles could have significant political and environmental consequences for the international community, as illustrated by the case studies of the Central Asian region and the East and South China Seas.

Nation state
A nation that has its own government and exercises sovereignty.

References

Allen, J. (2014) 'Supermarket power: winners and losers', in Allen, J and Blakeley, G. (eds) *Understanding Social Lives 1*, Milton Keynes, The Open University.

BBC (2014) 'How uninhabited islands soured China-Japan ties' [Online]. Available at www.bbc.co.uk/news/world-asia-pacific (Accessed 23 October 2014).

Buck, S. (1998) *The Global Commons: An Introduction*, Washington, Island Press.

Daoudy, M. (2007) 'Benefit-sharing as a tool of conflict transformation: applying the Inter-SEDE model to the Euphrates and Tigris river basins', *Economics of Peace and Security Journal*, vol. 2, no. 2, pp. 26–32.

Denmark, A. (2010) *Security and the Global Commons: Asia's Security and the Contested Global Commons*, Seattle, The National Bureau of Asian Research.

Gleick, P. (1993) 'Water and conflict: fresh water resources and international security', *International Security*, vol. 18, no. 1, pp. 79–112.

Hardin, G. (1968) 'The tragedy of the commons', *Science*, vol. 162, no. 3859, pp. 1243–8.

Homer-Dixon, T. (1994) 'Environmental scarcities and violent conflict: evidence from cases', *International Security*, vol. 19, no. 1, pp. 5–40.

Klare, T. (2012) 'Island grabbing in Asia: why the South China Seas are so tense', *Foreign Affairs* [Online]. Available at www.foreignaffairs.com/articles/138093/michael-t-klare/island-grabbing-in-asia (Accessed 23 October 2014).

Merco Press (2014) 'Spain doubles challenge on Gibraltar waters dispute: summons UK ambassador' [online]. Available at http://en.mercopress.com/2014/07/22/spain-doubles-challenge-on-gibraltar-waters-dispute-summons-uk-ambassador (Accessed 19 January 2015).

Mosello, B. (2008) 'Water in Central Asia: a prospect of conflict or cooperation?', *Journal of Public and International Affairs*, vol. 19, pp. 151–74.

Muckenhuber, D. (2013) 'Breaking the dam: waters politics in Central Asia', *IPI Global Observatory* [Online]. Available at http://theglobalobservatory.org/2013/02/breaking-the-dam-water-politics-in-central-asia/ (Accessed 25 may 2015).

Murphy, T. (2010) 'Security challenges in the 21st century global commons', *Yale Journal of International Affairs*, Spring/Summer, pp. 28–43.

Smith, J., Brandon, M. and Kurtz, M. (2009) 'Block 2: Arctic approach', in *U116 Environment: Journeys through a Changing World*, Milton Keynes: The Open University.

UNEP, UNDC, NATO and OSCE (2005) *Joint Report on Environment and Security: Transforming Risks into Cooperation – Central Asia* [Online]. Available at www.envsec.org/publications/ENVSEC.Transforming%20risks%20into%20cooperation.%20Central%20Asia.%20Ferghana-Osh-Khujand%20area_English.pdf (Accessed 20 January 2015).

Vogler, J. (2000) *The Global Commons: Environmental and Technological Governance* , (2nd edn), Chichester and New York, John Wiley & Sons.

Weinthal, E. (2002) 'The promises and pitfalls of environmental peacemaking in the Aral Sea Basin', in Conka, K. and Dabelko, G. (eds) *Environmental Peacemaking*, Washington, DC,Woodrow Wilson Centre Press, pp. 86–119.

Wolf, A. (1998) 'Conflict and cooperation along international waterways', *Water Policy*, vol. 1, no. 2, pp. 251–65.

Young, O. (1997) *Global Governance: Drawing Insights from Environmental Experience*, Cambridge, MA, MIT Press.

Chapter 4
Putting a price on common resources

by Alan Shipman

Contents

Introduction

What ensures that the self-interested actions of individuals produce harmony rather than conflict? This is a long-standing question among social scientists and some have found a surprisingly straightforward answer: the **price system**. The Austrian economist Friedrich Hayek (1899–1992) expressed the belief that prices set by **free markets** had created the opportunities and incentives that drove sustained wealth creation, especially in North America and Western Europe.

> By using prices as a guide, or as signals, we were led to serve the demands and enlist the powers and capacities of people of whom we knew nothing. It was because we relied on a system which we had never understood and which we never designed that we had been able to produce the wealth to sustain an enormous increase in the world's population, and to begin to realise our new ambitions of distributing wealth more justly.
>
> (Hayek, 1986, p. 1)

Hayek is a key figure in the Austrian school of economic thought, an approach that takes the motivations and actions of individuals as a basis for understanding society. This is associated with a free-market approach, which opposes interference in the setting of prices by agencies such as governments and large corporations. In this view, any efforts to regulate or plan the economy – even if undertaken with good intentions, such as reducing inequality or protecting the environment – are viewed as disturbing the harmony of market-coordinated activity, leading to less (and more unbalanced) wealth for all.

Markets put a price on the things that are bought and sold within a society. These include people's labour, which they can 'sell' to an employer in return for the income that lets them buy things. The advocates of free markets argue that they adjust to match the demand for any item with the supply of it. If demand goes up, prices will rise, encouraging more production. When more supply arrives, prices go down. The relationship between **supply and demand** is a fundamental idea in economics. As economies and populations grow, an increasing number of human interactions take place through markets. These also extend from operating locally to nationally, and ultimately across the

Price system
Prices set in unregulated, competitive markets, used to allocate resources.

Free markets
Assembly of many buyers and sellers who exchange goods and services at competitively set prices.

Supply and demand
A model of how the interaction of supply and demand for a resource determines its prices. Generally, high supply and low demand leads to lower prices, while low supply and high demand increases the price.

Free trade
Exchange of goods and services between countries without taxes (tariffs) or other barriers.

world (as countries commit to **free trade** and remove the barriers to it). The advocates of market economies argue that globalisation strengthens markets' abilities to coordinate people's activities in ways which bring mutual gain, without any need for interference. In this view, markets, the price mechanism, and supply and demand ensure that the self-interested behaviour of all individuals produces harmony and order rather than chaos and conflict. This school of thought does, of course, assume that 'rational self-interest' is the key motivation for all people.

This chapter will explore:

- the relationship between common resource problems and the 'free market'

- the 'tragedy of the commons' and the problem of putting the right price on common resources

- the concept of public goods, and how the problems surrounding them relate to the problem of common resources

- the relative merits of solutions to common resource and public goods problems.

Section 1, 'The tragedy of the commons', examines the concepts of social, external and private costs and benefits in free-market economics, with particular reference to public goods and common resources.

Section 2, 'Distinguishing common resources from public goods', looks at the differences (and similarities) between these two goods, and explores two ways of dealing with externalities here: taxes and privatisation.

Section 3, 'A contemporary application: "owning" carbon emissions', considers the ways carbon emissions, a threat to common resources, have been dealt with in the contemporary world.

Section 4, 'The drive to establish property rights', interrogates the ideas around the privatisation of shared resources further and outlines other ideas about managing common resources.

1   The tragedy of the commons

Free-market approaches are often criticised for allowing individuals to focus on their own interests, with no regard for the wider impact of what they do. This might lead to production and consumption decisions that make sense to the person (or organisation) that takes them, but are collectively disastrous when added to all the other decisions simultaneously taken by others. Supporters of the free market argue 'spontaneous' order arises because market prices give people all the information they need to coordinate and harmonise their behaviour. In the view of free-marketeers, even extreme coordination problems such as the 'tragedy of the commons' can be resolved – and are best resolved – by letting people organise themselves, without political intervention.

1.1   The problem of 'social cost'

Hayek never claimed his was an original view. He traced it to a long line of earlier economists, notably Adam Smith (1723–1790). Smith famously likened free markets and the price system to an 'invisible hand', which guided people's activities as producers and consumers, without any need for the 'visible hand' of government or corporate management. For Smith, free markets enable, and encourage, people to pursue their self-interest – producers seek the highest profits, and consumers seek the greatest satisfaction for the least expenditure (Smith, 1979 [1776]). He believed that free markets would harness the effort and creativity that results from this, and make sure that everyone gets the best deal: by doing what is best for themselves, people end up doing what is also best for society.

By the end of the 20th century, free-market ideas had gained wide currency. They had been taken up in many Eastern European, Asian and Latin American countries in place of attempts at centralised planning for faster development. Governments in Western Europe and the United States had also reaffirmed a commitment to free markets, retreating from models combining planning and a substantial welfare state. Yet as economies (and populations) continued to grow, the dominance of the free market encountered a challenge from the natural environment and its inherent limitations. The earth has scarce resources, whose value might not always be reflected in the price system. If such resources are wrongly priced, or not priced at all, they might not be efficiently allocated and sustainably used in the way that free-marketeers had always predicted.

Hardin's (1968) model of 'the tragedy of the commons', introduced in Chapter 1, turned directly against Smith's 'invisible hand'. Hardin described how freely acting agents could inadvertently ruin their economy, by over-using its common resources. 'The tendency to assume that decisions reached individually will, in fact, be the best decisions for the entire society' is undermined in relation to the commons, whose sad fate is 'the rebuttal to the invisible hand' (Hardin, 1968, p. 1244). For Hardin, the tragedy occurs because individuals' pursuit of their self-interest has damaging, unsustainable collective consequences.

The model of the invisible hand assumes that individuals' actions also provide an 'external benefit'; in other words, a benefit in addition to and beyond those that are just between the buyer and the seller, even if it is not intentional. In this model, companies' pursuit of profit, and consumers' pursuit of satisfaction, lead them to do things that also benefit others in society. For example, companies want to make money for their shareholders; but to do so they have to provide goods and services that consumers want to buy.

However, with a common resource that's in limited supply, one person's increasing consumption does not bring benefits to others: quite the reverse. Land and the natural resources it contains are prime examples, as already shown in Chapters 1 and 2. When one more sheep is grazed on the common, the farmer gets all the extra benefits, while other users lose out. There is a loss of space, and erosion of vegetation and soil, for the rest of the community. These are '**external costs**', imposed by the individual on everyone else outside the buyer–seller relationship.

External cost
An external cost occurs when producing or consuming a good or service imposes a cost upon a third party.

Hardin drew attention to problems that arise when individuals don't have to pay the full cost of their actions. It is then possible for an activity to be in one person's interest but against the collective interest. He suggested that leaving people free to pursue private profit would result in bad social outcomes, like the over-grazing of the commons and the excessive pollution of land, sea and air.

The car provides a way of illustrating this debate (as was introduced in Chapter 1). Individuals may prefer to travel by car because they think it's faster, cheaper and more enjoyable than travelling by train, but in what sense is it cheaper? Private costs – the amount that any one person pays to drive – are direct and clear. Yet these are only some of the costs that the activity – driving – involves. The full or '**social costs**' would include the indirect costs to the community when people drive. Cars create noise, air pollution, congestion and damage to the road. These represent 'external costs', which the whole of society suffers from, or has to pay to remedy.

Social costs
Social cost is the total cost to society. It includes both private costs plus any external costs.

Figure 4.1   Traffic gridlock grips Guiyang, in Guizhou province (China); car ownership levels are outpacing the new infrastructure needed to cope

Those external costs fall on the whole of society; the individual doesn't pay for them alone. This means that an action that is beneficial for the individual is damaging for society as a whole. In other words, the social costs (which are much higher than the individual's private costs) exceed social benefits (which are just the individual's private benefits).

Activity 1

In making a particular journey by car, an individual gets a benefit they value at £15 and pays a cost of £12. But the external costs imposed by their journey work out at around £4. Why might society want to restrict the individual's car use?

Discussion

In this example, the individual benefits from their car journey because private benefits of £15 exceed private costs of £12. Yet the journey causes a loss for society as a whole, because social benefits are £15 (the same as the individual's) whereas social costs are £12 (the private cost) + £4 (the external cost) = £16. The social costs of the car journey, which include both the private and external costs, outweigh the social benefits.

External costs, or 'negative **externalities**', drive a wedge between the **cost/benefit calculation** from an individual's viewpoint and a social viewpoint. The 'commons problem' can now be seen as one that arises when the social costs of one person's actions exceed the private costs (i.e. there are external costs). In this case, there will be a tendency for society's scarce resources to be over-used. Roads are congested, and the air around them polluted, because of the external costs imposed by adding another car.

Externalities
Costs imposed by an individual's activity that they do not pay for (and instead impose on society as an 'external cost'), or benefits conferred by an individual's activity that they do not receive payment for (and instead gift to society as an 'external benefit').

Cost/benefit calculation
A calculation of a course of action that states the action should only be taken if the extra benefit gained is greater than the extra cost.

To put this argument in summary form:

'negative externalities' mean that

social benefit = private benefit

while

social cost = private cost + external cost

So even if the private benefit exceeds the private cost, the social benefit can fall below the social cost (as this is bigger than the private cost).

1.2   Social benefits and externalities

The 'externalities' created by individual actions aren't always negative. Some can also confer external benefits – gains which flow to others too. If a programmer creates some useful 'freeware' that many others can download, or someone brightens up the neighbourhood with their front garden, they create positive externalities.

To put this argument in its simplest form:

'positive externalities' mean that

social benefit = private benefit + external benefit

while

social cost = private cost

So the social benefit can exceed the social cost, even if the private benefit does not exceed the private cost.

Let's suppose that I am worried about my home being flooded by the local river. The only way I can protect against this is to build a flood barrier, which can be raised to keep back the water when it gets unusually high. But the barrier will cost me £20,000 to build, whereas the flood damage will at most cost £10,000. The private benefit (a £10,000 saving) falls well below the private cost of £20,000, so it wouldn't be sensible for me to build the barrier. That's unfortunate – because as well as protecting my home, the barrier would protect 99 other houses in the area, each of which will also suffer £10,000 worth of damage if there's a flood. The *social* benefit of the barrier will be (100 × £10,000 =) £1,000,000. That's well above the social cost of building it, which is the same as the private cost, £20,000. But if everyone approaches this project on the basis of individual costs and benefits, this socially useful defence will not be built.

Whereas negative externalities can lead to individuals taking actions that are harmful from a social perspective, positive externalities can lead to individuals not taking actions that would be beneficial from a social perspective. If decisions are left to individual cost/benefit calculations, there will be too much production of goods and services which impose external costs, and too little production of goods and services which confer external benefits.

Figure 4.2   The Thames Barrier: a socially useful defence

Activity 2

In the example of the flood barrier, is there a way that the costs and/or benefits could be shared across the community, so that the project goes ahead?

Discussion

One way to rescue the flood-barrier project would be to spread the cost across all the 100 households that will benefit from its construction. The cost per home (including my own) will now be £20,000 / 100 = £200, while the benefit per home will still be £10,000. This even spread ensures that private benefits exceed private costs, reflecting the way that social benefits exceed social costs. Another approach might be that I build the barrier myself for £20,000 and then, when it successfully repels a flood, I try to collect contributions from all the other households that I've protected. But that's riskier: they might not pay up, even if they know that I've just spared each of them £10,000 of expense. It's much safer to agree a share-out of costs before the project begins.

Public goods
Goods or services whose production confers positive externalities, liable to be under-provided if people are asked to pay for them individually.

Products and processes that confer large social benefits, like the flood barrier, are often called **public goods.** The name hints at the solution often adopted in such situations: the cost of building them is taken over by the government, or other public authority, so that its cost can be shared (via taxation) across all who benefit. In the UK and other countries, public goods and services are often delivered by private-sector companies, but their provision is still financed by the state.

Unlike the flood barrier in the previous example, education and healthcare can often be bought privately. If they have the money, people can pay for an individual school place or for hospital treatment. Nevertheless, these services are also publicly provided in many countries. They are made free for users, and financed by tax or insurance contributions that are linked to people's income.

One reason for providing these services free of charge, or well below their costs, is that they confer external benefits. The whole community gains when an individual becomes more educated, and is kept free of infectious disease. Another reason is that even if people could pay individually, it is regarded as fairer for the cost to be met collectively. Many societies make a political choice to allocate education and healthcare on the basis of who merits them (which may be everyone), rather than who can afford them.

The existence of public goods isn't universally accepted. Some social scientists have argued that some, possibly all, of the goods and services described this way could actually be bought and sold privately through markets. In some cases a way could be found to 'internalise' any benefit, so that individuals will be willing to provide it privately.

Ronald Coase (1974) takes what seems to be one of the most obvious cases of a public service – a lighthouse whose beacon can be seen by all passing ships. He shows that in the past many were operated by private companies, which made a profit by collecting fees from ships that arrived in port. Similarly, there have in the past been subscription-based fire-fighting services, which would only put out fires in buildings whose owners had paid the necessary fee.

In these cases, it often became difficult or dangerous to restrict the service to individual payers, so private firms give way to public provision. Yet in other cases, goods and services once regarded as 'public' have now been taken over by the private sector. For example, the arrival of cable and satellite transmission made it possible to limit TV signals to households that had paid a subscription, allowing private companies to take over the transmission of televised sporting events, which used to be sent to all households by a public broadcaster.

Figure 4.3   In the past, lighthouses were often operated by private companies

Summary

- The 'tragedy of the commons' can be characterised as a type of problem with resources that are limited in supply. The private costs of someone using such an 'exhaustible' resource do not fully reflect the social cost. Individuals will over-use and exhaust the resource, unless something is done to make their private costs reflect the social costs.

- There is another important category of products for which the social benefits of usage exceed the private benefits. These 'public goods' are likely to be under-supplied if each user has to pay the full cost of consuming them without being rewarded for the external benefits of consuming them.

2   Distinguishing common resources from public goods

Common resources have been defined, so far, as those whose users or consumers impose 'external costs' on everyone else. They have been contrasted with 'public goods', whose providers confer 'external benefits' on everyone else. These external costs and benefits have important effects: if (as some economists and evolutionary psychologists tend to argue) individuals act mainly to promote their own interests, common resources will be over-used and public goods will be under-supplied. However, why do problems of 'external' cost or benefit affect some resources and not others? This can be understood by considering two important characteristics that all goods and services exhibit, to differing extents – exhaustibility and excludability.

2.1   Classifying goods: 'exhaustibility' and 'excludability'

As you saw in Chapter 2, environmentalists have drawn attention to individual actions that impose 'external costs', which the people around them are forced to pay. Such situations appear more frequently as economies and populations grow, making more demands on the planet's finite resources. The occurrence of social costs creates a particular problem with 'exhaustible' resources. Hardin's (1968) 'tragedy of the commons' model maintains that, when it is not possible to make individuals (or individual companies) pay the full cost of using such a resource, it is liable to be over-used and depleted. Such **collective action problems** have, Hardin argued, no 'technical' solution. There is no strategy that individuals can adopt within the 'rules' of the present game that will avert the tragedy. The only option is for the rules to be changed.

Collective action problem
The under-provision of a public good, or overuse of a common resource, caused by a group's inability to coordinate the actions of its members.

The occurrence of social benefits creates a problem with 'public goods'. These are products or services that one individual can't make or buy for themselves without also providing them to others free of charge. They provide an 'external benefit' as well as the private benefit to the person who procures them – such as the flood barrier in Section 1.2. When it is not possible to make those other beneficiaries pay for the external benefits they receive, the incentive to provide public goods is reduced.

Public goods and exhaustible resources can therefore be distinguished by two dimensions that other goods and services tend not to share. These are:

- 'exhaustibility'– the tendency for use by one person to diminish availability to all other people

- 'non-excludability'– the impossibility (except at great cost) of confining benefits to people who have individually paid for them.

Table 4.1 shows a classification of goods and services along these two dimensions.

Table 4.1 Distinguishing commons and public goods

		Exhaustibility	
		High	Low
Non-excludability	High	Common resources (e.g. atmosphere, oceans, national parks)	Public goods and services (e.g. healthcare, education, defence)
	Low	Private goods and services (e.g. shoes, cars)	Golf-course membership, after-school club membership

Public goods such as healthcare and education are affected by positive or negative externalities. The 'commons problem' arises with resources from which it is hard to exclude people (i.e. that are highly non-excludable), and which are exhaustible, so one person's use leaves less for the rest. This combination causes a problem of negative externality, leading to excessive demand and depletion.

People who want to use the resource, but don't want to pay for it, will be able to take a 'free ride' on those who have paid for the resource and can't stop others benefiting from it. So the amount that's provided (if any) is likely to be less than what people want, unless the provider can find a way to collect contributions from all the others who are getting the benefit.

Goods such as golf-course or after-school club membership do not encounter serious externality problems. These are the ones that can most easily be traded through private markets. A mass-produced product, such as shoes or a car, is highly exhaustible: when one person uses it, no one else can. Some products, such as a club membership, are in principle inexhaustible (any number could be issued), but they can still be made excludable (for example, by charging for membership) and this can prevent them losing value by having too many users.

Activity 3

The common resource problem can (in principle) be solved by restricting access to the resource, or by forcing everyone who uses the resource to pay the full cost of doing so. Returning to the example of cars and urban road space, the city of Athens in Greece tried to solve its city centre congestion (and pollution) problem by banning cars with odd- or even-number registration plates on alternate days (while admitting 'environmentally friendly' cars on any day). London has tried to solve the problem by imposing a congestion charge on any car entering the centre in peak periods.

Why is the first solution, which rations access to the scarce resource, often described as fairer than the second solution, which charges for access?

Discussion

The main reason for rationing, as with the odd- or even-number system, is that it gives the same rights of access to everyone; all are equally restricted (except for the rich Athenians who were able to buy two cars, or two sets of registration plates, and drive in every day). The charging approach, used in London, keeps out those drivers who cannot afford to pay, and still gives unrestricted access to those who can pay every time they want to enter the centre.

By definition, the public goods problem cannot be resolved by restricting access to the resource. So the two solutions usually adopted are forcing everyone who uses the resource to pay the full cost; or forcing everyone in the community, whether they use the resource or not, to pay the full cost of people's use. To appreciate the difference between these solutions, think of the ways that different countries pay for healthcare. In the United States, individuals make arrangements to pay the full cost of their treatment by having the appropriate insurance. In the UK, the full cost is met out of tax revenue raised from the whole community. Supporters of the UK system often argue that it is fairer, because people who need more expensive health treatment – for reasons that are usually beyond their control – do not have to pay more than people lucky enough to need little or no treatment. In contrast, both countries finance defence expenditure through taxation on the basis that everyone receives the same benefit from their armed forces.

Although Table 4.1 suggests a distinction between common resources and public goods, this is not always clear-cut. Some resources, such as healthcare or road space, as highlighted in Chapter 1, have elements of both, or move from one category to the other because of a changing balance between supply and demand. Many resources start out with the appearance of public goods, but as the amount of use expands faster than the supply, they might seem exhaustible after all. For example, state-owned motorways appear to be a public good and therefore have low exhaustability when there are comparatively few cars and lorries making long-distance journeys; but they become an exhaustible resource if too many vehicles try to use them.

2.2   Private intention and state intervention

'Externality' problems were already becoming noticeable in Smith's time in the 18th century. They rose in number and impact as industrialisation proceeded, but as well as observing the problem, economists came up with a solution. Private costs can be brought back into line with social costs, and private benefits with social benefits, by 'internalising' the externalities.

How can a society internalise an externality? The obvious solution was to impose a *tax* on individuals whose private costs were below the social cost, and offer a *subsidy* to individuals whose private benefit was below the social benefit. So a factory that dumps pollutants into the atmosphere could be forced to pay a tax equal to the cost of the pollution. This cost would then be 'internalised', in the same way as the costs of the fuel, raw materials and labour that the factory used. A school whose teaching made people into more productive employees, and couldn't recover the costs of this teaching by charging them fees, would expect to be given a subsidy reflecting that additional productivity, 'internalising' the benefit.

The problem of 'negative externality' is expressed as:

social cost = private cost + external cost

which means that

private cost = social cost − external cost

Setting a tax that is equal to the external cost ensures that private cost = social cost. Now (for example) the factory will pay the full cost of its pollution, and will reduce it accordingly. Similarly, in the case of 'positive externality':

social benefit = private benefit + external benefit

meaning

private benefit = social benefit − external benefit

Giving a subsidy equal to the external benefit ensures that private benefit = social benefit. With such a subsidy (for example) one dweller on low-lying land would find it worthwhile to build a flood barrier, from which the whole community will benefit.

Corrective taxes and subsidies are especially associated with the economist Arthur Pigou (1877–1959). The penalty charge on people generating external costs, designed to make polluters pay, is still often referred to as a 'Pigovian tax'. It appears to be a very neat solution to the problem of scarce resource being left out of (or mishandled by) the price system. From this perspective, once the appropriate taxes and subsidies are administered, all prices will properly reflect social costs and benefits, and free-market activity by individuals can once again be trusted to produce the best collective results.

However, Pigou's scheme, although enticing in principle, is difficult to put into practice. How do governments identify the appropriate levels of tax and subsidy? What happens if they get these wrong? The enhanced role of government, in 're-engineering' the price system before individuals started trading, also worried free-marketeers like Hayek, who preferred another approach that didn't require such intervention from the centre.

2.3   Privately owned 'commons'?

Figure 4.4   Ronald Coase (1910–2013)

Long before his interest in lighthouses, Ronald Coase examined the 'externality' problem that troubled Pigou and Hardin, and offered a far more optimistic assessment of how society might solve it. Coase (1960) argued that the tragedy of the commons arises *because* natural resources are treated as a commons. The problem is that when something belongs to everyone, it belongs to no one. Everyone who uses the commons wants it to be protected, but none profits individually from protecting it. The farmer who refrains from grazing another animal will just lose the space to a rival farmer, hurting their own welfare and doing nothing to preserve that of the community as a whole.

This problem can be resolved, Coase argued, if someone takes *ownership* of the commons. This could be one of the farmers, or perhaps a specialist landowner who rents out parts of it to farmers. The owner will then have an economic interest in preserving it, by ensuring its use is sustainable. Because it's now theirs, they will lose out from the destruction of the land. So they will reorganise production to prevent its destruction, even if they must expend time and money to provide that organisation.

Coase offers the example of an arable farmer whose crops are damaged when the neighbouring cattle farmer expands their herd. (Cows sometimes wander across and trample or eat the crops, and it's impossible to fence them in.) If the land is held in common, the problem is hard to resolve. However, if each farmer owns part of the land, they can bargain over it to reach the mutually best outcome. The arable farmer can impose a charge for the crop damage. As this cost rises with the size of the herd, the cattle farmer will limit the herd size to contain the damage. Alternatively, the arable farmer can pay the neighbouring farmer to limit the herd size. Both approaches will optimally limit the size of the herd, and of the external costs (of crop damage) that it imposes. The limit is set at the level where the arable farmer's losses exceed the cattle farmer's gains.

If the negotiations are costless, the outcomes in this example amount to the same, whether the cattle farmer *makes* a payment to compensate for crop damage or *receives* a payment as compensation for not causing damage. So Coase believes that private bargaining (motivated by private ownership of resources) can effectively eliminate a commons problem, regardless of how the rights and responsibilities are assigned. In economic terms it makes no difference whether responsibility falls on the cattle farmer (being made to compensate for crop damage), or on the arable farmer (being made to compensate for limiting the cattle farmer's herd).

Summary

- The many types of goods, services and other resources in a society can be usefully classified by their degrees of 'exhaustibility' and 'non-excludability'.

- Common resources are both highly non-excludable and exhaustible, creating a danger that societies will over-use them because individuals will neglect the external costs of using the resource.

- 'Public goods' are highly non-excludable, but have low exhaustibility, creating a danger that societies will be under-supplied with them because individuals are unwilling to pay for external benefits.

- 'Pigovian' taxes can be used to close the gap between private and social costs.

- In Coase's view, externality problems can be better solved by assigning common resources to a private owner, who can use the price system to bring social and private costs (and benefits) into line.

3   A contemporary application: 'owning' carbon emissions

Section 2 explained that advocates of the free market have always been sceptical towards 'Pigovian' taxes and subsidies, because, even if governments can correctly calculate them, it gives them an excuse to intervene in private transactions. They believe that the government might then be tempted to extend its 'visible hand' into markets that 'don't need' such regulation. Setting such taxes and subsidies at the right levels is difficult. Coase's argument suggested an alternative in which free markets could internalise social costs (and benefits) more reliably, and without state intervention. The influence of these arguments can be seen in the way that governments have sought to curb carbon emissions, since evidence began to grow (in the 1990s) that these were contributing to a serious global warming problem.

Activity 4

The Earth's soil, oceans and atmosphere seemed, for many centuries, to be 'global public goods'. Anyone could use them, and there appeared to be no limit to the resources that could be taken from them or the wastes and pollutants that could be discharged into them. How does the discovery of global warming, due to human activities' greenhouse-gas emissions, lead to a new understanding of the Earth's land, sea and air as common resources?

Discussion

According to scientists who study them, the oceans and atmosphere have reached the limit of their capacity to absorb greenhouse gases without cost. Their pollution-absorbing capacity once appeared infinite, but has now become exhaustible. Further emissions of carbon waste now have a significant social cost, imposed by the impact of global warming. Since it is not possible to bring down the high degree of exhaustibility that the sea and air (as 'carbon sinks') now exhibit, solutions to the problem centre on promoting excludability. This can be done by making polluters pay for what they emit, and/or restricting or banning some activities that lead to emissions.

One solution to greenhouse gas problems might be to impose a 'carbon tax' – an additional charge designed to raise the cost of carbon emissions to the level that polluters would pay if all the social costs were factored in to production. At the time of writing, few governments had put such a tax at the centre of their strategies to curb global warming. Most opted for putting a ceiling or 'cap' on the total amount of carbon emissions. The level at which carbon emissions are 'capped' is then divided into quotas for large emission-producing businesses. However, it is also possible for these quotas or permits to be freely traded between businesses so that one business's emissions 'allowance' can be increased if it purchases a quota from another business that doesn't itself use it.

Under this 'cap-and-trade' system, those producing the carbon emissions will stop doing so if it is cheaper to stop than to buy a permit to allow continuation. Yet if curbing the emission would be very costly in terms of production and profit, they will buy additional quotas to allow production and pollution to continue at the current level. They may also engage in seperate carbon-reduction projects for which an extra quota can be issued. Campaigners for emissions reduction can buy quotas, making them unavailable to potential polluters, if they view the cost of this as less than the social cost of allowing the pollution. In principle, the cap-and-trade approach sets a 'price' on pollution and reconfigures the pattern of production (and pollution) accordingly. The cap-and-trade 'carbon pricing' approach, as an alternative to carbon taxation, has been controversial. As the price of carbon quotas fell, it made it much cheaper to buy extra permissions for pollution than to take any steps to reduce that pollution.

Economists inspired by Coase's thinking developed a radical proposition regarding the tragedy of the commons, and other cases in which private activity has negative social costs. If everything (including the right to pollute) is costlessly tradable, then:

> It does not matter where you place the liability for, say, smoke pollution, because in a world of zero transactions costs the right to pollute will end up in the hands of those who value it most. If breathers value it most they will buy it. If steelmakers value it most they will keep it.

(McCloskey, 1998, p. 367)

When people are completely free to trade, through a system of competitive markets, they will then arrive at the most productive allocation of resources regardless of how property rights (and associated pollution liabilities) are initially allocated. This argument allows followers of Coase to reassert the Smith principle that Hardin called into question. In this view, individuals' pursuit of their self-interest will lead them to promote the collective good.

Once transaction costs (the cost of trading or allocating resources through a market) arise, however, it does start to matter who is made to pay for the pollution. Some penalty-charging or subscription-collecting arrangements will be more expensive and less effective than others. Coase himself drew attention to the pervasiveness of transaction costs, pointing out that corporations exist in order to administer the many exchanges that are too costly or inefficient to carry out in markets. Today, around half of world trade consists of flows through multinational corporations, rather than contractual exchanges between them, because of the extra cost that would arise from such exchanges if conducted through the market.

Coase's theorem shows that there may be more than one way to avert a 'tragedy of the commons' and have tried to show that private ownership would resolve some of the important problems that may arise from communal ownership or public ownership.

Summary

- Some economists believe that, in principle, problems of common resources and public goods can be resolved if their supply is entrusted to private owners, who then have an incentive to negotiate arrangements that 'internalise' the external costs and benefits.

- Two systems to deal with carbon pollution, a common resources problem, are:

  o a 'Pigovian' tax, an additional charge that carbon polluters pay (an example of a centralised solution)

  o a 'cap-and-trade' system, where polluters must pay for their emissions by buying pollution quotas whose supply is limited (an example of a free-market solution).

4   The drive to establish property rights

Chapter 1 suggested that the 'rights' that people first think of, and campaign for, tend to be those associated with fundamental freedoms – like the right to be treated equally, speak freely and enjoy basic security. However, the 'right' to private property is also regarded by some people as essential for the stability and progress of societies. They believe in the importance of letting individuals (and corporations) own resources, and treat them as private property. This is defended even when property holding is very unequal. They reinforce their arguments in favour of 'fundamental' private ownership with the possibility that this private ownership can help to resolve common-resource and public-goods problems, without what they see as politically dangerous and economically inefficient government involvement.

4.1   Privatisation and 'enclosure'

Hardin's suggestion that collectively owned resources were liable to depletion, and Coase's argument that clearly assigned private property rights could help to prevent this, have had a strong influence on national and international policy regarding 'externality' problems. A lesson from their work is that responsibility for the 'commons' must be clearly assigned to one agent (an individual or organisation), which can act as a gatekeeper. In Coase's view, if this agent has a financial interest in preserving the exhaustible resource, then they will manage it so that it does not become exhausted.

For example, consider the grounds and entrance area of a communally owned block of flats. For as long as they belong to no one, the trees and grass get trodden down, the doors bashed and the walls scratched. Any individual who looks after them and repairs them bears the full cost of this, while the benefits are spread across everyone. Yet if one person owns the block, and is allowed to impose a service charge on all the residents, the shared areas get repaired and preserved. As people generally want this, they might not mind paying the charge. For Coase, common ownership lacks the coordination needed to preserve common areas, whereas a private owner can provide this maintenace, and has the financial incentive to do so.

Figure 4.5   Are shared areas better maintained when privately owned?

Such observations have led policymakers in a number of countries to conclude that the absence of clearly assigned and enforceable property rights is a major cause of resources being depleted, or not being developed to their full potential. They have sought to remedy this by creating registers of existing property rights, formally assigning them where they do not already exist, and strengthening the legal system for protecting and enforcing these rights. Organisations that have a stated aim to promote economic development, including the World Bank, have in many countries promoted 'land titling' programmes, which seek to give people clearer property rights over the land they have been farming. Urban land-titling has been given a similar importance, because it gives people an incentive to use land and buildings efficiently. With legally protected ownership of land, buildings and machinery, the owners can (among other things):

- invest in improving or expanding them, knowing that they will be entitled to the extra profit

- use them as security for loans, raising capital to finance improvements

- use them sustainably, rather than running them down for immediate profit in case they are snatched away by people with rival ownership claims.

Rights of ownership may give people the ability and incentive to use resources more productively while managing them more sustainably. Some might argue that, by extension, private ownership is the key step for turning resources into 'capital', which they believe opens the way to modernisation and rising living standards.

Clearer assignment and stronger protection of property rights is often a double-edged sword. They enable the legal owner to protect and develop the resource, but they also exclude others who may have been using it informally and are now barred from doing so. In 16th-century England, landlords who had previously allowed small farmers to till their land began to reassert their title to it, expelling the tenants so as to engage in the increasingly profitable rearing of sheep for wool production. The resultant **enclosure** movement was deeply unpopular at the time – condemned by such observers as Thomas More (2012 [1516]) for pushing the landless peasants into poverty and criminality. However, it can also be argued that enclosure made the farmland more productive – notably by bringing together the smallholders' subdivided strips so that new technology (such as fertiliser and mechanical ploughs) could be applied to them, and by allowing coordinated shifts between cultivation and grazing that kept up the quality of soil, raising cattle weight and crop yields.

Enclosure
An area of land surrounded by a barrier excluding access to it. For example, a fenced compound is an enclosure whereas a village green is common land.

4.2   Ostrom's *Governing the Commons*

Like Coase, the economist Elinor Ostrom (Figure 4.6) also used empirical investigations to find out how different communities actually tackle the problem of over-using exhaustible resources, and under-providing public goods.

Ostrom's influential book *Governing the Commons* (Ostrom, 1990) contains many real-life examples of communities that have successfully rationed the use of exhaustible resources (which she calls common-pool resources (CPRs)) so as to avoid depleting them. Confounding Hardin's pessimism, she identifies 'many institutional arrangements that have been devised, modified, monitored, and sustained by the users of renewable CPRs to constrain individual behaviour that would, if unconstrained, reduce joint returns to the community of users' (Ostrom, 1990, p. 20). This important theory and evidence led to her becoming the first female winner of the Nobel Prize in Economics.

Figure 4.6   Elinor Ostrom (1933–2012) autographs a chair at Kafé Satir at the Nobel Museum in Stockholm, 6 December 2009

Ostrom agrees with Coase that a commons problem can be solved by limiting and assigning rights of access, so that whoever holds these rights has an interest in conserving the depletable resource. However, her research makes clear that limited rights of access need not involve private property rights. This distinction was, in fact, accepted by Coase. Ostrom presents cases in which rights to previous common property are assigned to individuals, and other cases in which the rights are given to collective (cooperative) agencies, or rotated across all community members, with equal effectiveness in preventing excessive depletion.

For example, fishers on the inshore waters of Alanya in Turkey realised in the early 1970s that unregulated fishing would permanently destroy their fish stock. They adopted a system in which, every September, all licensed fishers draw lots to decide on the location at which they can set their nets at the start of the season. They move one location eastwards every day for half the season, and then one location westwards every day for the second half. This ensures that the boats do not interfere with one another's catches, and cannot be moved to the location which is found to have the biggest fish clusters. Fishers were found to stick to this system of rules because they realised it gave them, on a daily basis, an equal chance of casting their nets where most of the fish were; and because it's very easy to detect if anyone has 'cheated' by moving their boat to a location when it isn't their turn (Ostrom, 1990).

Summary

- Assigning rights of ownership can provide a way of managing resources, and small communities can devise and enforce arrangements that ensure sustainable use of their scarce common resources, without needing either state intervention or private ownership.

- Ostrom's influential theory provides evidence that rights can be allocated to individuals and to communities – and that both can be equally effective in limiting resource depletion.

Conclusion

The 'tragedy of the commons' alerted social scientists to the external (social) costs and benefits of private action, and the possibility that negative externalities could cause serious environmental degradation. This challenged the widespread belief, traceable to Smith, that self-motivated individual action would generally have positive social effects. However, rather than changing their philosophical outlook away from private profit-motivated individualism, some economists have re-interpreted the commons problem as one in which profit-motivated action is derailed because private property rights have not been adequately assigned.

This chapter has investigated how 'commons' problems, and those relating to 'public' goods, can be traced to the external effects of individual action. Because 'externalities' are outcomes that are not fully priced, economists have suggested ways in which problems can be overcome by 'internalising' the effects, incorporating them into the price system. This leads these economists to argue that, contrary to the pessimism expressed by its discoverers, the 'commons' problem can be solved by comparatively simple adjustments, without fundamentally departing from a system of decentralised, unregulated private activity. This free-market view is strengthened if externalities are generally small, and if economic progress makes the problems of exhaustibility and non-excludability easier to tackle. Yet worsening environmental problems have led others to conclude that externalities are now pervasive, and require a fundamental departure from current ways of ordering individual behaviour.

> Environmental externalities are pervasive because property rights to prominent classes of natural capital are difficult to enforce and, worse, challenging to define. The wind blows, rivers flow, fish swim, deer flee, birds and insects fly, and even earthworms are known to move.
>
> (Dasgupta and Ehrlich, 2013, p. 326)

Hardin (1968), in framing the problem, argued that it has no 'technical' solution. Even modifying the price signals to encapsulate external costs, or giving people more information about their 'carbon footprint' and other global effects of local action, may not change people's behaviour to avert a tragedy within the current 'rules of the game'. This chapter has shown that some economists can point to suggestions for technical solutions – through the assignment of property rights, or consensual management of common resources. But as problems become wider, and ultimately global, such solutions may be harder to design and maintain.

References

Coase, R. (1960) 'The problem of social cost', *Journal of Law and Economics*, vol. 3, pp. 1–44.

Coase, R. (1974) 'The lighthouse in economics', *Journal of Law and Economics*, vol. 17, no. 2, pp. 357–76.

Dasgupta, P. and Ehrlich, P. (2013) 'Pervasive externalities at the population, consumption and environment nexus', *Science*, vol. 340, pp. 324–8.

Hardin, G. (1968) 'The tragedy of the commons', *Science*, vol. 162, no. 3859, pp. 1243–8.

Hayek, F. (1986) 'The moral imperative of the market', in Hayek, F. and Anderson, M. (eds) *The Unfinished Agenda: Essays in Honour of Arthur Seldon*, London, Institute of Economic Affairs.

McCloskey, D. (1998) 'Other things equal: the so-called Coase Theorem', *Eastern Economic Journal*, vol. 24, no. 3, pp. 367–71.

More, T. (2012 [1516]) *Utopia*, London, Penguin.

Ostrom, E. (1990) *Governing the Commons*, Cambridge, Cambridge University Press.

Smith, A. (1979 [1776]) *The Wealth of Nations*, Harmondsworth, Penguin.

Chapter 5

Indigenous lands and territories: mapping the commons

by Shonil Bhagwat, Nikoleta Jones and Giles Mohan

Contents

Introduction

At the World Conference on Indigenous Peoples held on 22 and 23 September 2014 in New York City, indigenous peoples' land rights were a central concern. This annual conference is hosted by the General Assembly of the United Nations, where the Member States make decisions on important global issues. At this conference, Rights and Resources, a global coalition of non-governmental organisations engaged in forest and land policy reform in Africa, Asia and Latin America, presented a report. This report argued, in the face of rampant tropical deforestation, that land rights of indigenous peoples are essential for the effective protection of many of the world's tropical forests (RRI, 2014). The report highlighted that the recognition of indigenous peoples' land rights can also benefit the mitigation of climate change, an important global environmental issue. It also pointed to the difficulties faced by the world's indigenous peoples whose land is increasingly claimed for industrial development – a kind of development that is beneficial for some but damaging for others.

Although the term 'indigenous peoples' is notoriously difficult to define, according to the United Nations Permanent Forum on Indigenous Issues, indigenous peoples have the following characteristics:

- self-identification as indigenous peoples at the individual level and accepted by the community as their member

- historical continuity with pre-colonial and/or pre-settler societies

- a strong link to territories and surrounding natural resources

- distinct social, economic or political systems

- distinct language, culture and beliefs

- forming non-dominant groups of society

- resolving to maintain and reproduce their ancestral environments and systems as distinctive peoples and communities.

Many indigenous lands and territories are owned, managed and used by communities. In most cases, the communities have a sense of belonging to these places and therefore such lands are seen and maintained as 'commons'. This view that is often challenged by claims from industries and corporations who want to make the land private –

creating enclosures and making the land excludable so that it can be exploited for profit.

The processes of enclosing and commoning occur across the globe. In this chapter you will explore these antagonistic processes, the actors and interests behind them, and the impact on those living in such areas. This chapter refers specifically to indigenous lands and territories, a majority of which are commons. However, not all commons are indigenous lands and are found in many other places. For example, public parks or national parks are also commons, as you read about in Chapter 1. ('Global commons', of course, have a much broader meaning and include, for example, the earth's atmosphere, deep oceans or even cyberspace.)

Common resources are governed in an economy that is increasingly based on private ownership. Being able to decide what happens to 'our' land is a matter of human rights. However, where laws are not equipped to deal with 'informal' ownership, external powers can start to exploit the land. Even seemingly well-meaning attempts at nature conservation that have declared many lands as 'protected' for the greater common good (such as you read about in Chapter 2) can conflict with the needs and wishes of indigenous communities. This chapter looks at the indigenous peoples' struggle in contesting and resisting enclosure. It examines different approaches to managing these resources and the extent to which greater inclusion of local communities in their management is desirable or possible.

Counter-mapping
A response from indigenous communities to challenge the 'official' version of a map that omits certain features of indigenous lands.

Representations of territories and resources are powerful tools in shaping how the use of land is intervened in and understood. The most common and powerful representations are maps and this chapter will develop the material introduced in Book 1, Chapter 4 in thinking critically about maps and processes of mapmaking to better understand the power embedded in them. One of the tools used to resist enclosure is something called '**counter-mapping**', which is also used as a tool for establishing the rights of indigenous peoples over their lands.

This chapter will:

- examine how some parts of the world are made excludable and exploited for profit even when they started off as commons

- look at how the commons can be governed in an economy that is increasingly based on private ownership

- think about maps as representations of territories and resources that help to shape the use of land.

Section 1, 'Counter-mapping indigenous lands', looks at a case study of Dongria Kondh, an indigenous group in Eastern India, to explore the processes of enclosing and commoning in relation to indigenous lands and territories. The case study focuses on the plight of these people who sought to save their sacred mountain and came into confrontation with a powerful multinational corporation. A long battle between the two ended with the indigenous group's victory.

Section 2, 'Governing the commons', focuses on community-conserved areas. These are areas that, in theory, should give greater management power to indigenous peoples but complex governance structures can work against them. These issues are framed using the work of Nobel Laureate Elinor Ostrom, to whom you were introduced in Chapter 4.

1   Counter-mapping indigenous lands

Indigenous peoples' traditional use of common land and Western notions of private property often come into conflict with each other. Demarcation of private property is motivated by the desire to have excludable rights over use and extraction of resources. This requires defining boundaries around privately owned land. The making of boundaries for declaring land private goes hand in hand with mapmaking because maps can help to legitimise boundaries. History is replete with examples of such mapmaking to claim territories. Roger Kain and Elizabeth Baigent in their 1992 book *The Cadastral Map in the Service of the State* trace the development and application of rural property mapping in Europe from the Renaissance through to the 19th century. Cadastral maps are records of property ownership. Kain and Baigent argue that these maps acted as tools for the consolidation and extension of land-based national power and played an important role in the rise of modern Europe. They demonstrate how cartography became a political instrument to serve national interests. Such mapmaking was further 'exported' to the European colonies throughout the 19th and 20th centuries in order to lay claims over valuable land resources. During this process, the European colonisers made detailed maps of these lands and the resources they contained, subsequently claiming a stake over them. The map of European settlements in West Africa in the early 18th century in Figure 5.1 shows how the land-based resources in West Africa were divided between the colonial powers of England, Holland and Denmark.

Forests were one of the most important resources mapped by the early colonisers because timber was an important commodity and one that was necessary for colonial expansion. Timber was used for ship building and the importance of timber as construction material continued well into the post-colonial period, when the newly independent states set out to develop their infrastructure. This infrastructure, however, came at a severe cost to indigenous peoples who lived in and depended on forests for their livelihood.

Nancy Peluso (1995) described a local response to the Indonesian government's disregard for customary forest rights and indiscriminate timber exploitation. This response involved 'counter-mapping' in order to delineate land that the indigenous peoples traditionally managed. Peluso argued that counter-mapping assists indigenous peoples to claim

Figure 5.1 Map of European settlements in West Africa in the early 18th century

their stake over land and resources by showing 'not only what is on a map but what is *not* on it' (Peluso, 1995, p. 386). Counter-mapping can be used to challenge the 'official' version of a map. For example, the official map may omit small settlements or it may alter categories of land or forest management that contradict indigenous peoples' modes of land use. Counter-mapping can be used to challenge these omissions or misrepresentations, proposing an alternative version that is different from the official map. Such counter-maps are often prepared by indigenous groups in collaboration with researchers and non-governmental organisations in an attempt to better represent indigenous knowledge related to resource management. The maps are seen to give an added advantage to communities to encourage them to stand up for their rights to their land, its resources and the right to manage those resources.

Figure 5.2 shows a counter-map prepared through collaboration between the Soliga people in South India and the Ashoka Trust for Research in Ecology and the Environment, India. This collaborative effort produced a counter-map showing six different types of sites that are sacred to the Soliga people. These sites were not recognised in the 'official' version of the map, which simply showed an 'empty' jungle

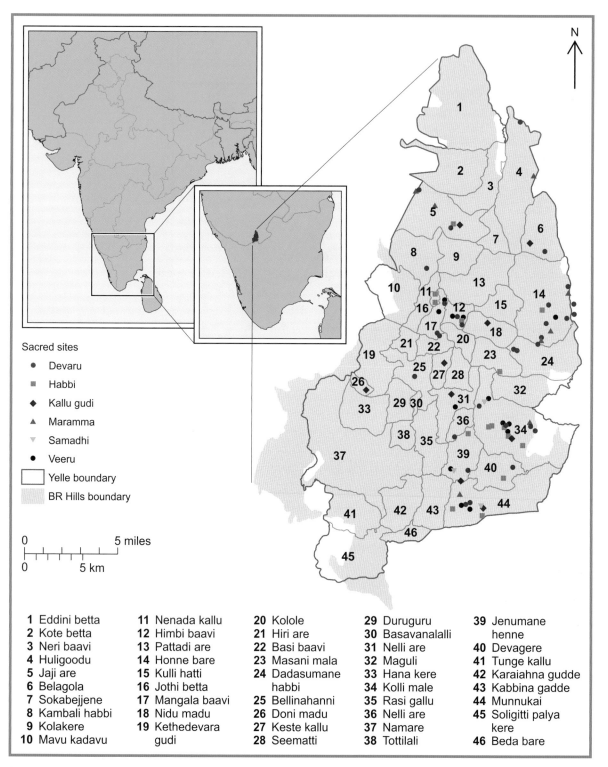

Sacred sites

- Devaru
- Habbi
- Kallu gudi
- Maramma
- Samadhi
- Veeru

Yelle boundary

BR Hills boundary

0   5 miles

0   5 km

1 Eddini betta	11 Nenada kallu	20 Kolole	29 Duruguru	39 Jenumane
2 Kote betta	12 Himbi baavi	21 Hiri are	30 Basavanalalli	henne
3 Neri baavi	13 Pattadi are	22 Basi baavi	31 Nelli are	40 Devagere
4 Huligoodu	14 Honne bare	23 Masani mala	32 Maguli	41 Tunge kallu
5 Jaji are	15 Kulli hatti	24 Dadasumane	33 Hana kere	42 Karaiahna gudde
6 Belagola	16 Jothi betta	habbi	34 Kolli male	43 Kabbina gadde
7 Sokabejjene	17 Mangala baavi	25 Bellinahanni	35 Rasi gallu	44 Munnukai
8 Kambali habbi	18 Nidu madu	26 Doni madu	36 Nelli are	45 Soligitti palya
9 Kolakere	19 Kethedevara	27 Keste kallu	37 Namare	kere
10 Mavu kadavu	gudi	28 Seematti	38 Tottilali	46 Beda bare

Figure 5.2   A counter-map of sacred sites prepared by the Soliga people in South India (Pareeth, 2010)

preserved by the state authorities as a protected area for tigers and other wildlife. The Soliga counter-map helped the group to assert its rights over land following the enactment of the Indian government's 'Recognition of Forest Rights Act' (FRA) in 2006.

1.1 Confronting claims over a sacred mountain

So what happens when indigenous peoples stand up against the forces of capitalist modernisation and fight a battle with powerful corporations offering to buy up their ancestral land to exploit mineral resources underneath it? The Dongria Kondh, an indigenous group of people in Eastern India, seeking to claim rights over their sacred mountain and ancestral land, confronted Vedanta, a powerful multinational mining corporation in 2002 (Figure 5.3). This led to local protests, which subsequently prompted the Indian government to declare that mining activities could only take place with consent from the indigenous group.

Figure 5.3 A general view of the Vedanta aluminum refinery at Lanjigarh, Odisha; note the sacred mountain in the background

Kundan Kumar (2013), a researcher at the University of Toronto, Canada, was involved in this case and describes the confrontation between the Dongria Kondh and Vedanta mining corporation between 2002 and 2013 (see Box 5.1).

Box 5.1   The Niyamgiri struggle

'You can chop off our heads, but you can't take Niyamgiri' (Lado Sikaka, Dongria leader).

Niyamgiri is topped by a rich bauxite deposit, the extraction of which was sought by the London-based Vedanta Resources PLC, a mining and metals multinational corporation. In 2002–2003, Vedanta, with the support of the Government of Odisha, started to build a 1.5 million tonne alumina refinery in Lanjigarh, and applied for permission to mine bauxite from the mountain top. The proposed refinery would lead to full displacement of 118 families, and partial displacement of 1,220 more families in local villages. The land acquisition for the refinery, carried out by the government, had been strongly opposed by the local people. This resistance was supported by local organizations. However, people were still forcibly removed from their houses before they were bulldozed. The freshly-bulldozed site was back-grounded by the brooding Niyamgiri. Repeatedly, people talked about the mountain as if it were a close friend or family member, a local and beloved perpetual presence.

Biswajit Mohanty, a Bhubaneswar-based conservationist, had already filed a complaint against the alumina refinery and the proposed mining with the Central Empowered Committee (CEC) of the Supreme Court of India, on the grounds of violations of forest and environmental laws. Mr. Ritwick Dutta, a young environmental lawyer based in Delhi, was involved in the forest rights movement. Prafulla Samantra, a Gandhian environmentalist used the analysis of the Environmental Impact Assessment Report for the alumina refinery and mining project, to draft a petition that was submitted to the CEC. The author, Kundan Kumar, prepared a brief report on the ecological and biodiversity importance of Niyamgiri. The report was released both through the email networks and on a website called www.epgorissa.org, managed by activists based in Bhubaneswar. These studies and the report documented the environmental and conservational importance of Niyamgiri.

These individuals and their activities eventually influenced the CEC's decision and a recommendation was made to the Supreme Court of India that the mining of Niyamgiri should not be allowed in view of its rich biodiversity. It also noted that the environmental clearance to the refinery was based on wrong information, and recommended withdrawal of this clearance. There was celebration amongst the local people and the activists, as the Supreme Court

(SC) generally tend to accept the recommendations of the CEC. However, additional reports commissioned by the Ministry of Environment and Forests (MOEF), Government of India said that mining could be taken up, with certain safeguards.

Two expert groups constituted by the MOEF subsequently visited the site, and were provided with information by both the company and the activist groups. These expert groups wrote scathing reports criticizing Vedanta, as well as the Government of Odisha, for having ignored the settlement of rights under the FRA. Based on these reports in 2010 the MOEF cancelled the forest clearance and refused to allow mining of Niyamgiri. The decision was challenged in the Supreme Court by Vedanta; and in April 2013 the Supreme Court, in a landmark judgement, said that Gram Sabhas (village assemblies) around Niyamgiri need to decide whether the proposed mining violates religious and other forest rights; and that the same must be considered by the government for forest clearance for mining. At the time of submission of this paper, the preparation for the Gram Sabha meetings is ongoing.

(Adapted from Kumar, 2013, pp. 199–200)

Activity 1

Having read the case study about the Dongria Kondh, think about the following questions:

1   Why was Vedanta, the mining corporation, able to start mining on the land that had spiritual importance to the Dongria Kondh?

2   How did a civil protest emerge to claim ancestral land rights and who was involved in this protest?

3   What factors empowered the Dongria Kondh to put up a fight against a powerful mining corporation?

Discussion

1   'Niyamgiri is topped by a rich bauxite deposit, the extraction of which was sought by the London-based Vedanta Resources PLC, a mining and metals multinational corporation' (Kumar, 2013, p. 199). Vedanta started mining the sacred mountain without consent from the Dongria Kondh because this land was assumed to belong to no one. The mountain clearly did have spiritual importance to the Dongria Kondh: 'Repeatedly, people talked about the mountain as if it were a close friend or family member, a local and beloved perpetual presence'

(Kumar, 2013, p. 199). However, the spiritual importance of the mountain to the Dongria Kondh was not obvious to the outsiders because the spiritual practices of the people did not require drawing boundaries around land.

2   In response to Vedanta's mining operation, the Dongria Kondh put up a fight: 'People were wailing and begging, holding onto their doors and posts, crying that we will go tomorrow … not today … but they were forcibly dragged out by goons hired by the company' (Kumar, 2013, p. 199). The indigenous group was able to gather support from NGOs and civil society, raising the profile of this issue in the media and taking it to the national and even international stage: 'Through our NGO contacts, we came to learn that Biswajit Mohanty, a Bhubaneswar-based conservationist, had already filed a complaint against the alumina refinery and the proposed mining with the Central Empowered Committee (CEC) of the Supreme Court, on the grounds of violations of forest and environmental laws' (Kumar, 2013, p. 199).

3   'Two expert groups constituted by the MOEF subsequently visited the site, and were provided with information by both the company and the activist groups. These expert groups wrote scathing reports criticizing Vedanta, as well as the Government of Odisha, for having ignored the settlement of rights under the FRA' (Kumar, 2013, p. 200). As this was becoming a high-profile case, India's Supreme Court had to take notice and its final verdict was in favour of the Dongria Kondh. The connections with NGOs and civil society organisations finally helped the Dongria Kondh in their struggle: 'In April 2013, the Supreme Court, in a landmark judgement, said that Gram Sabhas (village assemblies) around Niyamgiri need to decide whether the proposed mining violates religious and other forest rights; and that the same must be considered by the government for forest clearance for mining' (Kumar, 2013, p. 200).

1.2   The imbalance of power

The Niyamgiri struggle depicts a remarkable story of an indigenous group's success in claiming back land that it nearly lost to resource extraction by a multinational mining corporation. This is also a complex story that involves a chain of events that led to the Indian Supreme Court's decision not to allow mining to go ahead.

Kumar (2013) provides a detailed timeline of major events related to the Niyamgiri struggle during 1997–2013 (see Box 5.2).

Box 5.2   A timeline of the Niyamgiri struggle

1997: Memorandum of Understanding signed for a mining and alumina refinery project between Government of Odisha and Sterlite (later a subsidiary of Vedanta PLC)

2002: Land acquisition notice to twelve villages in the Lanjigarh area

2003: Land acquisition initiated in the Lanjigarh area, leading to local protests and mobilisation

2004: Rally against Vedanta attended by the affected people, Dongria Kondhs, the socialist leader Kishen Pattanaik, and Gandhian Prafulla Samantra

Petition filed against Vedanta PLC on environment and forest law violation in front of the Central Empowered Committee (CEC), Supreme Court

2005: CEC recommends that mining of Niyamgiri should not be allowed

The 'Vedanta Ravages Through India' report released

EPGOdisha's 'Brief Report on Ecological and Biodiversity Importance of Niyamgiri' issued

Dongria Kondhs come to Bhubaneswar to protest against proposed Niyamgiri mining

2007: The Norway Pension Fund divests in Vedanta on the basis of the recommendations of the Council of Ethics, Norway, in view of the poor environmental and human rights record of Vedanta

CEC issues another report, which recommends that mining of Niyamgiri should not be allowed, and the environmental clearance for the alumina refinery should be cancelled

2008: Protests outside Vedanta's Annual General Body Meeting in London, UK

Supreme Court ignores CEC recommendations and allows MOEF to give clearance for mining on Niyamgiri

MOEF gives clearance in principle for diversion of forest land for mining of Niyamgiri, with a number of conditions

---

Survival International names Vedanta as one of the worst three companies violating indigenous rights

Road blockades by local movement to stop mining equipment from reaching Niyamgiri hilltop

Rahul Gandhi visits Niyamgiri and assures Dongria Kondhs of his support for their fight to protect Niyamgiri

2009: MOEF gives environmental clearance for mining of Niyamgiri, contingent on final forestry clearance

Protests in front of Vedanta Refinery at Lanjigarh

Human chain of more than 10 000 people around Niyamgiri to protest against proposed mining

On recommendation of Forest Advisory Council, the MOEF constitutes the Ramanathan committee to examine whether the provisions in the Forest Rights Act have been followed before giving final clearance for the Niyamgiri forest diversion

UK National Contact Point (UKNCP) for the OCED Guidelines for Multinational Enterprises indicts Vedanta for rights and freedoms of Dongria Kondhs

2010: MOEF's Saxena Committee writes a scathing report citing violations of FRA and other forest and environmental laws by Vedanta and the state government

MOEF declines to give final forest clearance for mining Niyamgiri

2011: Writ petition filed by Odisha Mining Corporation in the Supreme Court to overturn the MOEF decision

2013: Supreme Court, based on its interpretation of the Forest Rights Act, 2006 and the Panchayati Raj Extension to Scheduled Areas Act, 1996, rules that the Gram Sabhas (village councils) shall have a say in whether mining should take place or not; and that MOEF will make its final decision based on the Gram Sabhas' recommendations

(Adapted from Kumar, 2013, p. 201)

This case study raises a number of issues about imbalances in political power. Before you go on to read about them in depth, consider the following questions:

- How does the political power of multinational corporations impact on indigenous stakeholders who are less powerful?

- How might these power imbalances be mitigated?

- How do indigenous communities mobilise support to put up a fight against multinational corporations?

- How might counter-mapping assist these communities to assert their land rights?

Much like the colonisers of the 18th and 19th centuries, Vedanta, the multinational corporation, assumed that the land it planned to mine for aluminium ore was *'terra nullius'*, but the land was in fact inhabited by an indigenous group. In everyday lives in the Western world, it is assumed that individuals have some rights to decide what happens to their own land. There may sometimes be compulsory purchase of land for road construction, for example, but in such circumstances the landowner is compensated. Barring such exceptional circumstances, however, people can in general exercise their right to decide how to use their own plot of land as long as they have obtained planning permission from the authorities. Once this permission is in place, it is normally guaranteed that individuals' rights will not be contravened by the state and that their land will not be trespassed upon by someone else. The right to decide what happens to an individual's land, even though constrained by certain rules and regulations, is partly because the legal systems can protect **property rights** by recognising land boundaries. Being able to decide what happens to their own land is also a matter of people's rights and those rights are strengthened by the legal system in place. The indigenous lands, on the other hand, often suffer from loosely defined boundaries and from the lack of named ownership. They then become vulnerable to exploitation.

The customary uses of land often remain unrecognised in the legal system, meaning that they do not afford the legal protection to the extent that private property does. In order to understand customary uses, the 'outsiders' need to understand how the local people use their land and what arrangements are in place for private or public ownership. Vedanta should have sought what is described as Free, Prior and Informed Consent (FPIC) from the Dongria Kondh, the key stakeholders and the guardians of the land in question, before conducting any resource extraction from the Niyamgiri mountain. This is in accordance with the United Nations Declaration on the Rights of Indigenous Peoples (UNDRIP) Article 10, which states: 'Indigenous

Terra nullius
'No man's land', in common parlance, a Latin expression meaning 'land belonging to no one'.

Property rights
A way of determining how land and its resources are used and owned.

peoples shall not be forcibly removed from their lands or territories. No relocation shall take place without the free, prior and informed consent of the indigenous peoples concerned and after agreement on just and fair compensation and, where possible, with the option of return' (United Nations, 2008).

FPIC is the principle that an indigenous group has the right to give or withhold its consent to proposed projects that may affect the lands it customarily owns, occupies or otherwise uses.

Free and Prior Informed Consent (FPIC)

FPIC implies informed, non-coercive negotiations between investors, companies or governments and indigenous peoples prior to the development and establishment of oil palm estates, timber plantations or other enterprises on their customary lands. This principle means that those who wish to use the customary lands belonging to indigenous communities must enter into negotiations with them. It is the communities who have the right to decide whether they will agree to the project or not once they have a full and accurate understanding of the implications of the project on them and their customary land. As most commonly interpreted, the right to FPIC is meant to allow for indigenous peoples to reach consensus and make decisions according to their customary systems of decision-making.

The right of FPIC is necessary to ensure a level playing field between communities and the government or companies and, where it results in negotiated agreements, provides companies with greater security and less risky investments. FPIC also implies careful and participatory impact assessments, project design and benefit-sharing agreements. FPIC has been widely accepted in the 'corporate social responsibility' policies of private companies working in sectors such as dam building, extractive industries, forestry, plantations, conservation, bio-prospecting and environmental impact assessment.

(FPP, 2014)

Activity 2

FPIC is a great principle in theory, but what are some of the obstacles to it?

Having read the description of FPIC above, list the obstacles that come to mind. Consider who might seek FPIC from the indigenous group in question and who might represent this group.

Comment

FPP (2014) identifies the following factors as some of the obstacles to FPIC: 'On the practical level of carrying out FPIC, it can be problematic identifying who should verify that the right to FPIC has been respected and how this should be done ... Another challenge for indigenous peoples in their efforts to exercise their right to FPIC is to ensure that their systems of decision-making are genuinely representative and made in ways that are inclusive of, and accountable to, members of their communities.'

Despite these obstacles, 'by insisting on their right to FPIC, forest peoples have been able to block plantations and dams planned for their lands and have been able to negotiate fairer deals with palm oil developers, loggers and local government land use planners'.

FPIC is now a key principle in international law and jurisprudence related to indigenous peoples. It is a way of addressing the power imbalance and mitigating the exploitation of the powerless by the powerful. A lack of consultation with the indigenous group meant that the mining activity on the Niyamgiri mountain went ahead without consent from the Dongria Kondh. This led the group to resist the mining activity, which was subsequently deemed illegal by the Supreme Court of India. In other situations the indigenous group would perhaps have agreed to mining if the mining operation avoided destroying a sacred site.

In either case, international law recognises indigenous peoples' right to self-determination – a fundamental principle of human rights law that is recognised by the United Nations Charter. It refers to an individual and collective right to 'freely determine ... political status and [to] freely pursue ... economic, social and cultural development' (Guide to Action, 2014). This recognition gives the indigenous people the right to decide whether or not to condemn the mining activity or to condone it. It also gives them the right to demand that the material benefits of such activity be shared with them.

1.3   The indigenous group's resistance

What could the Dongria Kondh have done to safeguard their sacred mountain before Vedanta came on the scene? From Vedanta's point of view, the 'official' version of the map of the Niyamgiri mountain in 2002 perhaps did not suggest that the mountain was sacred. This 'omission' of the cultural importance of the mountain from the official map meant that the Dongria Kondh had to go to great lengths to win back their claim over the mountain.

Imagine if counter-mapping (Peluso, 1995) had been carried out prior to 2002. Such an exercise would have challenged the official version of the map by representing an 'invisible' cultural tradition. However, counter-mapping commons such as the sacred mountain of the Dongria Kondh is challenging for two reasons:

1   The boundaries of such sacred sites are often fuzzy. Unlike well-defined boundaries of a privately owned property, the boundaries of the commons evolve over time through convention, rituals and practices associated with these sites.

2   The sacred attributes of such sites often relate to very individual or personal experiences of the indigenous peoples. The spiritual practices that take place there are often secretive and are intended to be practised without the knowledge of outsiders, making it very difficult to represent them on a conventional map.

To address these challenges, conventional maps are not sufficient, but new and emerging technologies in digital cartography hold promise. These technologies can facilitate the user to work beyond the two dimensions of a paper map and can also enable a 'mash-up' of various media and the map. Simultaneously, advances in participatory mapping offer opportunities for working with indigenous communities in collaborative ways. At the heart of these mapping methodologies is the spirit of collaboration between researchers and indigenous communities, where these communities are seen as co-researchers. The digital cartographic technology and participatory mapping together can help to address the challenges of mapping indigenous people's sacred sites. Such combinations of methods can help to recognise that indigenous sacred sites are more than points or shapes on the map. They are representations of indigenous cultural heritage – rituals, performances, offerings, folklores, narratives, stories and myths. The technological innovations, particularly the rise of easy-to-use online mapping tools to exploit location-based data, means that anyone can now map. The increasing accessibility of the mapping tools may be a way forward to address challenges of mapping sacred sites.

Robert Kitchin and Martin Dodge (2007) have highlighted the analytical potential of digital mapping to represent qualitative information such as stories and myths that accompany indigenous lands. This form of digital mapping can provide powerful tools for indigenous peoples to show information about their land which is not obvious from a two-dimensional map. However, there is often a mismatch between indigenous knowledge systems and Western digital technologies. Margaret Wickens Pearce and Renee Pualani Louis (2007), two geographers who also have their roots in Native American communities, argue that the challenge for indigenous peoples across the world is to find a way of incorporating digital technologies in their mapping efforts without mistranslating the rich qualitative information that goes hand-in-hand with the maps. Overcoming this mismatch requires close collaboration between the researchers and the indigenous peoples who are most engaged with their ancestral land and have intimate knowledge of it.

It is not just the mapping of indigenous lands that can benefit from these digital technologies. Everyday maps aimed at the motorist or walker, for example, also suffer from omissions because they cannot represent the users' engagement with the space in a two-dimensional form. Also, official maps, such as the British Ordnance Survey maps, have restrictions on their use. For example, the Ordnance Survey website says: 'Ordnance Survey paper mapping is protected by Crown Copyright. We have delegated authority from The Controller of Her Majesty's Stationery Office to decide the terms and conditions under which our customers can copy our paper maps' (Ordnance Survey, 2015). Copying these maps is allowed only if you hold the correct licence. Similar licences are also required to use digital versions of Ordnance Survey maps.

To address these issues, in 2004, British entrepreneur Steve Coast came up with the idea of OpenStreetMap. He was inspired by the success of Wikipedia and applied the principles of free, online, user-generated content to everyday street maps. At the time of writing, the

OpenStreetMap community has grown to over 2 million registered users who can collect data using GPS devices, aerial photography and other free sources, and update Open Street Map to include features that are missing from places they are familiar with (OpenStreetMap, 2015).

Cyber-cartography
The use of mapping tools on the internet to create, edit and modify maps.

Could this '**cyber-cartography**' and digital mapping be of help to indigenous peoples to represent their own version of how their lands are used? These technological innovations hold tremendous power to create more accurate maps of indigenous lands and territories, but the challenge is that such maps, despite their interactive properties, may not always represent everything on the map, particularly the wide variety of ways in which users engage with their everyday spaces, some of which are hard to represent on a map.

Summary

- The process of enclosing and commoning in relation to indigenous lands and territories was illustrated through the case study of Dongria Kondh, an indigenous group in Eastern India.

- The Dongria Kondh people sought to save their sacred mountain and came into confrontation with a powerful multinational mining corporation. A long battle between the two finally ended with the indigenous group's victory.

- The tool of counter-mapping can be used for establishing the rights of indigenous peoples over their lands.

2   Governing the commons

So far you have looked at conflicts arising from the extraction of natural resources from indigenous peoples' lands and some solutions to reconciling these conflicts. Ironically, it is the contemporary approach to nature conservation that comes into conflict with indigenous lands most often. Protected areas are cornerstones of modern-day nature conservation. The Yellowstone National Park in Wyoming, United States, set up in 1872, is credited for being the first protected area in the world (Figure 5.4). Since then this network of nature reserves has expanded rapidly with nearly 160 000 protected areas now covering an area of nearly 25 million km^2 – more than 13 per cent of the earth's land surface according to the World Database of Protected Areas (WCMC, 2014). The focus of this network of protected areas is the conservation of biological diversity, and the argument is that this protection is necessary for saving numerous other species with which humans share this planet. However, many of these areas have often antagonised indigenous peoples, some of whom depend on natural resources from these protected areas for their livelihoods. In this case, one form of governance has unseen or unintended consequences for other forms of land use on which local communities depend. So how can protected areas work with, rather than against, local communities?

Figure 5.4   A US National Park Service sign welcoming visitors to Yellowstone National Park in Wyoming. Established in 1872, this is considered the world's first protected area

A protected area is 'a clearly defined geographical space, recognised, dedicated and managed, through legal or other effective means, to achieve the long-term conservation of nature with associated **ecosystem services** and cultural values' (Dudley, 2008, pp. 8–9).

Ecosystem services
Benefits people derive from ecological processes, for example, freshwater provision, decomposition of wastes, removal of carbon dioxide from the air and production of oxygen by plants, and nutrient cycling.

In 2012, Gustavo Andrade and Jonathan Rhodes carried out an analysis of 55 published case studies from developing countries where local communities lived in the close vicinity of formally protected areas. They wanted to discover factors that minimise conflict between the regulations of protected areas and the interests of the local people. They assessed these case studies for a variety of measures:

- how old the protected areas is

- how large the protected areas is

- whether or not there is a 'buffer' zone around the protected area

- what level of protection is enforced within the protected area

- what is the per-head wealth within the community

- what is the population density in the immediate vicinity of the protected area

- how involved the local community is in the management of protected area.

Their quantitative analysis indicated that the greater the participation of the local community in making decisions about the protected area, the less was the conflict between people and the protected area. For example, in Roviana, Solomon Islands, women in the community decided to get closely involved in managing and monitoring natural resources and set their own rules for access to these resources. This helped to halt illegal activities by members of the community inside strict resource use zones, which were common before the women took charge (Aswani and Weiant, 2004). This and other studies reviewed by Andrade and Rhodes suggest that, if protected areas are to work for nature, then they also need to work for people. Does this mean different forms of protected areas and different ways of managing them?

One of the recommendations that came out of the fifth World Parks Congress of the International Union for Conservation of Nature (IUCN) held in Durban in 2003 was about Community Conserved

Areas, which subsequently became known as 'Indigenous and Community Conserved Areas' (ICCAs). These areas are defined as 'natural and modified ecosystems including significant biodiversity, ecological services and cultural values voluntarily conserved by indigenous and local communities through customary laws or other effective means' (Kothari, 2006, p. 1). What distinguishes these sites from protected areas is that they are predominantly controlled and managed by communities; and there is often a commitment on the part of the stakeholder communities to conserve biodiversity at these sites. This commitment takes the form of various informal means, such as cultural taboos or community protocols regarding access to, or harvesting of, resources at these sites. While this type of informal conservation had been recognised through other international instruments, such as the Convention on Biological Diversity or the UN Declaration of the Rights of Indigenous Peoples, the appreciation of these informal practices as an instrument for conservation of biological diversity was first proposed at the 2003 World Parks Congress.

ICCAs are present on all continents except Antarctica and these sites are privileged over others in providing relatively secure spaces for biological diversity on a human-dominated planet (Bhagwat and Rutte, 2006). Despite the small size of these sites, they are widely distributed; and as unmanaged habitats within highly managed landscapes they provide so-called ecosystem services – benefits that people derive from natural ecosystems. For example, a distributed network of sacred groves might provide the ecosystem service of pollination, beneficial for many agricultural crops. As unmanaged habitats, they might also provide benefits in the form of groundwater storage. In addition, they are also repositories of non-wood forest products, particularly medicinal herbs, which are very important in local healthcare systems.

ICCAs such as the community forest in Figure 5.5 form a network of protected areas informally protected by the communities. These networks are often located in places where no other form of forest protection is possible. As such, they provide valuable ecosystem services to activities such as farming and food production that take place in landscapes surrounding these areas.

Figure 5.5   Villagers from Deulahudi in Odisha District, India, map their community forest to claim their land under the Indian government's 'Recognition of Forest Rights Act', 2006

Therefore, as 'informal' protected areas, ICCAs offer a large number of benefits to local people. While complementing the formal protected area networks, they also provide shelter to species, habitats and ecosystems that are not sufficiently protected within the formal reserve networks. ICCAs, however, are still struggling to be recognised by their state authorities because they are largely governed by customary laws, norms and institutions that are not formally or legally recognised in many countries. As a result, ICCAs are facing a number of threats (discussed in recommendation V.26 from the IUCN World Parks Congress (IUCN, 2005)):

- The ownership of these lands is unclear and insecure.

- The state authorities plan community development projects on these lands that often fail.

- The state authorities can easily de-legitimise customary rights associated with these lands.

- The state authorities do not consult communities when making decisions about the future of these areas.

- The stakeholders of these areas are often seriously disadvantaged in social, economic and political terms.

- The lack of long-term security of these areas is leading to cultural change and the loss of knowledge.

- The commercialisation of resources is challenging some of the traditional modes of resource extraction practised at these sites.

These continuing threats have been attributed to differences between the interests of indigenous peoples and those of state authorities. These differences are reflected in the approach to management of conservation areas by the two groups. The lack of legal recognition of many of these areas also means that they may not always be recognised and respected beyond the stakeholder community. Despite calls for their recognition in international conservation policies, therefore, there are still serious hurdles to their effective and appropriate recognition in national policies and practices.

The well-established models on which present-day economic decisions are made are among the primary reasons why the commons and their governance have not been recognised in natural resource management. Science writer Wendee Nicole contends that:

> policymakers opted for two opposite solutions to protecting the commons: privatize natural resources (leading to '**payment for ecosystem services**' type projects), or have governments lock natural areas up in preserves. The latter usually meant stripping rights from locals who had long used these commons for subsistence fishing or hunting, or in the case of forests, gathering firewood, medicinal plants, and other forest products. Many governments (supported by large conservation organizations) evicted indigenous peoples from their homeland in the belief they damaged ecosystems.

> (Nicole, 2014)

Payment for ecosystem services
A mechanism to pay local people to conserve nature and natural resources on their land so that they continue to provide ecosystem services to the rest of humanity.

Writing about an alternative world-view expounded by Elinor Ostrom, Nicole goes on to suggest that Ostrom's research found that such policies to make natural resources private are unhelpful for their conservation. Ostrom's work on governing the commons highlighted that 'many of the evicted people receive little or no government assistance and end up as **conservation refugees** adrift with nowhere to go and no means to support themselves' (Nicole, 2014).

Conservation refugees
People displaced by the establishment of protected areas for nature conservation.

This demands a change in the outlook towards indigenous lands and territories, and the modes of their management informed by traditional methods. As such, Ostrom (1990) proposed eight design principles for governing the commons (Box 5.3).

Box 5.3   Ostrom's eight design principles for governing the commons

1   Define clear group boundaries.

2   Match rules governing use of common goods to local needs and conditions.

3   Ensure that those affected by the rules can participate in modifying the rules.

4   Make sure the rule-making rights of community members are respected by outside authorities.

5   Develop a system, carried out by community members, for monitoring members' behaviour.

6   Use graduated sanctions for rule violators.

7   Provide accessible, low-cost means for dispute resolution.

8   Build responsibility for governing the common resource in nested tiers from the lowest level up to the entire interconnected system.

(Ostrom, 1990)

Polycentric governance
Having multiple levels of governance in place – with legal frameworks and regulations at regional, national and international levels – alongside local people devising their own systems of natural resource management based on traditional methods and principles of cooperation.

Ostrom used the concept of '**polycentric governance**' to examine the usefulness of her eight design principles. Talking in her Nobel lecture, Ostrom argued:

Designing institutions to force (or nudge) entirely self-interested individuals to achieve better outcomes has been the major goal posited by policy analysts for governments to accomplish for much of the past half century. Extensive empirical research leads me to argue that instead, a core goal of public policy should be to facilitate the development of institutions that bring out the best in humans. We need to ask how diverse polycentric institutions help or hinder the innovativeness, learning, adapting, trustworthiness, levels of cooperation of participants, and the achievement of

more effective, equitable, and sustainable outcomes at multiple
scales.

(Ostrom, 2009, pp. 435–6)

The governance of indigenous lands and territories requires polycentric
arrangements as described by Ostrom. For this to happen, the regional,
national and international policies, laws and regulations need to work
in sync with local governance structures. Such a multilevel approach is
necessary for the governance of these complex 'social–ecological
systems', which have historically come under threat from top-down
modes of regulation.

Summary

- Areas formally protected for nature conservation can come into
  conflict with the commons, such as indigenous lands and territories,
  and specifically community-conserved areas.

- The complex governance structures involved in governing the
  commons can work against allocating greater power to indigenous
  peoples.

- Ostrom proposed the idea of polycentric governance of these
  complex social–ecological systems.

Conclusion

This chapter started by looking at how some parts of the world are made 'excludable' and exploited for profit and, by contrast, how some communities seek to maintain access to land or resources. These commons often come into conflict with enclosures claimed by the politically powerful for profit. The case studies of such conflicts highlighted the fight that 'commoners' have put up against the forces who strive to restrict access to land and its resources.

In many places, laws are not equipped to deal with 'informal' ownership of land, making it easy for external powers to exploit the land. This has been the plight of many indigenous communities around the world. The struggle of the Dongria Kondh with Vedanta was examined in this chapter, as were the practices of 'counter-mapping', which, in many such cases, have proven useful for showing on a map what the 'official' version of the map often ignores. These alternative representations of territories and resources are powerful tools in shaping how the use of land is understood and intervened in.

Ironically, protected areas that are set aside for nature conservation are often the ones that conflict with the rights of indigenous peoples to manage their lands and to use them for subsistence or cultural practices. Research conducted with local communities has examined the possibility of greater inclusion of local communities in the management of protected areas. In doing this, the concept of 'polycentric governance' is commonly put forward, where legal frameworks and regulations at regional, national and international levels operate alongside local frameworks. At the local level, people devise their own systems of natural resource management based on traditional methods and principles of cooperation, as opposed to authoritative governance from the state. This form of authority is better suited to governing the complexity of actors, landscapes and practices that characterise indigenous lands and territories.

References

Andrade, G.S.M., and Rhodes, J.R. (2012) 'Protected areas and local communities: an inevitable partnership toward successful conservation strategies?', *Ecology and Society*, vol. 17, no. 4, p. 14.

Aswani, S., and Weiant, P. (2004) 'Scientific evaluation in women's participatory management: monitoring marine invertebrate refugia in the Solomon Islands', *Human Organization*, vol. 63, no. 3, pp. 301–19.

Bhagwat, S.A. and Rutte, C. (2006) 'Sacred groves: potential for biodiversity management', *Frontiers in Ecology and the Environment*, vol. 4, no. 10, pp. 519–24.

Dudley, N. (2008) *Guidelines for Applying Protected Area Management Categories*, Gland, Switzerland, IUCN.

FPP (Forest Peoples Programme) (2014) *Free and Prior Informed Consent* [Online]. Available at www.forestpeoples.org/guiding-principles/free-prior-and-informed-consent-fpic (Accessed 13 December 2014).

Guide to Action (2014) *Guide to Action* [Online]. Available at www.guidetoaction.org/parker/selfdet.html (Accessed 13 December 2014).

IUCN (International Union for Conservation of Nature) (2005) 'Benefits beyond boundaries: proceedings of the Vth IUCN World Parks Congress', Gland, Switzerland and Cambridge, IUCN.

Kain, R.J.P. and Baigent, E. (1992) *Cadastral Maps in the Service of the State: A History of Property Mapping*, Chicago, IL, Chicago University Press.

Kitchin, R. and Dodge, M. (2007) 'Rethinking maps', *Progress in Human Geography*, vol. 31, pp. 331–44.

Kothari, A. (2006) 'Community conserved areas', *Protected Areas Programme: Parks Magazine*, vol. 16, no. 1, IUCN and UNEP-WCMC, Cambridge [Online]. Available at http://cmsdata.iucn.org/downloads/parks_16_1_forweb.pdf (Accessed 13 December 2014).

Kumar, K. (2013) 'The sacred mountain: confronting global capital at Niyamgiri', *Geoforum*, vol. 54, pp. 196–206.

Nicole, W. (2014) 'Special reporting initiative fellow', *Tipping the Scale: How a Political Economist Could Save the World's Forests* [Online]. Available at http://news.mongabay.com/2014/0529-sri-nicole-ostrom-principles.html (Accessed 13 December 2014).

OpenStreetMap (2015) 'OpenStreetMap stats report run at 2015-04-22' [Online]. Available at www.openstreetmap.org/stats/data_stats.html (Accessed 22 April 2015).

Ordnance Survey (2015) 'Copying Ordnance Survey paper maps' [Online]. Available at www.ordnancesurvey.co.uk/business-and-government/licensing/licences/paper-map-copying.html (Accessed 3 February 2015).

Ostrom, E. (1990) *Governing the Commons: The Evolution of Institutions for Collective Action*, Cambridge, Cambridge University Press.

Ostrom, E. (2009) *Beyond Markets and States: Polycentric Governance of Complex Economic Systems* [Online]. Available at www.nobelprize.org/nobel_prizes/economic-sciences/laureates/2009/ostrom_lecture.pdf (Accessed 13 December 2014).

Pareeth, S. (2010) *Biligiri Rangaswamy Temple Wildlife Sanctuary: Home of the Soligas*, Ashoka Trust for Research in Ecology and the Environment [Online]. Available at www.atree.org/sites/default/files/brt/brtmap_eng.pdf (Accessed 4 June 2015).

Pearce, M.W. and Louis, R. (2007) 'Mapping indigenous depth of place', *American Indian Culture and Research Journal*, vol. 32, pp. 107–26.

Peluso, N.L. (1995) 'Whose woods are these? Counter-mapping forest territories in Kalimantan, Indonesia', *Antipode*, vol. 4, no. 27, pp. 383–406.

RRI (Rights and Resources Initiative) (2014) *Recognising Indigenous and Community Rights* [Online]. Available at www.rightsandresources.org/wp-content/uploads/Securing-Indigenous-and-Communtiy-Lands_Final_Formatted.pdf [*sic*] (Accessed 13 December 2014).

United Nations (2008) *United Nations Declaration on the Rights of Indigenous Peoples* [Online]. Available at www.un.org/esa/socdev/unpfii/documents/DRIPS_en.pdf (Accessed 1 June 2015).

WCMC (World Conservation Monitoring Centre) (2014) *World Database on Protected Areas* [Online]. Available at www.protectedplanet.net/ (Accessed 13 December 2014).

Block 4
Exploring boundaries

Chapter 6

Introducing boundaries and justice

by Sophie Watson

Contents

Introduction

In the first half of this book you have considered how the relationship between human populations and common resources is understood, debated, politicised and managed. You have learnt there is a complex relationship between the notion of 'natural' resources and 'social' resources, and that the boundaries between these can shift and change over time and place. In the second half of this book, the focus moves to the topic of boundaries and their significance in making social worlds. This will entail distinguishing between physical and symbolic components of boundaries and learning how these different types of boundary create senses of proximity and distance, identification and difference. You will see how boundaries can be visible to some people and invisible to others, and also how they can have different meanings for, and effects on, different people depending on gender, race, ethnicity, class, age and many other social characteristics. Through the cases explored, you will discover how boundaries are governed, controlled, regulated and managed in different ways across time and place.

Let's consider a graphic illustration of such a difference, taking the example of a border between countries, which is one specific kind of boundary. The United States shares borders with Mexico in the south and Canada in the north. Yet this is where the similarity ends. The border with Canada is relatively easy to cross, with the appropriate passports. It passes through miles of forests, prairies and mountains, with little sign of high security measures along most of its length (Figure 6.1).

The border between Mexico and the United States offers a stark contrast (Figure 6.2). In order to restrict and contain what is defined as unlawful immigration from Central and Latin America, the border is guarded by more than 20,000 border patrol agents, marked by insurmountable wire fences and is highly militarised with the explicit intention of keeping people out. It is estimated that '300,000 people still enter the United States illegally each year' (Khazan, 2013) and many people are killed on the border attempting to cross from south to north.

Figure 6.1   The border between the United States and Canada

Figure 6.2   The border between the United States and Mexico

Some boundaries are hard, impermeable and fixed, while others are soft and permeable. Important here, as you will discover, is the question of power; who has the power to define boundaries, and who has the power to contest and resist them. The social sciences provide different routes into understanding how boundaries divide the social world, and make distinctions between social groups.

In the chapters that follow you will consider the topic of boundaries through the notion of justice, a concept closely related to rights. Justice is a complex idea that has many meanings and is understood from different theoretical perspectives. Many definitions of justice begin from an understanding of fairness. You will probably all have heard a child crying out 'but it's not FAIR!' and the parent's common answer is 'darling, life is not meant to be fair'. In the following chapters, the specific focus will be on social, criminological, environmental and trade justice, with each chapter paying attention to the various ways that ideas of justice play out in particular contexts. These contexts include the borders between countries, or in the soundscapes of daily life that demarcate public and private places, or in the practices of fair trade. You will be considering the interconnections between these different forms of justice and in so doing you will be learning to employ the valuable social science skills of *debating* and *communicating*. As a social scientist, you need to learn how to explore different perspectives, weigh up their relative merits and participate within debates about them. Part of your role as a social scientist is to be able to communicate effectively and to make an informed intervention into debates.

In this chapter you will be focusing on the city as a way to explore diverse boundaries, the theme of justice and the usefulness of debate.

This chapter will:

- introduce the complex nature of boundaries
- develop an understanding of different notions of justice
- begin to explore the importance of debating and communicating as social science skills.

1 Boundaries and the city

In this chapter, and the four that follow, you will encounter different kinds of boundaries. You will discover that boundaries are complex and can be physical or symbolic, fixed or fluid, and visible or invisible.

Activity 1

Can you think of one example of each of the following types of boundary:

- physical – a boundary that has a material presence

- symbolic – a boundary that exists in the imagination, or through an individual or group giving it a meaning

- fixed and impermeable – a boundary that is permanent and difficult to cross

- fluid and permeable – a boundary that shifts and can be passed through

- visible – a boundary that can be seen

- invisible – a boundary that cannot be seen?

For each of these examples, think about for whom your particular example might matter, such as women or older people. In the sections that follow, you will find answers to this question.

Boundaries are constructed and maintained across almost every setting in the social world, offering a way of ordering and regulating social life. This chapter takes as its setting the contemporary city to explore diverse and varied forms of boundary. In particular, you will be encouraged to explore physical and symbolic boundaries.

- Physical boundaries are those that have a material presence, such as walls or bollards. These are usually visible, although there are instances where you might not see them, and more often they are fixed rather than permeable.

- Symbolic boundaries are boundaries that are imagined or are created by the particular meaning we attach to them, such as the qualities we assign to people that belong to different social groups. Symbolic boundaries are not typically visible.

1.1 How boundaries operate

The city can be thought of as a space that concentrates differences through its density of people interacting in their daily lives, often with a high intensity. This high intensity of interaction was considered by an early German sociologist, Georg Simmel (1903), who argued that city living resulted in over-stimulation and an excess of emotion for individuals, leading them to withdraw from city life. Living in cities today does indeed demand a high level of interaction – in the streets as pedestrians, in our cars as motorists, as well as in our work and consumption activities.

For individuals, groups or communities seeking to make sense of city living, drawing boundaries around the home or the community to which they belong is one response. In such circumstances, erecting boundaries might be a matter of choice. For example, people who choose to live in privately owned gated communities represent this kind of boundary-making in the city (which shall be discussed further later in the chapter), while gay people who choose to live and work in a defined part of the city in close proximity to each other might represent another.

Are these two cases the same? Both are clear examples of people segregating themselves out of choice, but their reasons for doing so may be different, as might be their power to do so. Historically (and sometimes still today), gay people were harassed in public, so separating themselves into specific localities in the city might be as much about self-protection as about the celebration of a minority lifestyle.

Other examples include that of a council housing estate that has a reputation (which may or may not be an 'urban myth') for high levels of crime, where few outsiders choose to cross the boundary into the estate. Is this boundary operating to protect those who are resident, or to keep people out? Or what about a disused piece of land that becomes popular for young skateboarders, and which gradually becomes 'their territory'? Why might an older woman feel unable to enter? These are just some illustrations of the different kinds of boundary you might encounter in the city.

An important question for you to consider is how and why boundaries operate in different ways.

Peter Marcuse (2000) makes the point that the bases of separation between different parts of the contemporary city – ethnicity, lifestyle, class, race, religion and sexuality – have very different impacts on the city. Marcuse suggests that as a general rule:

- divisions by class and race tend to be hierarchical, involuntary, socially determined, rigid, exclusionary and incompatible with a democratic city life – although often legitimated as cultural divisions

- divisions by ethnicity and lifestyle tend to be cultural and voluntary, individually determined, fluid and non-exclusionary, and consistent with a democratic city life.

Activity 2

Marcuse's framework is useful, although there are some problems with this formulation as it stands. Can you think what these might be?

Discussion

In the first set of divisions, it depends what side of the divide you are on. If you are the group to impose the boundary, then the divisions are not involuntary. Similarly, where groups can choose to live separately on the basis of life style or ethnicity, it is different from the situation where it is the only route to feeling safe in the city. Central to these divisions are questions of power and income.

Summary

- Boundaries divide groups from one another.

- They are used by different groups for different purposes and with different effects depending on who the groups are and where the boundaries are placed.

- Boundaries can be matters of choice, or forms of enforced segregation.

- Boundaries might operate to provide protection for some people while being spaces of exclusion for others.

The chapter will turn now to explore some specific cases of boundaries and boundary making in the city.

2   Physical boundaries

Physical boundaries come in many forms such as walls, barriers, gates and barricades. This section looks in particular at a type of physical boundary that separates private residential housing from the wider urban environment.

Figure 6.3   An example of a gated community

An increasingly popular trend across the globe is the flight of households from mixed city spaces into self-segregated homogeneous housing enclaves – gated communities (Figure 6.3). This section considers how these gated communities create physical boundaries between different groups living within the city. Sarah Blandy et al. (2003, p. 3) provides this definition of the gated community: 'Walled or fenced housing developments to which public access is restricted, often guarded using CCTV and/or security personnel, and usually characterised by legal agreements (tenancy or leasehold) which tie the residents to a common code of conduct.'

Activity 3

Jot down what you think are the attractions of these gated communities. What kind of boundaries do they illustrate? Do they have different meanings for different people?

Discussion

What you might have considered is that gated communities provide safe and secure spaces for people away from the turmoil of the city, where people perceive others who are different from them as threatening and potentially dangerous.

The boundaries that exclude others from these residential enclaves are several: at the physical level, there are usually gates or high, electrified fences. These boundaries are visible, fixed and not at all permeable. There is also a whole suite of material practices that construct boundaries, from the showing of identity cards at the gates to driving into an electronically controlled private garage. These practices work to minimise contact with threatening, unknown others, thereby building an imagined sense of security and community. Yet there is another kind of boundary at stake here that is less visible, and this is economic: the people who can afford to live in these gated communities are those with high incomes, since these are usually expensive places to live. This represents a boundary of exclusion that is invisible but equally powerful.

In 2004, there were 1000 gated communities in England (Atkinson and Flint, 2004, p. 9), with most clustered in the South East. The segregation of residential areas represents an attractive commercial venture for developers, who can increase their profits with the promise of safety and security to their residents. According to *Building Balanced Communities* (Minton, 2002), 65 per cent of 18–24 year olds, and 44 per cent of those over 65, think that gated communities are a 'good thing', acting to provide greater security. Some residents claim that concern about crime was their main reason for choosing to live in a gated community (Minton, 2002).

The new popularity of gated communities is thus profoundly embedded in a climate of fear and the search for greater security that characterises the contemporary city.

Mixophilia
A term coined by the sociologist Zygmunt Bauman to refer to the ways in which the city prompts the feelings of attraction and tolerance toward strangers.

Mixophobia
A term coined by the sociologist Zygmunt Bauman to refer to the fears brought about by spatial planning that separates, isolates and homogenises, causing people to not want to mix with others.

Zygmunt Bauman is a significant figure in sociology and, in his terms, the attraction of these residential enclaves, as they are sometimes called, represents a spatial shift in the city from '**mixophilia**' to '**mixophobia**', where city residents are increasingly reluctant to live alongside those who are different from themselves (Bauman, 2003). According to Bauman, mixophobia is a widespread response to the overwhelming variety of lifestyles and differences that people encounter each day in the city streets, and to those 'accumulated anxieties [which] tend to unload against the selected category of "aliens", picked up to epitomise "strangeness as such". In chasing them away from one's homes and shops, the frightening ghost of uncertainty is, for a time, exorcised' (2003, p. 26). It is mixophobia, he suggests, that drives individuals into self-segregation in walled and fortified enclaves. Like many others, Bauman attributes this drive towards similarity and sameness to the fact that people in cities are overwhelmed and discomforted by the strangeness and unknowability of others.

Summary

- Boundaries in gated communities that exclude others are visible and fixed.

- Gated communities can be seen as embedded in a climate of fear and a result of the search for greater security.

3 Symbolic boundaries

In this section, you will be looking at symbolic boundaries – those boundaries that may not be as visible as physical ones, but which have particular significance and meaning to certain groups or individuals in the community.

Activity 4

You have begun to see how one kind of boundary (around a gated community) operates in the city to exclude some groups but include others – those who we think of as more like ourselves.

Now take a moment to reflect on some examples of *symbolic* boundaries in your nearest city and jot these down. How do these boundaries operate to exclude some groups and not others?

Discussion

There are many boundaries that are symbolic and less visible in the city. These kinds of boundaries operate in different ways.

There might be visual signs that you are entering an area which belongs to a particular community; for example, rainbow flags in a gay area (Figure 6.4), or different languages on shop fronts, such as in Chinatown. A group of people might frequent an area on a regular basis and be highly visibly present, making it 'their own'. You could think here of public spaces that young people take over for skateboarding and which many people are fearful of entering. Though there is no visible or physical boundary of exclusion, the fact that the space has been claimed by a particular group perceived as threatening operates to construct a boundary.

The Jewish *eruv* offers a fascinating illustration of a symbolic boundary. For Orthodox Jews, Sabbath is the day that is set aside for rest and calm away from the fast pace of weekday life, which involves a cessation of labour of various kinds. Various restrictions are laid down in Jewish law imposing prohibitions on the Sabbath, which include the carrying of objects from private domains to public domains and vice versa. These public domains include streets, thoroughfares, open areas, highways and so on. Private domains are homes and flats in residential

Figure 6.4   Birmingham Gay Village

areas that are enclosed and surrounded by a wall. In these private areas, carrying of objects on the Sabbath is permitted.

The purpose of the *eruv* (or enclosure), which in Hebrew means 'mixing' or 'joining together', is to integrate a number of private and public properties into one larger private domain for the purposes of the Sabbath so that activities normally allowed only in the private domain can be performed (Valins, 2000, p. 579; Watson, 2005). Once an *eruv* is constructed, individuals within the designated area are permitted to carry and move objects across what was hitherto a private/public boundary. This may include anything from the carrying of house keys, to the pushing of a stroller or wheelchair. The construction of an *eruv* is thus of particular relevance to women with small children and people who are frail or disabled, or in other words those effectively excluded by age, gender or infirmity from public spaces on the Sabbath.

The practice of demarcating an *eruv* has been used by Orthodox Jews for 2000 years. For an area to be reconstituted as a private domain, it must cover a minimum of 12 square feet and be demarcated from its surroundings by a wall or boundary of some sort. Already existing boundaries such as fences, rivers, railways or even rows of houses can serve as the basis for the *eruv*, but where the boundary is not continuous or is broken, for instance, by a highway, a boundary line must be constructed to maintain the enclosed space. To construct the enclosure, an *eruv* can use existing poles in the street (such as telephone or electric cable poles) or new poles can be erected. These are joined either by existing wires (usually the lowest in place) or by a new wire, made from material such as fishing line or plastic cable, which is usually very difficult to see (Figure 6.5).

Figure 6.5   An example of an *eruv* wire

In the construction of *eruvin* (the plural of *eruv*) in the UK and the United States, these almost invisible boundaries have become sites of contestation even though their intrusion on the street landscape is minimal (Vincent and Warf, 2002). There are *eruvin* in many urban areas across the globe and they vary in size from a small front yard of a single household to a large building such as a hospital (allowing Orthodox Jewish medical staff to work on the Sabbath), to ones that match the boundaries of whole cities, as is often the case in Israel. The largest *eruv* in the UK is in Barnet in North London (Figure 6.6).

Figure 6.6   Map of the *eruv* in Barnet, North London

Typically, *eruvin* are patrolled the day before the Sabbath to ensure the enclosure is intact and wires are not broken, as they cease to function once a gap has emerged. The *eruv* boundary is unlike other boundaries in that when it ruptures, nowhere inside is safe or unaffected.

In many cities the formation of the *eruv* has been hotly contested by different groups for different kinds of reasons, even though it is largely symbolic and usually very difficult to see. The arguments are many and various, including from non-Jewish people who don't want their area to be defined by a boundary not of their making, even if it is a symbolic one. Orthodox Jews have argued that this is a boundary that is not supported by the true Jewish religious texts, and is simply being used by the more liberal Jews to give them permission to go out into the public arena on a Saturday rather than observe traditional customs. The fierceness of the debate illustrates how powerful symbolic boundaries can be. What the *eruv* also reveals is how boundaries can have different meanings for different people depending on who they are. Though the boundary can barely be seen, the fact that it matters to people makes it as forceful as a boundary that is physical and clearly visible.

Summary

- This section has shown two very different examples of boundaries in the city: one physical, visible and hard to permeate; the other symbolic, permeable and largely invisible.

- Despite these differences, both mean different things to different people, and have the potential to allow some people in and keep others out.

4   Justice

Justice comes in many forms. If you think back to the discussion so far, the question of justice in the city is ever present. Is it, for example, just and fair that those with higher incomes separate themselves off into protected residential areas? Or should governments intervene to oppose these developments and encourage people to intermingle in the residential spaces of the city? With the example of the *eruv*, you saw how different ideas about the right to create this symbolic boundary had the power to define and restrict the movements of certain groups of people on the Sabbath. Justice is a complex issue that is open to debate with many different ways of interpreting justice or judging what is fair. What is deemed fair for one individual or one society may not be considered fair if one takes into account the needs or experiences of another person or society. Context matters.

For Nancy Fraser (a leading social scientist in the field of politics and philosophy, depicted in Figure 6.7), justice means 'parity of participation' or, put another way, justice means that all individuals ought to be in a position 'to participate as peers in social life' (Fraser, 2009, p. 16). Many people see the equal distribution of resources as a key dimension of justice. Yet the objective of seeking equality for all does not always mean distributing resources equally, as individuals and groups of individuals are different. For someone to participate equally in society, they may need access to different resources or given differential treatment to be on a level playing field with others. For example, special resources might need to be allocated to disabled people in particular circumstances for their full participation in social life.

So it is important to remember that when justice is mobilised as an idea that applies to everyone – a universal notion of justice – there is always the potential that some groups in the population are marginalised or excluded. Women have often contested notions of justice on the basis of gender, while racial minorities have sought to show how notions of justice might only apply to, for example, white people and ignore racial and other inequalities.

Figure 6.7   Nancy Fraser, New School for Social Research in New York

Fraser has gone on to argue that, as the world becomes more globalised, it is no longer possible to treat justice in one state alone. Rather, issues of justice cross national boundaries and borders:

> …decisions taken in one territorial state often have an impact on the lives of those outside it, as do the actions of transnational corporations, international currency speculators, and large institutional investors…Faced with global warming, the spread of AIDS, international terrorism and superpower unilateralism, many believe that their chances for living good lives depend at least as much on processes that trespass the borders of territorial states as on those contained within them.

> (Fraser, 2005, p. 70)

Fraser's arguments here are particularly salient for the topics that you will be exploring in the rest of this book, where issues such as border crossing or fair trade are very much situated in the wider global, rather than national, context.

Another well-known theorist on justice is John Rawls. In his influential text, *Theory of Justice*, he argues:

...no one knows his place in society, his class position or social status, nor does anyone know his fortune in the distribution of natural assets and abilities, his intelligence, strength, and the like. I shall even assume that the parties do not know their conceptions of the good or their special psychological propensities. The principles of justice are chosen behind a veil of ignorance... They are the principles that rational and free persons concerned to further their own interests would accept in an initial position of equality as defining the fundamentals of the terms of their association.

(Rawls, 1971, p. 11)

Activity 5

Reflect for a moment on how you might define your own place in society compared with those around you. Do you find it difficult to imagine where you are likely to be in 20 years' time?

Do you make your mind up about what is fair on the basis of your own interests, or on the basis of aiming for wider equality?

In Rawls' view, not knowing these facts about oneself – what he calls a 'veil of ignorance' – leads to principles that are fair to everyone, since if we do not know where we are going to end up in our own society, we are likely to try to cooperate in developing a system of justice that will treat everyone fairly and which will be mutually acceptable.

Rawls' views have been widely discussed among philosophers and political theorists. One critique of his position comes from Amartya Sen, another prominent theorist, who argues that:

Rawls' idealized theory excludes too much of what we should care about: the person's real position in the world, as well as parts of the world which are not included in Rawls' closed system of the state.

(Bird-Pollan, 2002, p. 102)

These multiple perspectives on justice pose interesting challenges for the social scientist. As you move through the chapters that follow, remember that justice is debated and it is your role to draw on social science evidence to interrogate and substantiate claims about fairness in the social world.

Summary

- The notion of justice is complex and contested.
- Justice involves ideas about redistribution and equality.

5   Overview of Chapters 7 to 10

This introduction has covered:

- the complex nature of boundaries which act to both include and exclude people

- two different types of boundaries: physical boundaries and symbolic boundaries

- the complex and contested notion of justice

- the role of the social scientist to debate and communicate, drawing on social science evidence to interrogate and substantiate claims.

This chapter has presented some of the challenges and tensions that characterise debates about boundaries: the different forms of boundaries in the city, which have differentiated effects on people's daily lives. It has also introduced the complex and contested notion of justice, which can be used in different contexts with different meanings. The chapters ahead will explore these issues in more detail and, in doing so, will draw on, and encourage, a debate on a range of environmental, political and economic ideas. You will also be introduced to several different notions of justice:

- **Social justice**: this sees justice in terms of the distribution of wealth, opportunities and privileges within a society, where social institutions such as health, welfare and education exist to enable people to live a rewarding life and contribute fully to society. Central to this version of justice is mutual obligation and responsibility. In Chapter 7, Steve Garner and Sophie Watson explore how immigration borders operate unfairly to give some people freedom of movement and opportunities while restricting others.

- **Criminal justice**: this defines the institutions and practices that are concerned with preventing and mitigating crime, administering punishment and rehabilitation to those who contravene the laws of a specific country, as well as protecting those accused of committing crimes against the potentially abusive powers of the police or institutions of prosecution. In Chapter 8, Victoria Canning explores 'border criminologies' and 'crimmigration', and you will look at the growing trends in the criminalisation of immigrants. In particular, you will explore how this impacts on women, men and children fleeing persecution and seeking asylum.

- **Environmental justice**: environmental harms and hazards impact different groups in society in differentiated ways across time and space. Environmental justice aims to mitigate these harms through the enforcement of environmental regulations, laws and policies. In Chapter 9, George Revill explores soundscapes and you will see how symbolic boundaries formed through sound have differentiated and unequal social and spatial impacts.

- **Trade justice**: this concept refers to giving all countries fair and equal access to international trading markets because it is believed that trade is fundamental to lifting people out of poverty and distributing wealth and resources within and between countries. In Chapter 10, Katy Wheeler explores the notion of fair trade and asks you to evaluate different pathways to trade justice.

References

Atkinson, R. and Flint, J. (2004) *Fortress UK? Gated Communities: The Spatial Revolt of the Elites and Time–Space Trajectories of Segregation*, Research Paper 17, Bristol, ESRC Centre for Neighbourhood Research.

Bauman, Z. (2003) *Liquid Love: On the Frailty of Human Bonds*, Cambridge, Polity.

Bird-Pollan, S. (2010) 'Review of Amartya Sen, *The Idea of Justice*', *Public Reason*, vol. 2, no. 2, pp. 102–8.

Blandy, S., Lister, D., Atkinson, R. and Flint, J. (2003) *Gated Communities: A Systematic Review of the Research Evidence*, CNR paper 12, Bristol, ESRC Centre for Neighbourhood Research.

Fraser, N. (2005) 'Reframing justice in a globalizing world', *New Left Review*, vol. 36, pp. 69–88.

Fraser, N. (2009) *Scales of Justice: Reimagining Political Space in a Globalizing World*, New York, Colombia University Press.

Khazan, O. (2013) 'Mexico is getting better, and fewer Mexicans want to leave', *The Atlantic* [Online]. Available at www.theatlantic.com/international/archive/2013/04/mexico-is-getting-better-and-fewer-mexicans-want-to-leave/275064/ (Accessed 2 June 2015).

Marcuse, P. (2000) 'Cities in quarters', in Bridge, G. and Watson, S. (eds) *The Companion to the City*, Oxford, Blackwell.

Minton, A. (2002) *Building Balanced Communities: The US and UK Compared*, London, Royal Institute of Chartered Surveyors.

Rawls, J. (1971) *Theory of Justice*, Cambridge, MA, Harvard University Press.

Sen, A. (2009) *The Idea of Justice*, Cambridge, MA, Belknap Press.

Simmel, G. (1903) 'The metropolis and mental life', in Bridge, G. and Watson, S. (eds) *The Blackwell City Reader* (2002) Oxford, Wiley-Blackwell.

Valins, O. (2000) 'Institutionalised religion: sacred texts and Jewish spatial practice', *Geoforum*, vol. 31, pp. 575–86.

Vincent, P. and Warf, B. (2002) '*Eruvim*: Talmudic places in a postmodern world', *Transactions of the Institute of British Geographers*, New Series vol. 27, pp. 30–51.

Watson, S. (2005) 'Symbolic spaces of difference: contesting the *eruv* in Barnet, London and Tenafly, New Jersey', *Environment and Planning D: Society and Space*, vol. 23, pp. 597–613.

Chapter 7

Immigration and borders: people, policies and processes

by Steve Garner and Sophie Watson

Contents

Introduction

There are few areas of social policy which inspire as much debate and argument as immigration. It is frequently a topic that appears in the headlines of the tabloid newspapers, such as this one in the *Daily Mail*: 'Immigration – what a mess! 50,000 in Britain illegally are missing, minister says we'll never control our borders' (Drury, 2014) or this one, in the *Sun*: 'You're a soft touch: Immigrant on £14k benefits refuses full-time job' (the *Sun*, 2013). If you read tabloid newspapers, you might well have the impression that all British people are against immigration. Those against immigration might mobilise all sorts of arguments, such as the claim that there aren't enough jobs to go round for those already in Britain or that there isn't enough housing or welfare provision to extend access to those who have only recently arrived. In contrast, policymakers and others arguing for immigration might do so on the basis that there are gaps in the labour market to be filled, or that there is a need to increase the population. Arguments in favour of immigration vary across different historical periods and different countries. However, immigration policy is never neutral and almost always contested in one way or another, as you will see.

Activity 1

Take a moment to note down your views about immigration to the UK at the current time. What do you think the important issues are to consider in an immigration policy? Keep your notes and when you have finished the chapter look back to see if your views have remained the same.

In this chapter, you will be exploring this contentious issue in social policy, and hopefully will come to understand that immigration is far more complicated than some of the tabloid headlines would have us think. The chapter will look at immigration as an area for social policy and ask a number of questions:

- What is at stake in immigration and for whom?

- How did immigration become a topic that was regulated by government policies?

- What factors impact on immigration policy?

Throughout the chapter, you will see that immigration centrally concerns borders, which themselves are intimately connected to the notion of boundaries. As you saw in Chapter 6, *Introducing boundaries and justice*, borders can be physical in the hard sense of fences and barriers, such as those cutting across the United States where it connects to Mexico. Or the borders might be softer, with a material and physical presence in the form of, say, counters where passports must be shown, but where, if you have the right passport for travel, you may be quickly waved through. Immigration policy plays a key role in boundary making, acting to construct, police and defend borders. However, as you will see, sometimes those defended borders may not correspond to the geographical ones.

You will also learn that borders shape people's lives in ways that are to a greater or lesser extent fair and just, and as such are an important component of what is called 'social justice'. This is a term which is used in a number of different ways to describe the fair distribution of wealth, opportunities and privileges in society. It concerns public services, such as education, social welfare, healthcare and employment rights, which can lead to a fairer and more equal society. Social justice can also be enabled through forms of regulation of free markets and progressive taxation directed at a fairer distribution of wealth, resources and equality of opportunity.

This chapter will develop your understanding that:

- immigration is a complex process which is never neutral
- borders mean different things to different people
- borders are implicated in relations of power
- immigration policy changes over time and place and has to be understood in specific political and social contexts
- immigration policy is a social justice issue where people are treated differently from one another.

Section 1, 'Immigration as social policy', explores colonial and European migrations.

Section 2, 'Immigration policy in practice: filtering entry across borders', looks at North America and the UK in relation to the role of immigration policies in nation building.

Section 3, 'Policy-making and postwar migrations', examines **postcolonial** migration into Europe and North America, including the Schengen Agreement.

Section 4, 'What policy does to immigrants: categories, boundaries and justice', considers how government policy produces different categories of immigrant, where some migrants have greater rights than others or greater access to resources.

Section 5, 'The controlling state? Border control in the 21st century', briefly highlights some emerging trends in the ways that governments manage immigration in the early 21st century.

Postcolonial
(1) Dating from the period of decolonisation ending in the 1960s.

(2) Relating to an area of multidisciplinary study that analyses the variety of ongoing cultural legacies of colonialism and imperialism.

1   Immigration as social policy

For centuries, people have been moving from one part of the world to another for a wide range of reasons. For example, for some people, moving to a new country offers the promise of new and greater economic opportunities. For others, however, moving out of the country in which they were born is their only hope for survival. Those who live in war-torn countries sometimes need to seek refuge in another country. The patterns of movement between different countries have changed over the course of history and are shaped by different factors. For many centuries, Europeans migrated to other parts of the world such as America, Canada and Australia. Since the Second World War, the direction of migration has changed as a result of persecution and poverty, which have brought people to Europe seeking survival and safety.

At one time, migrants typically had a colonial relationship with their chosen country, but increasingly, as a result of cheap airfares, recruitment practices and refugee policies, there are new immigrant communities who have had no prior connection to the countries in which they settle. For example, countries such as South Korea and Malaysia, which are economically successful and have growing labour-market opportunities, are increasingly places where in-migration exceeds out-migration, i.e. there is net immigration.

The national context where immigration takes place is always different and so is important to explore. In more wealthy and developed countries, there is usually a system of social welfare in place for those who pay taxes, although this was not the case before the second half of the 20th century. Much of the heated debate about immigration, as you saw from the headlines at the start of the chapter, is around whether it is fair or not to allow migrants access to welfare resources. Yet there is another side to this debate, which does not hinge on immigrants' access to welfare benefits, but which concerns the positive benefits of immigration for the general welfare of the longer-established population. Many Western societies of high economic development have an aging population and a low birth rate. This means that as the population gets older, more people of working age are required to pay the contributions that provide for pensions and more health services. Immigrants to these countries can thus play a positive role in this regard, if they are in employment.

Figure 7.1 Lampedusa, October 2013 – the bodies of more than 360 shipwrecked migrants await burial

As the gaps between the most developed and the most underdeveloped countries in the world grow, the stakes of crossing borders for those from the least developed countries rise. It is becoming more difficult to obtain visas to access the EU and North America and, as a result, immigration without the proper documents has increased. There has been a rise in human smuggling as people are forced into finding more dangerous methods of entry. You may well have read stories about the migrants in Calais waiting to jump onto lorries at night, or even hiding themselves in the undercarriages of aeroplanes, or being packed into leaky boats to cross rough seas. People are literally dying – on a regular basis – to get into Europe, North America and Australia. So while most nations' decisions about their own immigration policies are often insular, there are significant global and regional dimensions to the issues that are unlikely to be resolved at national levels.

1.1 Colonialism and European migrations

It could be argued that the history of mankind is the history of migration. Various theories about the geographical origins of human social life suggest that people first migrated out of Africa into other continents between 100,000 and 600,000 years ago. According to these theories, the Americas were the last continents to be inhabited by people and this happened between 12,000 and 16,000 years ago.

These theories give us a very different perspective on the migration that has taken place in more recent centuries, notably the mass movement of people out of Europe into the 'New World' between 1500 and 1945. Looking back to these mass movements of early humans, these more recent migrations could be seen as simply another stage in a process that has been taking place since humans inhabited the earth, rather than as an exceptional phenomenon; though of course, each historical period differs and has differing implications for the migrants involved.

The principal direction of mass migration for four and a half centuries was from Europe into the 'New World' of colonies such as Australia and the United States. Historian David Eltis (1983) estimates that over 50 million Europeans emigrated to the Americas in the 19th century alone, and 60 million in the period 1815–1932. Many of these early migrants left home never to return. One Irish writer describes what a hard life it was:

> Though life in Ireland was cruel, emigrating to America was not a joyful event … it was referred to as the American Wake for these people knew they would never see Ireland again. Those who pursued this path did so only because they knew their future in Ireland would only be more poverty, disease, and English oppression. America became their dream … They left in droves on ships that were so crowded, with conditions so terrible, that they were referred to as Coffin Ships.

> Even as the boat was docking, these immigrants to America learned that life in America was going to be a battle for survival. Hundreds of runners, usually large greedy men, swarmed aboard the ship grabbing immigrants and their bags trying to force them to their favorite tenement house and then exact an outrageous fee for their services. As the poor immigrant had no means of moving on, they settled in the port of arrival. Almshouses were filled with these Irish immigrants. They begged on every street … No group was considered lower than an Irishman in America during the 1850s.

> (Kinsella, 1996)

Estimates of total global migration in the colonial period (1500–1945) are well over 100 million.

Why, you might ask, did so many Europeans migrate to unknown lands?

Activity 2

Before reading the next section, take a moment to jot down what you think the reasons might have been for European migration during this period.

Discussion

There were many reasons for migration. As trade and commerce began to develop between European nations and the developing colonies, migration was fuelled by people looking for economic opportunities or taking up new job possibilities in the administration or government of the new colonies. In many other places in the Americas, the voluntary migrant population was supplemented, then overtaken, by enslaved labour drawn from the West coast of Africa.

Indeed, migration was not always a choice, and the link between punishment and mobility goes back centuries (maybe millennia if we include the Israelites of the Old Testament). Migration has always been on a spectrum between the free and unfree – the convicts, the Africans forcibly removed as slaves and to a lesser extent, the poor Europeans who worked alongside them for short periods before they were given pay-offs (indentured labour). Even after the abolition of slavery, people from Asia, especially India and China, migrated under similar circumstances (unpaid labour followed by grant of land or a cash sum).

Summary

- Migration is a complex process that is all about power – the power to choose and cross borders and then settle, or the lack of power to do so.

- Migration is by no means a neutral process and borders operate like other boundaries – to include some people while excluding others.

2   Immigration policy in practice: filtering entry across borders

Figure 7.2   A travel document issued under the Canadian Head Tax Act (1885)

Despite all the migration from one part of the world to another, historically it was not an issue that was discussed much publicly. In the last part of the 20th century, everything began to change as immigration became an object of public discussion and legislation – in other words, *immigration policy* was born.

The first immigration policies were:

- very much to do with **race**

- sometimes about exclusion

- sometimes about nation-building.

When trying to understand modern immigration policies, it is important to try to unravel the intentions behind them.

At the time when immigration policies became central to public discussion, there was a dominant view that different races had different characteristics and capacities. Many believed that the current political

Race
A very contested term, the dominant social science understanding of 'race' is that it is the social interpretation of biology and culture. Race is thus social rather than biological, and therefore can differ in meaning from one site to another and from one period to another.

and global balance of power reflected a natural hierarchy of races, with people in the most developed countries at the top. As a result, some elites, such as politicians, understood the world as being mostly driven by the distinctions between people (and their cultures) and based policies on them. Rationales for economic development co-existed with the idea of either keeping your country's population racially homogenous or expressly improving its composition.

In the next section you will be introduced to the notion of immigration policies as both forms of exclusion and as examples of nation-building.

2.1   Exclusionary immigration policies

Let's look at the first batch of immigration policies: the 1882 Chinese Exclusion Act (United States) and the 1905 Aliens Act (UK).

2.1.1   The North American 1882 Chinese Exclusion Act

In the United States and Canada in the 1880s, immigration legislation was federal (involving all the states) policy and was motivated by public opinion and some labour unrest over Chinese immigrants being employed on public works in the Pacific states (California and British Columbia). Chinese migration had been going on for decades, specifically as people were recruited to build roads and railways, while others prospected for gold, or set up small businesses, such as laundries. Campaigns against these migration streams argued that not only were the Chinese taking work from US citizens and Canadians, but also corrupting their lifestyles (US Department of State, 2015).

Activity 3

Can you think of which groups in the UK are being blamed for taking work away from British-born people in the early part of the 21st century?

In what ways are they seen as corrupting what some call the 'British way of life'?

Comment

The groups that are blamed for taking work from British-born people are often those who have arrived most recently to undertake jobs that British-born people are not prepared to do. Thus, for example, many Eastern Europeans in the first decade of the century came to the UK to work as agricultural labourers, picking fruit or digging potatoes for very low wages.

New immigrants are often blamed for corrupting the 'British way of life' when they engage in their own cultural or religious practices, which differ from those of the dominant culture.

Indeed, by the mid-1870s there was already an exclusion act (1875 Page Act) in place that sought to limit the number of Chinese immigrants, which effectively linked Chinese women to prostitution and therefore a moral threat to US men. This Act reduced the number of Asian women migrants. In 1882, the US government banned Chinese migration for ten years, though the ban actually remained in place until the 1940s.

Public opinion thus had, and continues to have, an important impact on the decisions to implement policy – combining racist ideas with economic imperatives. As you saw in the tabloid headline at the beginning of the chapter, the *Sun* newspaper was mobilising public opinion in an attempt to persuade politicians to change their immigration policy.

As the numbers of migrants to North America rose, so the need for an immigration policy became more pressing. The Ellis Island (New York) processing facility opened its doors in the 1890s to formalise immigration procedures. This was the busiest immigration portal for over 60 years.

2.1.2   The British 1905 Aliens Act

The UK has had a long history of migration in addition to waves of settlement from other parts of Europe. London had a population of people from the African, Caribbean and the Indian sub-continents numbering in the thousands as early as the 18th century. The British 1905 Aliens Act was the first immigration legislation in the UK. It had a different objective from that of the United States – here the aim was to stem the flow of poor Jewish refugees from Eastern Europe (which was then part of the Russian empire), who had been fleeing the pogroms (violent concerted attacks on Jewish communities) since the 1880s. Many fled to North America and Western Europe. Some escaped to Britain.

In the early 20th century, immigrants were once again seen as undercutting wages in some industries, leading to demands and lobbying by the trade unions and some politicians for immigration legislation to stop this flow. Others feared the development of 'ghettos' in London, Leeds and Manchester where the opponents of Jewish immigration alleged that 'alien customs', such as working on Sundays, were challenging the 'British way of life'. You might have heard similar comments about migrants living in your area.

The campaign gathered cross-class support and in 1905, the Aliens Act enabled customs officials to refuse entry to Jewish arrivals in 'steerage class' (those with the cheapest tickets) on boats, who could not prove they had sufficient funds to sustain themselves in Britain. The 1905 Act was superseded by a much more restrictive update in 1914, aimed at keeping out potential fifth columnists (e.g. spies and subversive groups) in wartime.

2.2   Policies for populating land

Not all immigration policies were aimed at keeping people out; some were intended to draw people in, and a preference for European migrants was expressed. In the UK, as a result of British colonialism where countries such as India were subject to British rule, channels were opened up for migration from former colonies.

Elsewhere, newly independent Latin American states (like Brazil, Uruguay and Argentina) sought to expand their economies through massive immigration. In this period of overtly racial ideologies, moves to Europeanise the population by encouraging immigrants were not generally viewed as impractical or unethical. European migrants were associated with industriousness, civilisation and modernity, in contrast to the elites' view of indigenous Americans, Africans and Mestizos (those of mixed European and indigenous American heritage) as uncivilised, backward and lazy. Argentina, for example, encouraged the immigration of Europeans in the second half the 19th and early 20th centuries. It attracted 6.5 million people (1840–1930), increasing its labour force by 86 per cent in the period 1870–1910 (in the United States, it was 24 per cent). European migration to the rest of the world continues to this day, mainly in the form of highly skilled migration, as the next section will explore.

Thus immigration policies are a relatively new idea aimed at filtering entrants to territory and regulating their conditions of stay. The precise rationale of the filter is specific to each country's historical experiences, but racialised difference was a key variable spoken about freely, which was the case until the postwar period.

Activity 4

1   Which one of these was *not* a rationale for early immigration policy?

   (a) Protecting the labour market

   (b) Keeping the population stock racially European

   (c) Responding to public campaigns against immigration

   (d) Overpopulation.

2   Which one of these statements about immigration is true?

   (a) Race was not a factor in deciding immigration policy until the postwar period.

   (b) Immigration has been a policy area since Europeans first arrived in the Americas.

   (c) Britain's first immigration act was a response to lobbying.

Answer

1 D; 2 C

Summary

- Immigration policies involve hierarchies of power consisting of those who make the immigration policies and those who are subject to them.

- Immigration policies were often concerned with race, and sometimes exclusion or nation-building.

- Immigration policies had different rationales in different places at different times.

3   Policy-making and postwar migrations

The post-Second World War migration picture is quite different from that of the pre-war period for several reasons:

- large-scale immigration from the developing world into the economically developed world takes off

- immigration policy constructs official categories of migrant that are internationally recognised, and treated differently in law

- destination countries have strong welfare states where benefits are available to those making contributions.

In other words, the migration picture becomes much more complex and more regulated from this point onwards.

Immigration policy-making is not a discrete area, but connects with issues of employment, residence and citizenship, and social integration. Policy regulates the crossing of borders and the conditions under which those crossing remain in this new territory. In this chapter, however, the focus is on the border-crossing element of policy.

Analyses of policy-making tend to stress a number of factors, or variables, such as which actors are involved in the process, whether policies are made at local, national or supranational levels, and the immigration history/culture of the receiving country. In the following sections, you will look at examples of policy from the EU and the UK, where national and supranational levels of regulation work together.

3.1   Postcolonial migration into Europe

In the postwar period, many colonial countries began to claim independence. Nevertheless, from the late 1940s into the 1960s, countries such as the UK, France, Belgium and the Netherlands recruited migrants from former colonies to help rebuild, and gradually expand, their economies. The migration to these countries thus built on already established linguistic and cultural ties. Those countries which had had small colonial empires, such as Germany, developed new lines of migration with nations which had weaker economies such as Turkey, Italy and Yugoslavia, making bilateral agreements with their governments to allow workers to come to Germany on fixed-term contracts. In most cases, it was the Ministry of Labour or Employment that oversaw migration. This demonstrates that in policy terms, immigration was viewed essentially as a solution to labour-force shortages at this time.

3.2   Europe and the Schengen Agreement

A union of European nations was established in the 1950s (as the Common Market) to avoid further war in Europe and realise the free movement of goods and people. In 1986, some of the member states of this union (now known as the EU) set up a pilot scheme in which internal borders were abolished, so that movement between those nations was easier. This was called the '**Schengen Area**' (see Figure 7.3) and was later extended. Further agreements mean that for EU nationals, movement, residence and employment within the Schengen Area (plus the UK and Ireland, which are not signatories to the Schengen agreements) is very easy. Even if you have never heard of this agreement, if you have ever travelled to Europe, you will probably have noticed that EU nationals are given access to a faster route through passport control where the officials look at all EU documents together.

Schengen Area
According to the European Commission Directorate General for Migration and Home Affairs, the Schengen Area affords 'free movement of persons as a fundamental right guaranteed by the European Union to its citizens. It entitles every EU citizen to travel, work and live in any EU country without special formalities. Schengen cooperation enhances this freedom by enabling citizens to cross internal borders without being subjected to border checks' (DG Migration, n.d.).

What impact has this had on immigration policy?

1   All the EU nations, to some extent, have their immigration policy set at a level above the national parliament (i.e. the *supranational* level). All the regulations applying to Schengen, such as residence rights for other EU nationals, are agreed by a Council of Ministers at EU meetings.

2   EU countries cannot easily limit the right of other EU nationals to cross their national borders.

3   While the internal borders of the EU (inside the Schengen Area) have become easier to cross for European citizens, the external borders have become much more difficult to cross for people without EU passports ('non-EU nationals', or 'Third Country nationals' in official language).

Figure 7.3 The original Schengen Area, 1986

You have now seen that immigration policies are rather complicated and rule-bound, but what is the reality for real people in real places? The next section looks in more depth at the UK's policies on Eastern European migration, which should give you a better sense of the more complicated and messy realities of policy over a period of time.

3.3 Case study: Polish migration to the UK

The 2011 census showed that more than 500,000 people in the UK speak Polish, making it the third most-spoken language after English and Welsh. While the majority of Polish migrants arrived after 2004, what many people don't realise is that the story goes back to the early postwar period. Many Polish people ended up in the UK during the Second World War and joined the British armed forces, or had their own sections of them. When the war ended, many settled here and others, mainly people displaced by the fighting, came under various public works schemes as 'European Volunteer Workers' (EVWs). In 1947, Parliament passed a 'one-off' law, the Polish Resettlement Act, granting rights of residence to around 200,000 Polish nationals. At that stage, Poles constituted the largest single group of migrants to the UK.

In 2004, the European Union admitted ten new 'accession' countries, eight of which are in Central or Eastern Europe. Polish people made up the majority of migrants in all three of the countries that immediately granted access to the labour markets that year (the UK, Ireland and Sweden). It is difficult to precisely measure the inflow and outflow of EU nationals (who no longer require visas to cross the UK border). At the 20111 census (ONS, 2011), there were just over 500,000 Poles resident in th UK, with a workforce of 450,000. However, it is important as a social scientist to interrogate the evidence presented and to question statistics that you read in newspapers or hear on the television. This 500,000 figure includes people who settle permanently, those who work for a short period then return to Poland, and those who come frequently to do seasonal labour.

You might well have heard stories of Polish migrants as 'welfare scroungers', but the evidence contradicts these negative stereotypes. The figures also showed that people from Poland have the highest employment rate of any group in the UK (81.2 per cent), which is almost 20 points higher than the figure for people born in the UK (ONS, 2014). Moreover, EU migrants since 2001 are far more likely to have a degree than other groups. Other research (Dustman and Frattini, 2014) demonstrates that migrants as a whole tend to pay more into social security than they take out, suggesting that EU migrants arriving since 2001 have added almost £5 billion into social security. Not surprisingly, there are always criticisms of such surveys, which revolve around what is included or not included in the calculations. Though these more technical issues might be the subject of debate, what often lies behind the discussions are strong emotions and personal viewpoints: immigration is a subject of intense and controversial political debate. As social scientists, it is important to be aware of the ways in which different political narratives emphasise different elements of the data and evidence to strengthen their argument.

Since 2004, one of the main immigration debates has concerned Central and Eastern European migrants taking 'British jobs' and accessing welfare. As the largest national group (at least 0.5 million UK residents), Polish migrants are at the heart of this debate. Typically these arguments flourish in times of economic insecurity when people perceive public resources to be dwindling, and the perceived competition by migrants for jobs is likely to be the source of tension. Polish people are spread quite evenly across the country, with larger pockets in London, Leeds and Manchester, but also in less urbanised areas, where there was little migration in the postwar period until the early 21st century, when EU migrants arrived to work in agriculture.

Figure 7.4 Polish people form the largest group of Eastern European migrants in the UK

Though Polish people are seen by the UK population as generally hardworking and in some ways easily integrated, they are also associated with driving down wages, drinking too much (and then driving), generating mess and symbolising stigmatised ways of living (Dawney, 2008). The picture of Polish people's experience is similarly ambivalent. They identify the UK as a place where they can, with the right language skills, progress and make a better life than in Poland, but they face hostility, and verbal and physical violence (Lee-Treweek, 2010). They are also aware of their position in British society, sometimes being considered 'white', and therefore higher up the racialised hierarchy than black and Asian British people, but also liable to be categorised as 'backward foreigners' (Ryan, 2010; Moore, 2013).

The experiences of Polish migrants in Britain illustrate that migrants can simultaneously be:

- useful to the economy – placed in specific sectors in the 1940s and then filling lower-skilled jobs in the 21st century

but also

- the subject of controversy and hostility – for some, Polish people represent how EU rules for migration override those of the UK (no controls can be placed on this migration), and therefore symbolise the state's failure to protect British workers' jobs and social security. The establishment of Polish as an important language underscores some popular arguments that the UK is changing character.

Summary

- After the Second World War, immigration from less economically developed countries to the developed countries takes off, constructing internationally recognised official categories of migrants.

- The Schengen Agreement (1986) allows free movement of people in member states within Europe.

- Polish immigrants, though useful to the UK economy, are the subject of controversy and hostility.

4   What policy does to immigrants: categories, boundaries and justice

You will now have some idea of how the rationales for immigration policy differ from one place and time to another, even contradicting each other at some points.

In Chapter 6, 'Introducing borders and justice', you were introduced to the block theme of justice. How boundaries are made, who has the power to make them, and the effects of this boundary-making are questions that concern social justice because of the way they include and exclude certain people. In order to understand immigration policy, it is important to acknowledge that the policy itself creates distinctions between immigrants and then categorises them as such. Though the system purports to be 'fair', inevitably judgements are made which favour some groups and individuals over others. In this sense, immigration is squarely in the field of social justice, where access to resources and freedom of movement and settlement are unequally distributed.

Activity 5

What do you think should be the main criteria used for allowing migrants to settle in the country?

Note down your answers and look back at them after you have read the whole of this section.

In the next sections, you will explore the four principal categories of migrant:

- economic migrants

- highly skilled migrants

- asylum seekers and refugees

- students.

4.1   Economic migrants

These are people who migrate in order to work. Typically, this category accounts for most migrants and comprises those requiring a visa and those not requiring one. Nations usually have agreements with other nations about whether their citizens require visas to travel, work and reside in them. The European Union currently practises a system of allowing freedom of movement to other EU nations' citizens as part of the Schengen Agreement (see Section 3.2).

Activity 6

What is now the main distinction made between groups of migrants in the European Union's immigration policy?

Discussion

The main distinction is between EU nationals (who do not need visas to travel, reside or work) and non-EU nationals (who do).

The United States, on the other hand, has a 'green card' (residence and work permit) lottery every year, with millions of entrants, and where tens of thousands of green cards are distributed. As a guide, the United States admitted just under half a million green-card holders to permanent residence in the country in 2012.

Historically, visas have been issued on the basis of gaps in the labour force, and of the nationality of the applicants. Some countries are excluded from access to visas and others are subject to more scrutiny than others. Indeed, for applicants from nations subject to extra scrutiny (for reasons to do with political instability, security, etc.), the border is in reality the embassy where they are interviewed by an immigration official. So there is a significant divide between nationals needing visas (for whom the application process is costly in terms of time and money), and those who do not need a visa. Policy creates these categories and policy changes over time. Do you think this is fair?

4.2   Highly skilled migrants

Some markets for labour are international and some economic migrants (often requiring a visa) are recruited via 'skilled migration schemes'. States compete to attract migrants with particular skills, often related to engineering, health, computer programming or other specialised fields. It could be argued that countries with points-based systems (e.g. Canada, Australia) already operate this type of filtering as the standard. Indeed, there are often age limits and salary thresholds attached to the filtering in the first place.

Many countries use special schemes (in addition to the existing visa schemes) for attracting migrants who have skills that are in relatively short supply. Typically these sought-after migrants will be identified by qualifications and salaries, then offered different conditions to entice them in, such as tax breaks; visas that are attached to the migrant rather than the employer (so they do not have to reapply if they change employers); some family reunification; the option to apply for citizenship, etc. The UK has long operated such schemes to recruit specialised medical staff into the National Health Service, while Germany's 'Blue Card' scheme and the Netherlands' ExpatCenter procedure are examples of this in practice elsewhere.

4.3   Asylum seekers and refugees

In the aftermath of the Second World War, thousands of people displaced by fighting had been housed in temporary camps. The United Nations produced an international agreement about what to do with refugees in the future. This 'Convention and Protocols' (1951) contained a definition of a refugee, as someone with:

> a well-founded fear of being persecuted for reasons of race, religion, nationality, membership of a particular social group or political opinion, if he/she returned to their country.

As the 1951 Convention referred specifically to the aftermath of the Second World War, it was reframed and expanded in the 1967 New York Protocol. These agreements basically created a new official category of migrant who moves to escape persecution. Governments agreed to standardise procedures and recognise 'refugee' status granted in other states. From this point on, there were two new and connected official categories: an 'asylum seeker' (who has lodged an official case to be considered as a refugee), and a 'refugee' (who has been granted this official status).

As the numbers of asylum seekers are largely determined by political instability, it is not possible to arbitrarily limit their numbers, or spread out applications evenly. So in the course of wars and natural disasters, many people are displaced. However, 'asylum seekers' and 'refugees' have very different entitlements. Each country has the right to set rules around what benefits asylum seekers receive, while refugees usually receive a level of rights approaching that of citizens. You will learn much more about this category of migrant in the next chapter.

4.4   Students

Due to differential fee regimes, foreign students are highly sought after by Western universities, particularly those from growing economies in Asia, as they represent lucrative markets. In the 2012–13 academic year, there were 425,000 students in UK higher education institutions of whom 300,000 came from outside the EU (UK Council for International Student Affairs, 2015). The United States had around one million foreign students in 2014, more than 250,000 of whom were Chinese nationals (US Immigration and Customs Enforcement, 2014). Students typically enjoy a different migration regime from other migrants: they are allowed entry to the nation to study and there is often some latitude for them to take paid work, depending on the country issuing the visa.

Summary

- Immigration policy differs across time and place, and how borders are constructed is a question of social justice.

- At the time of writing, there are four principal categories of migrant – asylum seekers and refugees; economic migrants; highly skilled migrants; and students.

5   The controlling state? Border control in the 21st century

Immigration policies change frequently as different governments reprioritise and use different rationales aimed at reducing particular forms of immigration and opening up others. Typically, in the 21st century, Western governments have tended to narrow the grounds for economic immigration and treat asylum-seeking as an area needing further attention, while student and highly skilled migrant schemes have been expanding. Changing the rules means that some previously legal situations and activities become categorised as illegal.

There are a number of ways of breaching immigration rules, mainly:

- crossing a border without the required documentation

- staying beyond the date stamped in a visa (overstaying)

- undertaking activities (such as paid work or claiming social-security benefits) that are not allowed under the conditions of a particular type of visa.

All of these are civil offences rather than criminal ones, as you will see in more detail in the following chapter. This section will explicitly raise the idea of a dynamic field of policy where changes can lead to a significantly different immmigration picture.

In the 21st century, a range of technologies and agencies (including some from the private sector) are used in immigration control. In the postwar period, immigration in most countries was the responsibility of the Ministry of Labour or Employment. Now, it is usually Justice and/ or Security. This demonstrates an important reframing of immigration: from a tool for rebuilding the economy, to a problem that must be seen to be managed in order to placate public opinion. In this section, you will look at four emerging trends that illustrate this re-framing of migrants crossing borders:

- surveillance

- **outsourcing**

- detention

- deportation.

Outsourcing
The practice of commissioning external service providers to carry out functions within a company (usually accomplished in-house previously).

5.1   Surveillance

Borders are made by policy and, as you have seen, this form of boundary making is not neutral, but means different things to different people. The United States/Mexican border is a result of a war fought in the 19th century, while the same can be said of the Franco-German border. If the border is defined as the place where you have to show ID, it can effectively exist in places other than the physical border, for example, embassies (Guild et al., 2009; Bigo, 2009), residential areas and workplaces hundreds of miles from a border (Aguirre, 2012), or universities.

To enable surveillance of these types of border, technology such as fingerprinting, eye recognition and the storage of data in internationally-shared databases is deployed. The European Union even has an agency – Frontex – charged with guarding the European borders and sharing information. It also trains agencies of countries outside Europe to make the international cross-border surveillance of border-crossing more manageable.

In a cruel twist, formal border-crossing has become an entertainment spectacle on cable television, as a set of reality television shows have emerged in the Anglophone world since around 2004, portraying the work of border officials: *Border Security: Australia's Front Line*; *UK Border Force*; *Border Patrol* (New Zealand); *Border Security* (Canada); *Border Wars* and *Border Patrol* (United States).

5.2   Outsourcing

Another trend is the employment by the state of a range of traditionally non-immigration agencies for immigration purposes. These include:

- increasing use of the police by state border agencies
- the addition of immigration-status checking duties to a variety of public and private-sector jobs
- contracting private security companies to fulfil border control and associated responsibilities, such as deportations, detention centres and prisons.

Sharon Pickering and Leanne Weber, in their 2013 study of this phenomenon in Australia, call this 'transversal practices', presenting the image of a range of people across a set of different agencies and levels, all involved in immigration verification and surveillance: a far cry from the old model of the customs officer stamping passports at the border.

Having private companies run immigration-related detention centres and providing other services – won through lucrative government contracts – has led to the growth of private security companies like Corrections Corporation of America (CCA) and Group 4 Security (**G4S**). The latter is the third-largest private company in the world, and the largest employer on the African continent. It is involved in providing services to governments from the United States to Australia, the UK and Israel.

G4S
A large private security firm that merged Group 4 and Securicor. Securicor had worked in immigration removal centres (IRCs) since the opening of the first centre, IRC Harmondsworth, in 1970. The agency has been accused of a range of abuses across the Middle East, in IRCs in the UK and Australia, and in prisons.

Figure 7.5   HMP Oakwood in the English Midlands, a prison privately managed by G4S

5.3 Detention

The use of detention for immigration offences is increasing. A major change since the late 1990s is the development of detention as an option for holding migrants. French NGO (non-governmental organisation) Migreurop, which monitors the development of the detention-camp complex, notes that the number of camps in Europe (and the non-European countries bordering the Mediterranean, but which are part of the EU's network) grew from 324 in 2000 to 473 in 2012. Mostly the inmates have neither been charged with, nor convicted of, any crime: they are held as a deterrent, as a form of exclusion or to ensure they do not abscond before a decision is made on their status.

A clear example of this logic at play is the Australian government's use of detention centres in the desert, and on the islands surrounding the country, since the early 2000s. People arriving in Australia by boat – usually after a dangerous journey across the ocean – and who have no documentation are currently held in a centre on Christmas Island, with no opportunity to apply for asylum, and are then deported. This practice of holding and return is widespread on islands belonging to larger nation states, which Alison Mountz (2011) calls 'the enforcement archipelago'.

Finally, in terms of social policy, the privatisation of the state's responsibilities increases the potential for making detention into a profit-making business. As noted earlier, private security companies like CCA and G4S are heavily implicated in the detention process across the world.

5.4 Deportation

The ultimate logical conclusion of defending borders is to physically eject unwanted people from national territory. Deportation is supposed to be used at the end of legal processes, but it is now increasingly used *instead of them*. National security is used as a rationale, with its permissible exceptions to the rules. This does not necessarily equate to more deportations, but changes how they come about.

As more acts become illegal, because laws change, deportation is increasingly used as a punishment for offences that were previously dealt with under civil law (e.g. infringements of immigration law). Although it is primarily used against foreign nationals, deportation can now also be used to punish naturalised citizens who break particular rules, as is the case in the UK (Gibney, 2013).

Increasing surveillance, outsourcing, detention and deportation are all trends that are changing what immigration policy is, how it is implemented and by whom. It is leading to overlaps between the public and private sectors; between trained and untrained people checking documents; and significantly, to the convergence of criminal and immigration law, in what US legal scholar Juliet Stumpf (2006) has termed 'crimmigration'. This will be the focus of the next chapter.

Figure 7.6   A deportation from the UK

Borders are the staples of immigration, and crossing them is the subject of policy. However, borders are not always where they are marked on a map, and sometimes they change place. As you have seen, borders play an important role in demarcating different categories of migrant, and in constructing their rights and their access to just treatment.

Summary

- There are various ways of breaching immigration rules that are civil offences rather than criminal ones.

- A range of technologies and agencies are involved in controlling immigration.

- Borders play an important role in demarcating different categories of migrant and in constructing their access to just treatment.

Conclusion

Immigration is a subject of public debate in which different ideas about justice, rights and entitlements often come into conflict with one another. It is the role of the social scientist to carefully evaluate popular claims made about migrants (like those you read in the tabloid headlines at the beginning of the chapter), consider how rationales underpinning immigration policies are constructed, and what their consequences may be. In this chapter, you have explored immigration as an important area of social policy which constructs boundaries between people in the form of borders. You have seen how there are different rationales for controlling borders which principally concern economic or social engineering (control of demography), and sometimes many rationales are in play at the same time. The chapter has introduced the different categories of immigration (and immigrants), all of which are dealt with in separate ways through different policies.

At the beginning of the chapter, you learnt that controls on immigration have only been in operation for a relatively short time and were introduced as a way of controlling population movement at the end of the 19th century. Following the Second World War, the character of immigration policy changed considerably for several reasons. Immigration was understood as a way of rebuilding economies and enabling people to move to find work and prosperity. Yet because of the introduction of welfare systems around this time, there was also much debate about who had the right to stay and access these benefits. As the EU and the Schengen Area have expanded since the 1980s, the distinction between EU nationals and non-EU nationals is now the most significant one in Europe, including some people while excluding others. In recent years, changes to immigration policy have meant that the line between 'legal' and 'illegal' actions has shifted (partly through the use of methods of control such as surveillance, detention and deportation), which has led to some migration behaviours becoming criminalised. It is because of the capacity of immigration policy to include/exclude people from accessing valued resources that it is strongly connected to systems of social justice.

In the next chapter, these issues of criminalisation will be explored more fully. You will see that the criminalisation of immigrants is growing and that this has particular impacts on different groups fleeing persecution and seeking asylum. You will be looking at changes in border security, and the system of border controls and detention centres utilised to prevent illegal immigration into Europe. The concept of 'crimmigration' will be introduced, which refers to the use of the criminal law (as opposed to the use of social policies) to manage immigrants.

References

Aguirre, A. (2012) 'Arizona's SB1070, Latino immigrants and the framing of anti-immigrant policies', *Latino Studies*, vol. 10, no. 3, pp. 385–94.

Bigo, D. (2009) 'Immigration controls and free movement in Europe', *International Review of the Red Cross*, vol. 91, no. 875, pp. 579–591[Online]. Available at www.icrc.org/eng/assets/files/other/irrc-875-bigo.pdf (Accessed 14 March 2015).

Dawney, L. (2008) 'Racialisation of central and east European migrants in Herefordshire', *Sussex Centre for Migration Research*, Working Paper, vol. 53, pp. 1–17.

Drury, I. (2014) 'Immigration – what a mess! 50,000 in Britain illegally are missing, minister says we'll never control our borders while in EU, and France says we are migrant "El Dorado"', *Daily Mail*, 29 October.

Dustman, C. and Frattini, T. (2014) 'The fiscal effects of immigration to the UK', *The Economic Journal* [Online]. Available at www.cream-migration.org/files/FiscalEJ.pdf (Accessed 14 March 2015).

Eltis, D. (1983) 'Free and coerced transatlantic migrations: some comparisons', *American Historical Review*, vol. 88, pp. 251–80.

European Commission Directorate General for Migration and Home Affairs (n.d.) *Schengen Area* [Online] Available at http://ec.europa.eu/dgs/home-affairs/what-we-do/policies/borders-and-visas/schengen/index_en.htm (Accessed 1 June 2015)

Gibney, M.J. (2013) '"A very transcendental power": denaturalisation and the liberalisation of citizenship in the United Kingdom', *Political Studies*, vol. 61, no. 3, pp. 637–55.

Guild, E., Groenendijk, C.A. and Carrera, S. (eds) (2009) *Illiberal Liberal States: Immigration, Citizenship, and Integration in the EU*, Aldershot, Ashgate.

Kinsella, J. (1996) 'Irish immigrants in America in the 19th century' [Online]. Available at www.kinsella.org/history/histira.htm (Accessed 8 February 2015).

Lee-Treweek, G. (2010) '"Be tough, never let them see what it does to you": towards an understanding of the emotional lives of economic migrants', *International Journal of Work Organisation and Emotion*, vol. 3, no. 3, pp. 206–26.

Moore, H. (2013) 'Shades of whiteness? English villagers, eastern European migrants and the intersection of race and class in rural England', *Critical Race and Whiteness Studies*, vol. 9, no. 1, pp. 1–19.

Mountz, A. (2011) 'The enforcement archipelago: detention, haunting, and asylum on islands', *Political Geography*, vol. 30, no. 3, pp. 118–28.

ONS (Office of National Statistics) (2011) *Polish People in the UK - Half a million Polish Residents* [Online], London, ONS. Available at www.ons.gov.uk/ons/dcp171780_229910.pdf (Accessed 1 June 2015).

ONS (2014) *2011 Census Analysis: Social and Economic Characteristics by Length of Residence of Migrant Populations in England and Wales*, [Online], London, ONS. Available at www.ons.gov.uk/ons/dcp171776_381447.pdf (Accessed 1 June 2015).

Pickering, S. and Weber, L. (2013) 'Policing transversal borders', in Aas, K. F. and Bosworth, M. (eds) *The Borders of Punishment: Migration, Citizenship, and Social Exclusion*, Oxford, Oxford University Press, p. 93.

Ryan, L. (2010) 'Becoming Polish in London: negotiating ethnicity through migration', *Social Identities*, vol. 16, no. 3, pp. 359–76.

Stumpf, J. (2006) 'The crimmigration crisis: immigrants, crime, and sovereign power', *The American University Law Review*, vol. 56, p. 367.

The *Sun* (2013) 'You're a soft touch: immigrant on £14k benefits refuses full-time job', The *Sun*.

UK Council for International Student Affairs (2015) *International Students in UK HE by Domicile, Level and Mode, European Union (EU) (Excluding UK) and Non-EU, 2012–13* [Online]. Available at www.ukcisa.org.uk/Info-for-universities-colleges–schools/Policy-research–statistics/Research–statistics/International-students-in-UK-HE/

US Department of State, Office of the Historian (2015) 'Chinese immigration and the Chinese Exclusion Acts' [Online]. Available at https://history.state.gov/milestones/1866-1898/chinese-immigration (Accessed 8 February 2015).

US Immigration and Customs Enforcement (2014) *Enforcement Student and Exchange Visitor Programme, Student and Exchange Visitor Information System*, Quarterly Review, July [Online]. Available at www.ice.gov/doclib/sevis/pdf/by-the-numbers.pdf (Accessed 20 March 2015).

Chapter 8
Border criminologies and crimmigration

by Victoria Canning

Contents

Introduction

The previous chapter outlined the importance of social policy in understanding immigration and asylum. Towards the end of the chapter, you considered some critical criminological issues in relation to immigration, specifically the criminalisation of migrant groups and key aspects within this, such as detention. This chapter develops these issues by looking at growing trends in the criminalisation of immigrants and ways in which this can impact on women, men and children fleeing persecution and seeking asylum. It considers the impacts that policy and law have on the lives of asylum seekers living at borders or awaiting asylum decisions.

This chapter will mainly focus on people seeking asylum in the United Kingdom. However, as a number of trends across Europe relate directly to changes in the UK, the broader European context will be set in relation to what has been called 'border criminologies' and the idea of '**crimmigration**'. 'Crimmigration' refers to the use of the criminal law to manage immigrants. Expanding on ideas you encountered in the previous chapter, this unpacks contentious issues in the politics of asylum such as detention in immigration removal centres, the treatment of women seeking asylum, welfare and poverty, and **securitisation**. You will also look at the gendered implications of asylum policy, and consider the experiences of women and children who have been detained.

Crimmigration
A term coined by Juliet Stumpf (2006) to describe the increased entanglements between immigration and criminal justice procedures.

Securitisation
Refers to social control measures that increase security in our everyday lives, such as surveillance, as well as border controls and policing.

This chapter will explore:

- the background development of what are known as 'border criminologies' in relation to social control

- ways in which immigrants and asylum seekers are controlled, as well as the problems related to such controls

- the role of criminal justice in immigration control and the debates that surround this relationship

- the concept of 'crimmigration' in relation to the criminalisation of asylum seekers in Western Europe, specifically the UK

- problem areas created by border control agendas, such as immigration detention, dispersal, destitution and deportation.

Section 1, 'Controlling immigration', begins by looking at changes in border security that have been made possible by increased legal and social controls on immigration, and introduces the concept of 'Fortress Europe'.

Section 2, 'The politics of seeking asylum in the UK', examines issues of welfare restrictions and gender inequality that can arise in the complex UK asylum system.

Section 3, 'The crimmigration crisis', looks at the politics of immigration removal centres and the impact on those detained in them, particularly women and children.

1   Controlling immigration

Immigration is a highly debated issue in contemporary politics and society. Government representatives and Members of Parliament in the UK commonly focus on reducing or controlling immigration, usually based on political factors such as economic migration flows between European Union countries. As you saw in Chapter 7, mass media, particularly tabloid newspapers, place a lot of focus on problems surrounding immigration, sometimes distorting the realities of asylum seeking, economic migration and net migration (defined later). Immigrants are often represented as illegal or 'bogus' (deceptive), and such tabloid stories seldom explore accurate patterns in migration.

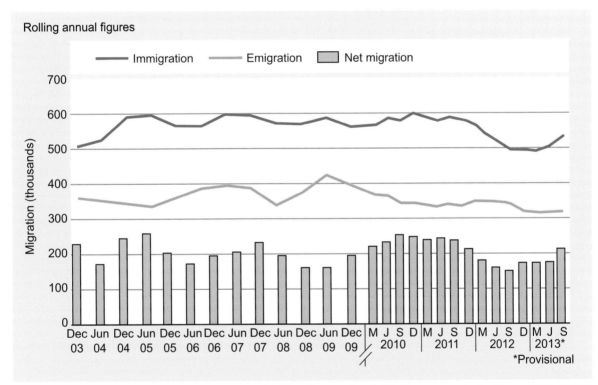

Figure 8.1   UK migration figures, December 2003 to September 2013 (Source: adapted from BBC, 2014)

The term 'net migration' refers to the number of people per year immigrating to and emigrating from (leaving) a certain country. This includes applications for asylum in a country, which will be a major focus of this chapter, as well as student visas and temporary work permits. Although it may not necessarily be that migrants will leave or stay permanently, recent growths in net migration in the UK, where more people have immigrated and fewer emigrated, have led key political parties to increase controls on the number of people coming into the country. These controls include attempts to cap net migration targets to less than half the current number of just over 200,000 people leaving and entering per year (see Figure 8.1).

Activity 1

From looking at the chart in Figure 8.1, would you say that immigration and emigration figures have risen or fallen in the period shown?

Discussion

Overall, people moving out of and coming into the country have both remained fairly steady considering the length of time examined. However, as you can see, there are higher rates of people entering the UK than those leaving during this period. From 2008, fewer people moved away from the UK, which is likely related to the economic recession that developed in the same year, when people's financial ability to leave became more limited. Immigration also steadily fell in this time, but began to increase again towards the end of 2013. This means that net migration increased, as you can see from the bar chart at the bottom of the graph in Figure 8.1.

Since the early 1990s, there has been an increase in border controls, and this has had a number of major impacts on people seeking asylum. As you saw in the previous chapter, asylum seekers are people claiming to be fleeing persecution under the 1951 Refugee Convention. Reasons for doing so are often related to violence during conflict or periods of political unrest where people who identify as being part of a specific ethnic, national or political group have been deliberately targeted for systematic abuses. A number of major conflicts, such as the wars and conflicts in Iraq, Afghanistan, Syria, the former Yugoslavia, Libya, Egypt, Ethiopia and Somalia (to name but a few) led to increases in people travelling to European countries to apply for refugee status.

However, in light of the increase in people seeking asylum, political parties across Europe, particularly in Western Europe, made a number of legislative and policy changes aimed at controlling the flow of migrants. These included the Dublin II Regulation, which requires the first country that an asylum seeker arrives in to take responsibility for their claim for refugee status, meaning they should not attempt to claim in a second country and may be returned to the first European country they arrived in if they do so. Since many people move overland from Middle Eastern or North African regions, this can mean that countries such as Italy and Greece are held responsible for a high number of applicants. Other changes in policy include the expansion of measures to detain asylum seekers and **undocumented migrants** in immigration removal centres. This latter issue will be discussed more thoroughly throughout this chapter.

Undocumented migrants
Generally refers to migrants who have entered a country without acquiring the legal authorisation to do so.

Activity 2

Take a few minutes to think about what impact the implementation of net migration targets might have on the rights of people seeking asylum on the basis of refuge from persecution. Think, for example, about the kinds of cases that might be advantaged or disadvantaged through an immigration system that focuses only on the numbers of migrants and not on the reasons why people immigrate.

Discussion

Having targets in the immigration system can mean that the number of people entering is the main focus of border control agencies, rather than each individual case. Therefore, some people's claims might be overlooked in favour of being processed quickly, rather than being thoroughly considered. For example, although applicants with heavily documented evidence of persecution may have their cases resolved easily and be granted asylum, it can also mean that people who have complex cases or who may struggle to provide evidence of persecution (such as people who have been sexually tortured) have their claims rejected or unfairly considered.

Criminal justice
A system made up of agencies and institutions such as the prison service, courts and the police. Border controls have increasingly mirrored the criminal justice system, especially in the expansion of asylum detention, the increase in laws that work to criminalise more aspects of immigration, and the surge in numbers of asylum seekers and immigrants held in custody.

1.1 Border criminologies

In light of concerns about border controls, there has been an increase in the study of what has become known as 'border criminologies'. In the wider field of criminology, the idea of border criminologies has developed in response to the growing use of detention centres and increased numbers of immigrants being viewed as 'criminals'. This has invited questions and debate in **criminal justice** arenas, as more

Critical criminology
A strand of criminology developed in the 1970s. It is concerned with structures in society that limit equality and access to human rights for some groups of people. Critical criminologists are mainly interested in the experiences of people with less power in society.

Othering
A key concept in the social sciences used to refer to processes that make distinctions between groups of people. For example, migrants are seen as 'different' – whether through nationality, place of birth, work ethic or access to welfare – developing an 'us and them' social mentality. Particular social groups or individuals can then become marginalised by cultural processes that exclude or 'other' them.

people have begun to be targeted and processed by the criminal justice system, which in turn has meant more people are confined in prisons and immigration removal centres (as you will see in more depth in Section 3). Criminology generally, and **critical criminology** in particular, is often concerned with many of the issues inherent to border controls, such as the use of surveillance and related technologies, surges in the criminalisation of certain social groups, and intensified processes of '**othering**' through media sources and news reports. At the same time, social policy has become increasingly geared towards restricting the entry or internal movements of migrants, and has been strengthened through the use of the criminal law to prosecute people for immigration-related offences, such as working without a permit. However, as criminologists Aas and Bosworth (2013) argue, although scholarly interest in the role of criminal justice in immigration processes developed from the 1990s in areas such as refugee studies, human geography and sociology, criminology has been slower to pay attention.

1.2 Regulation, policy and control

A number of key changes have been made across Europe, North America and Australasia since the early 1990s that move immigration law closer to the realms of criminal law. While asylum and immigration have historically focused on the rights of those fleeing poverty or persecution (see the 1951 Refugee Convention), recent moves in policy and practice have impacted on those seen to be 'legal' in host countries, such as increasing the uses of detention for asylum seekers, and limiting routes and opportunities for people seeking asylum to move across borders to safety.

Frances Webber, a legal practitioner who works on asylum case law in the UK, identified a number of ways that asylum seekers are controlled by the state and other security agencies. Webber points out examples of how social control and criminalisation have expanded, particularly in responding to immigration through criminal justice processes. These examples include increased fines and prison sentences for people found smuggling immigrants, and the extension of border controls to areas affected by conflict or unrest that restrict people's capacity to migrate. Webber also includes increases in detention and criminalising entry without relevant visas or documentation (Webber, 2012, pp. 19–34). She specifically points out the following:

(a) The 1951 Refugee Convention requires refugees to have left their country of origin before seeking asylum. However, some countries require people to have visas before they enter. Therefore, countries which ask individuals to apply for visas prior to leaving their country of origin limit whether people will be considered as refugees if they apply for asylum. Instead they can be criminalised or deported for entering without the appropriate visa if they reach the UK and other areas.

(b) Since 1987, airlines and shipping companies have been liable to receive fines if they transport individuals who do not have valid passports or visas for travel to the UK. This has been extended to lorry drivers (aimed at those travelling through Calais), which deters companies and individuals from bringing in undocumented migrants or people who may claim asylum.

(c) Criminalising humanitarian smugglers: smugglers are people or groups who may or may not charge to help undocumented migrants gain entry to a country. Although some do this to help people flee persecution who have no alternative, European governments have focused on this as acts by criminal and organised gangs. While this is the case for some, there is a difference between a *smuggler* and a *trafficker*, the latter being someone who moves people for financial benefit through selling bodies or body parts.

(d) Extension of borders: increased information gathering has meant that the Home Office has extended borders to areas where high volumes of asylum seekers or undocumented migrants may move through; for example, from North Africa or at the crossing between Calais and Dover.

(e) Outsourcing border controls: some areas across the Middle East and Northern Africa have arguably become 'buffer states' that act to reduce, detain and deter people from crossing overland or by sea to reach Southern and Western Europe. Agencies funded by the European Union, such as Frontex, outsource some functions to private companies (see Section 1.3) and police migration across the Mediterranean Sea and Atlantic Ocean.

(f) Criminalising refugees: this will be the focus of Section 2.

1.3   'Fortress Europe'

'Fortress Europe' was historically a military term used during the Second World War, but it is also often used to describe the ways in which European borders are policed to keep migrants out or to criminalise those who do not fit the regulations outlined in the legislations and policies discussed throughout this chapter. It mainly refers to countries in the European Union's Schengen Area. As you saw in the last chapter, this agreement allows free movement of EU migration but presents numerous difficulties for people entering from outside this area. This is managed through EU policy and policing, and member states are encouraged to share data and information regarding other forms of migration. It is worth noting that, although there are some standard European policies, they are not necessarily applied in the same way and can vary from country to country. For example, countries such as France, the UK and Italy have quite limited welfare rights for asylum seekers in comparison to some Nordic countries, such as Sweden. Therefore policy can (to some degree) be open to interpretation, which is often led by the political agenda of each country's governments.

According to Human Rights Watch, which is a non-government organisation (NGO) concerned with investigating and defending the human rights of people worldwide, there has been evidence in countries such as Greece that private agencies, such as Frontex, have worked with state agencies to transport and detain migrants entering the country, despite being informed of possible abuses and violations of fundamental rights. This raises questions in criminology on the role of surveillance amongst outsourced agencies, where states (in this case, EU member states) can and do use people's personal information for social control and detention purposes. For critical criminologists, this relates to Stanley Cohen's idea of the 'dispersal of discipline' (1985) through which he raised concerns about social control becoming a business-like enterprise rather than the responsibility of a government or state.

1.4   Precarious life on borders

Before moving on to look at ways in which migrants are criminalised or deterred from entering a country, it is important to consider the human cost of the concept of 'Fortress Europe'. For example, the

'Borders Project', which is part of the work of the European network UNITED for Intercultural Action, has documented 17,306 migrant deaths in or at the borders of European countries between 1993 and 2012 (United Against Racism, 2012). In 2014 alone, the office of the United Nations High Commissioner for Refugees (UNHCR, 1951; 1967) estimated 2500 people lost their lives attempting to cross the Mediterranean to gain entry to Europe, most of whom are thought to have been fleeing conflict or persecution.

Often people who are fleeing poverty, conflict or persecution feel they have little option but to risk their lives to save themselves, but with severe consequences. Poor health and safety on boats and overcrowded carriers contribute to migrant deaths, but there are two other key considerations. Firstly, the criminalisation of humanitarian smugglers has led some to approach islands, such as Lampedusa off the coast of Italy, but not anchor the boat there so as to avoid prosecution. This attempt at avoiding criminalisation means migrant women, men and children have to swim to the safety of shore, which is when many lives are lost. Secondly, the increases in border controls have limited the number of migrants entering legitimately, and thus many find more dangerous ways to flee their country of origin. Some organisations, such as Amnesty International, argue that by creating barriers through surveillance and European policing, some countries are failing to protect the human rights of migrants or provide safety to those who need it most.

Summary

- 'Border criminologies' is a constantly developing area of criminology that focuses specifically on the controls placed on the movements, welfare, rights and criminalisation of migrants, asylum seekers and refugees.

- Both the movements of migrants and the policies for their welfare are controlled by increasingly restrictive measures that impact on the lives of asylum seekers and immigrants to varying extents across Europe.

- These restrictions can have serious consequences for people fleeing persecution and seeking asylum.

2   Case study: the politics of seeking asylum in the United Kingdom

Imogen Tyler (2013, pp. 85–6) argues, 'if you arrive in the UK today to claim refugee status under the 1951 Convention, you enter an extremely complex bureaucratic system'. By this, she is pointing to the multitude of processes in the asylum system that make it very difficult for most people to claim asylum, and particularly difficult if the individual or family cannot speak, read or write in English. People often arrive with limited knowledge of how or where to apply for refugee status, how the system works, or what her/his entitlements are (such as welfare allowances or housing). Indeed, they may not be aware of their rights under the Refugee Convention or the Universal Declaration of Human Rights.

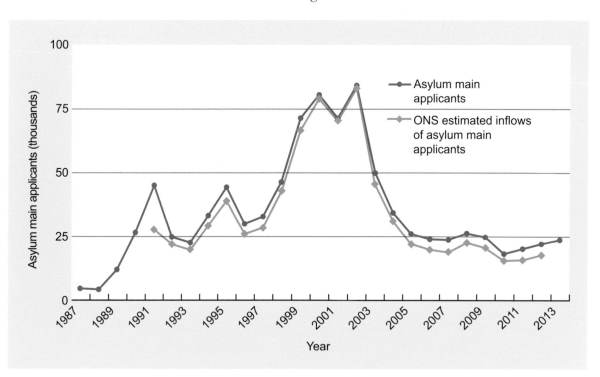

Figure 8.2   Asylum applications and estimated inflows, 1987–2013 (Source: adapted from Blinder, 2014, p. 3)

Like other Schengen Area countries in Europe, the UK has been working to reduce net migration. As Figure 8.2 demonstrates, immigration, and specifically asylum applications, increased from the mid-1990s toward the early 2000s. This was related to a number of conflicts in areas such as the former Yugoslavia and Iraq, from which people were fleeing and requesting asylum in other Middle Eastern and European countries. As you can see from the graph in Figure 8.2, asylum applications began to drop from the early 2000s. The aftermath of 9/11 in the United States, and subsequently the 7/7 London bombings, led to increases in border controls, security checks, punitive measures for undocumented migrants, and a general tightening of borders in the United Kingdom and further afield.

2.1   Who seeks asylum in the UK?

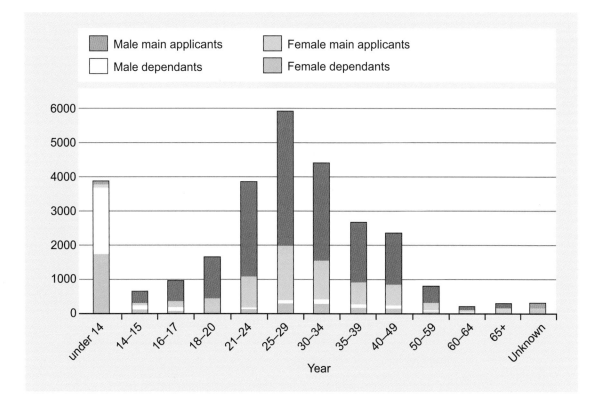

Figure 8.3   Asylum applicants by age and sex, 2012 (Source: adapted from Blinder, 2014, p. 6)

As you can see from Figure 8.3, the majority of asylum seekers in the UK are men, and most are between the ages of 21 and 29. This is largely related to men's economic and political ability to migrate as they are less likely to be primary carers of children and more likely to be politically active. This does not mean that women do not flee persecution, but rather that the forms of persecution that women are more often subjected to, such as sexual violence or domestic abuse, are mostly perpetrated by husbands, partners or friends. Since these are not necessarily state actors (such as soldiers or police officers) they are therefore not always seen as political acts. It is worth noting that this is questioned by many feminist scholars and activists who argue that violence against women in society is related to a number of inequalities, which are inherently political and result from cultural and social values and the way societies are structured.

Some of the reasons people seek asylum are due to:

- fleeing areas affected by war, conflict or civil unrest

- fleeing direct persecution based on their religious or political beliefs

- fleeing on the grounds of sexuality, sexual orientation or sexual identity where it may be legally or socially prohibited to identify as lesbian, gay, bisexual or transgender.

2.2   The asylum process

In the UK, the Home Office is responsible for processing asylum applications. Even though the United Kingdom is made up of England and Wales, Scotland and Northern Ireland, the Home Office retains power over immigration and asylum.

People entering the UK can apply for asylum at any port of entry, such as airports or ferry ports, but full applications are made in Croydon in London where the applicant will be interviewed, or 'screened', at the asylum screening unit. Applicants are expected to provide a range of documents, including passports, birth certificates, police registration certificates, other supporting documents and evidence of accommodation. A basic outline of the procedure is documented in Figure 8.4.

On making an application for asylum, the first interview is undertaken during the 'screening' process, which may involve discussing reasons for the application, including information on persecution. During this, fingerprints and photographs are taken and the individual's passport and any documentation will be retained. At this point, asylum seekers are given their asylum registration card and all individuals should be allocated a 'case owner' who is, in theory, responsible for their application until the final decision. Once the initial statements are taken and the interview has been completed, the case description

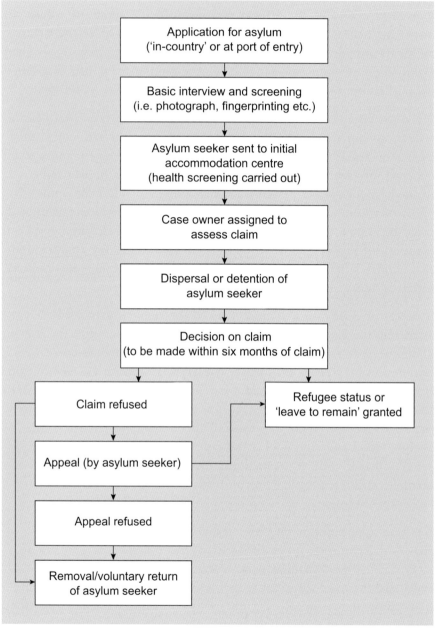

Figure 8.4   An example outline of the British asylum process (Source: adapted from Haroon, 2008, p. 2)

becomes dependent on what the Home Office deem as the 'merits' of the story, such as the depth in which information is given and its consistency through multiple interviews.

As well as extracting the information given by the applicant, a case owner has access to 'Country of Origin Information' (COI), which is meant to provide reliable, up-to-date information regarding the country from which the applicant has fled. This should cover a wide range of political issues, including the status of women.

While awaiting an asylum decision, or if the decision taken has been a refusal, asylum seekers are not entitled to work in the UK unless they have been resident or the application has been ongoing for more than one year, despite access to employment being a basic human right (United Nations, 1948). Even then, dependants of the main applicant (most of whom are women or children) cannot apply to work either. It could be argued that this further increases the social isolation and exclusion of people and their ability to integrate into the country, and also ultimately leaves individuals state-dependent and increases poverty within asylum communities.

In terms of depriving asylum seekers of the right to work and increasing the likelihood of destitution, the Joint Committee on Human Rights went as far as to say that, 'the government's treatment of asylum seekers reaches the Article 3 ECHR (European Convention on Human Rights) threshold of inhuman and degrading treatment' (JCHR, 2007, p. 5). In 2013, individual asylum seekers over the age of 18 were eligible to receive £36.62 per week. This money is to pay for food, clothes, travel and any other expenses, which amounts to just over £5 per day. Importantly, it is much less than other benefit recipients. For example, in 2015, people living as British citizens and receiving Jobseeker's Allowance received between £57.35 and £72.40 per week.

While an application is ongoing, asylum seekers will usually be dispersed, or moved, to another part of the UK. This is generally to areas such as the North West or North East of England, or Scotland, which are the main dispersal areas outside of London. If an applicant is accepted, they may gain asylum status that can have limitations (for example, the right to remain for up to five years, after which the case may be reviewed) or their claim may be rejected. If rejected they have the chance to appeal the decision. Many initial decisions are overturned at the appeal stage (see Section 2.4).

Activity 3

Make some notes on the problems you think adult asylum seekers may have if they are not able to work. Compare them to the list in the discussion below.

Discussion

Although there are many points you may have considered, your answer may include one or more of the following:

- Destitution: asylum seekers receive very little money and so cannot always afford to live to a standard that is deemed acceptable in the UK.

- State dependency: people seeking asylum are made to depend on the state for money, rather than being able to earn an income. This can include being given food vouchers (rather than actual money) that determine where asylum seekers can shop and what kind of goods they can buy.

- Impact on skills: people seeking asylum may have worked in a profession or skilled job before seeking asylum. Not being able to work can leave people unable to maintain the skills they need to subsequently secure employment.

- Boredom: although there are some opportunities to study or volunteer, people seeking asylum sometimes report feeling lost or bored.

- Travel: travelling, even by bus, can be impossible due to lack of money. Asylum seekers do not have travel paid for, and not being able to work to bring in extra income can limit their mobility, even within the town or city in which they are living.

2.3   Issues in the asylum system

Although the process of seeking asylum seems fairly straightforward, there are some issues that are seen as problematic for criminologists. These include access to welfare benefits, credibility, the Fast Track system, and detention at immigration removal centres. Some of these concerns are summed up by Tyler, who points out that:

once an asylum-seeker is identified, they are issued with an asylum-seeker's identity card, become subject to detention, dispersal and electronic tagging, barred from access to paid work and have limited (if any) access to education, health care, social housing and income support. For the asylum-seeker, the first and most critical stage in this process is being identified as an asylum-seeker.

(Tyler, 2006, p. 188)

Some of the key issues that can affect asylum claims, and that can impact on the lives of people seeking asylum in the UK, include:

(a) **Policy changes such as the New Asylum Model (2007) and Fast Track:** The New Asylum Model was introduced with the key aim being to speed up asylum decisions, thus accepting, rejecting or returning applicants based on their claims. It was also to ensure that the same case owner would follow the whole application and thus know the application well enough to present a fully informed case. Although it initially set out to reduce the time people spent in the system, in reality it has meant complex cases have not been given enough time for due investigation. For example, Stonewall (a UK-based lesbian, gay and bisexual charity) found that people applying for asylum under humanitarian grounds based on sexual orientation persecution were often given very little time to develop their claims (Stonewall, 2010).

(b) **Welfare:** Although asylum seekers do receive some benefits while awaiting a decision, this amounts to very little financial support and leaves some people living below the poverty line. Since applicants do not have the right to employment, they generally have no alternative but to depend on welfare allowances.

(c) **Merits and credibility:** To be granted asylum, it is up to applicants to prove they have a well-founded fear of being persecuted in their country of origin for reasons of race, religion, nationality, membership of a particular social group, or political opinion. A number of problems arise in this process. Firstly, country-of-origin information files can be out of date or inaccurate. Secondly, interviews may not be sensitively carried out, as will be discussed in Section 2.4. Thirdly, not all abuses can be easily evidenced. Finally, sexual violence and 'silent' forms of torture (which are used purposely to leave no evidence) might not leave any physical scars, but that does not mean it has not occurred.

(d) **Cuts to legal aid:** To make a case for asylum, an applicant should have access to a solicitor. Cuts in legal aid, which offers state-supported legal representation to people who have little funds themselves, have meant that fewer people seeking asylum can gain representation.

Activity 4

Do the issues raised in this section challenge any ideas or assumptions you previously held about seeking asylum in the UK? Take a few minutes to reflect on your own ideas on immigration in light of this material.

Discussion

Often the knowledge or insight people have about seeking asylum is heavily informed by the media. This regularly focuses on welfare claimants, crime or the blurring between asylum and immigration statistics more generally. It is very seldom that the reality of seeking asylum is represented accurately and in an unbiased way, especially in relation to the process of application and decision making, or the problem of destitution for many asylum seekers.

2.4   Gaps in responding to gendered violence

One key issue for feminist activists and criminologists alike has been the treatment of women seeking asylum in the UK, as well as other parts of the world. Research shows that women and men who seek asylum often do so for different reasons. For example, during conflict or political unrest, men may more commonly be politically targeted for systematic abuse by state actors. In these kinds of circumstances, men may claim asylum based on factors such as torture by the state, cruel or inhuman treatment or because of their political affiliation. While many women are targeted for similar abuses, women and girls are disproportionately affected by sexual abuse, rape, domestic abuse and other violent acts often attributed to gendered cultural practices such as **female genital mutilation (FGM)**.

Female genital mutilation (FGM) Procedures that intentionally alter or cause injury to the female genital organs for non-medical reasons. The procedure has no health benefits for girls and women.

There has been a growing concern for the rights of women seeking asylum, especially since the 1990s when asylum applications were at a high. During this period, the extent of conflict-related sexual violence increasingly became a focus for international bodies such as the United Nations. Organisations working with asylum seekers and refugees became increasingly aware that asylum policies and the system itself did not have a 'gendered lens', meaning they did not adequately consider the forms of violence that women may be subjected to. Likewise, the process did not consider appropriate ways for women as a particular social group to make claims related to sexual violence, 'extreme' domestic violence or other gendered forms of violence that may lead to 'leave to remain' under humanitarian grounds. In 2004, the then UK Border Agency established a policy called 'Gender Issues in the Asylum Claim' (followed up in 2010). This recognised that women who have experienced sexual or domestic violence may have reservations about disclosing sensitive information about instances of abuse. The policy required UK Border Agency staff to offer a female interviewer and interpreter, and highlighted forms of violence against women that may be common across many countries.

While these were positive steps, a number of agencies have found gaps in the way women's cases are handled that can affect their claims. As a feminist criminologist, I have found that if women do not disclose sexual violence in the initial interview, but do so later on in the process, the application is likely to be refused. This is particularly complex as women (and men) may take a long time to build enough trust in a person to disclose intimate violence, as it can be seen as particularly shameful or stigmatising (Canning, 2014). Looking at the process, the first interview aims to determine an applicant's identity and lodge the asylum claim. To do this, asylum seekers are required to give a brief overview of why they are seeking asylum, although not in any great depth until the 'substantive', or full, interview.

Summary

- The number of people seeking asylum in the UK was at a high in the mid-1990s but decreased over a ten-year period.

- Those who claim asylum are usually fleeing conflict or persecution, and most applicants are male; the gendered nature of asylum can mean there are gaps in responding to women who apply.

- The asylum system in the UK is complex and can take a long time for people to move through, although the Home Office has attempted to address this by the introducing a 'Fast Track' system; most applications are refused, although many of these refusals are overturned at appeal and 'asylum' or 'leave to remain' are granted.

- Welfare restrictions and practices such as dispersal are used as means of controlling asylum seekers.

3   The crimmigration crisis

Now that you have explored the experiences of asylum seekers and refugees, the focus will move to looking at the topic of 'crimmigration', a term coined by Juliet Stumpf. Referring to state responses to immigration patterns in North America, Stumpf (2006) argued that:

> Both criminal and immigration law are, at their core, systems of inclusion and exclusion. They are similarly designed to determine whether and how to include individuals as members of society or exclude them from it. Both create insiders and outsiders. Both are designed to create distinct categories of people – innocent versus guilty, admitted versus excluded or, as some say, 'legal' versus 'illegal'.

> (Stumpf, 2006, p. 380)

Punitive

Inflicting punishment, particularly harsh forms of punishment, such as lengthy prison sentences.

Stumpf's main concerns are twofold: that immigration law and policy have been gradually incorporating criminal law over a number of years, which has meant an increase in crimes related to immigration (thereby swelling the immigrant representation in prison populations); and that routine practices in the US immigration system have become more **punitive**, such as incorporating mandatory detention.

These are valid concerns and can be seen echoed by other commentators. For example, according to Aas and Bosworth (2013, p. vii), in Europe alone 'rapidly growing foreign populations represent on average 20 per cent of prison inmates, reaching extraordinary highs in countries such as Switzerland (71.4 per cent), Luxembourg (68.8 per cent), Cyprus (58.9 per cent), Greece (57.1 per cent) and Belgium (44.2 per cent)'. Importantly, many of those are imprisoned based on immigration policy or legislation violations rather than for violent crimes or other offences. Thus border control policies have significant impacts on the criminalisation of immigrants.

Likewise, law and social policy have become increasingly punitive toward immigrants. Looking at the UK as an example, Aliverti has shown that, while 70 types of immigration offence were passed in the UK from 1905 to 1996, 84 new immigration offences were created from 1997 to 2010 (in Zedner, 2013, p. 410). This takes us some way to seeing how the 'crimmigration' crisis is developing in some other areas of the globe. Rather than dealing with immigration as a matter mainly related to social policy, law has created more ways for immigrants to be taken into the criminal justice system. In this sense, the extent to which 'justice' is served through a criminal justice approach to immigration must be called into question by criminologists and those with an interest in the role of social policies in responding to complex social problems and issues.

Social policy also has a wider role in the 'crimmigration crisis' in that reductions and stagnations in welfare benefit allowance, for example, can mean asylum seekers live on or below the poverty line. For example, the level of financial support for asylum seekers was frozen for three years in the UK from 2011 to 2014. This policy was challenged by the High Court in 2014, and through this challenge it was demonstrated that government policies regarding welfare were pushing asylum seekers into severe poverty. Such barriers to financial support can lead some people, who may otherwise not be able to afford to survive legally with such stringent financial limitations, to engage in 'crimes of survival', such as shoplifting or stealing food, or working illegally to gain enough money to live above the poverty line. Therefore, people who may genuinely fear return to their country of origin, but whose claims have been refused, may continue to live in a country outside immigration rules and regulations, and so can fall into the criminal justice system due to immigration offences.

3.1   Detaining immigrants: the politics of immigration removal centres

Immigration removal centres ('IRCs', named detention centres until 2003 but often still referred to as this) have been a growing area of interest in criminology. One obvious reason is that detention is a form of imprisonment, and since many criminological studies have found prisons to be harmful or detrimental to the health of those confined within them, concerns are raised about the growth in detention populations, particularly across Europe, Australasia and North America. Immigration detention differs from most regular forms of imprisonment in that the person detained does not have to be accused or guilty of a crime, and does not know how long the period of detention will last (Webber, 2012). This section explores some wider concerns regarding life in detention, as well as the treatment of people being detained.

It is worth beginning our analysis of IRCs by looking to the work of Mary Bosworth, a key criminologist working in the area of immigration control. Her study of IRCs in the UK was the first systematic research project to investigate life in detention centres, and included undertaking interviews with asylum seekers, undocumented migrants and convicted foreign nationals, most of whom were awaiting deportation to their country of origin. She also interviewed IRC staff and spent 20 months recording field notes in and around the centres. Bosworth points out the political division in opinion on the use of detention for immigrants:

> For its proponents, immigration detention is a necessary part of border control, both a right and an obligation of the British sovereign state. Those without visas and immigration status are not entitled to stay and, if they will not go voluntarily, they must be detained to prompt their deportation. For critics, however, immigration removal centres should be abolished. They cause long-term psychological distress, are used in an arbitrary fashion, and are expensive and inefficient. Notwithstanding official claims that people are detained only briefly prior to their departure, such opponents point out a growing number of people languish in detention for months and even years.
>
> (Bosworth, 2014, p. 5)

Therefore, the detention of asylum seekers is a highly debated issue. On one side, some argue that governments have the right to detain and then remove those who do not fit their citizenship or asylum requirements. On the other, commentators argue that the removal of liberty is at best a violation of the Universal Declaration of Human Rights, which states that all people have the right to liberty, and at worst a form of abuse in and of itself.

Activity 5

List some of the key issues that are raised in the debate about the detention of asylum seekers.

Discussion

On one hand:

- Some people argue that the numbers of immigrants entering countries (in this case, the nations that make up the United Kingdom) are too high.

- The economic climate in the aftermath of the global recession has impacted on the number of people able to move away from the UK, while inclusion in the European Union has increased EU migration to the UK.

- People who support immigration detention often argue that asylum seekers who have had their claims rejected by the Home Office should be detained and then deported, since they are not considered to be in fear of persecution on return to their country of origin.

On the other hand:

- Sometimes the rights of individuals are not upheld when they are detained or imprisoned without having committed a crime or being found guilty of criminal wrongdoings.

- Confinement can be harmful for many people (including prisoners more generally) in the long term.

- For those working in the field of refugee studies, immigration detention for asylum seekers goes against the principles of the Universal Declaration of Human Rights and the 1951 Refugee Convention since it responds to people seeking asylum through criminalisation, rather than treating them as survivors of persecution.

- At the same time, serious conflicts (such as in Afghanistan, Iraq and Syria) have increased the need for asylum for many people fleeing violence in these areas.

- There are a number of appeals that lead to original decisions by the Home Office being overturned, and asylum then being granted (up to a third of rejections are overturned when appeals are made (Asylum Aid, 2011)), which calls into question the use of detention and deportation.

3.2   Privatisation and IRCs

As Stumpf (2006) has argued, criminal law and asylum law have gradually merged. Increases in privatisation are mirrored in border controls, including IRCs, with some controversial outcomes. The privatisation of state-led facilities, such as prisons and healthcare, has been a concern for criminologists for many decades. Nils Christie, a key thinker in critical criminology, has argued that privatisation allows crime control measures to become an industry where money could be made and contracts are sold to the highest bidder, thus promoting a business model by increasing profit and so encouraging increased target setting (2000). Others have shown that this can have an impact on the quality of care for people depending on, or living in, such institutions or facilities. For example, businesses require facilities to make a profit, and as such may find ways to save money in areas such as staffing. In IRCs, this has been found to be detrimental to people living in detention who have complex healthcare needs, as staff may not be on hand at all times to provide appropriate care.

Importantly, criminologists are concerned about the use of such agencies as they are seldom held accountable if and when abuses or problems do occur. Medical Justice, for example, reported around 300 allegations of abuse by security staff, including use of excessive force (Medical Justice, 2010). The death of Jimmy Mubenga in 2010 at the hands of three G4S guards led to investigations into the use of excessive force and restraint during removal.

3.3   Women in detention

As with other areas of asylum, IRC populations are mostly made up of men. In the UK, out of ten centres, one (IRC Yarl's Wood) is purpose-built for women and some families. Two others, IRC Tinsley House and the Cedars Unit, have been built for families. The others mostly (or only) detain men. This has meant that the limited information and research available to those studying asylum detention has, more often than not, focused on men's experiences. However, in Yarl's Wood alone, up to 405 women can be living in detention at any given time. As a number of feminist criminologists have argued in relation to prisons, it is not only the numbers of women in confinement that should be of interest, but the specific experiences and problems that women face during imprisonment or, in this case, detention.

The work of 'Women for Refugee Women' helps fill in this gap in knowledge. In 2014, they reported a number of important findings from their research with women who had previously been detained in IRCs in the UK, mostly in Yarl's Wood. Overall they interviewed 46 women, 72 per cent of whom said they had been raped as a form of persecution before seeking asylum, and 41 per cent said that they had been tortured (Girma et al., 2014). Survivors of these forms of violence should not be detained, yet all had been subject to detention.

3.4   Children in detention

Another controversial issue in relation to IRCs is the detention of children. People working in the area of children's rights, such as Patricia Hynes (2010) in the UK and Edith Montgomery (2008) in Denmark, have highlighted problems in responding to child migrants and unaccompanied minors without due consideration of their age. They have pointed out that immigration policies can at times contravene, or do not uphold, the United Nations Convention of the Rights of the Child (1989). For example, countries that have signed the Convention are required to hold the best interests of a child as their top priority, should protect their wider rights (including refugee rights) and protect them from all forms of violence.

A number of studies have brought the rights of children into question where immigration is concerned. It is useful to recognise at least two key issues: the question of age determination in asylum; and the treatment of detained children in the UK. As you have seen, not all immigrants or asylum seekers have the identity documentation that is required by border control agencies, such as passports or visas. This can make it difficult to know the person's country of origin, name or even their date of birth. The last issue is important for deciding how a person's status is approached – that is whether they should be treated as a child or an adult – and whether or not they are seen to be accompanied by parents or they are unaccompanied minors. For example, young people who claim to be children are sometimes disbelieved, especially those who are teenagers. This can affect whether a child will be detained or deported in some countries.

In 2010, the UK government promised to end the detention of child migrants based on evidence given that demonstrated the harms of incarceration, including witnessing violence and racism, attempted suicides and self-harm by children, as well as the longer-lasting impacts of detention on children's mental health after they are released (Burnett et al., 2010). Organisations such as Medical Justice have long been critics of the immigration of children in detention. In 2010, they reported that many children had been subjected to 'dawn raids', where immigration officers and/or police entered the home early in the morning to conduct immigration raids that led to detention. They found that, while in detention, food was regularly of a poor standard, schooling was poorer than regular education, and some children experienced violence by parents, other detainees or security guards while in the IRC (Burnett et al., 2010). Bosworth points out, however, that although the detention of children has been officially halted, family units still detain some children (2014).

As this section has shown, there are some serious problems linked with immigration removal centres and the issue of detention more broadly. These include abuses against women, children and men seeking asylum, the expansion of detention industries, and issues linked with privatisation. As Zedner (2013), Aas and Bosworth (2013) and Bosworth (2014) show, these provide good reason for human rights campaigners to be concerned about the treatment of people seeking asylum, particularly in terms of their criminalisation. This again draws us back to questions about 'justice', and concerns raised about the increased representation of asylum seekers (and immigrants more broadly) in Britain's criminal justice system. Furthermore, the way in which the asylum system itself increasingly mirrors the criminal justice system remains a site of contention in this area, particularly for critical criminologists.

Summary

- Changes in policy since the 1990s have made it more difficult for asylum seekers to gain entry to the UK, and easier to be processed through the criminal justice system due to increasingly restrictive policies and punitive laws in the area of immigration.

- Migration policy and practice have gradually shifted towards criminal justice approaches, resulting in the increased criminalisation of immigrants.

- The use of detention is controversial and strongly debated in immigration politics. It can have serious implications for the rights of migrants, as well as long-term impacts on mental health. This, coupled with issues in privatisation, has made immigration a site of debate in the UK and further afield.

Conclusion

This chapter has documented issues in terms of how asylum seekers and immigrants are controlled. It has shown the ways in which this can be done, namely through social policy, increased border security and through the blending of asylum and criminal law. Key ideas, such as Stumpf's concept of 'crimmigration', have been explored, which gives some way of understanding the wider landscape of these changes.

It has been important to consider the impacts that some outcomes of control, such as 'Fortress Europe', can have on the lives of people fleeing persecution and seeking asylum, and to question the extent to which current approaches achieve just outcomes for people in need of help. Many people's lives have been lost trying to gain entry to safer European countries through dangerous overland travel or unsafe migration by sea. For those who reach safer shores, the prospect of detention, dispersal or deportation can leave people feeling depressed and anxious about the future.

As you have seen, seeking asylum is a highly debated subject and is often represented in political forums or through the media as a serious problem, particularly in terms of increases in net migration. However, it is also clear that applications for asylum in the UK have decreased, partly because of the kinds of controls put in place that make it difficult to reach. As this chapter has shown, this does not mean fewer people flee conflict or persecution, but that many are deterred from applying for asylum because of offshore controls, the implementation of key policies such as the Dublin II Regulation, and by private border police. All of these issues are of great concern to criminologists who are interested in questions of justice and in upholding key legislative principles, such as those which protect human rights or the 1951 Refugee Convention, as well as to those who have shown that detention and incarceration can be particularly harmful for people seeking asylum.

References

Aas, K.F. and Bosworth, M. (2013) *The Borders of Punishment: Migration, Citizenship and Social Exclusion*, Oxford, Oxford University Press.

Asylum Aid (2011) *Unsustainable: The Quality of Initial Decision Making in Women's Asylum Claims*, London, Asylum Aid.

BBC (2014) *Big increase in net migration to UK* [Online]. Available at www.bbc.co.uk/news/uk-politics-26367391 (Accessed 3 June 2015).

Blinder, S. (2014) *Briefing: Migration to the UK: Asylum*, 3rd Revision [Online]. Available at www.migrationobservatory.ox.ac.uk/sites/files/migobs/Briefing%20-%20Migration%20to%20the%20UK%20-%20Asylum_0.pdf (Accessed 3 June 2015).

Bosworth, M. (2014) *Inside Immigration Detention*, Oxford, Oxford University Press.

Burnett, J., Carter, J., Evershed, J., Bell Kohli, M., Powell, C. and de Wilde, G. (2010) *State Sponsored Cruelty: Children in Immigration Detention*, London, Medical Justice.

Canning, V. (2014) 'International conflict, sexual violence and asylum policy: Merseyside as a case study', *Critical Social Policy*, vol. 34, no. 23, pp. 23–45.

Christie, N. (2000) *Crime Control as Industry: Towards Gulags, Western Style*, London, Routledge.

Cohen, S. (1985) *Visions of Social Control*, Cambridge, Polity Press.

Girma, M., Radice, S., Tsangarides, N. and Walter, N. (2014) *Detained: Women Asylum Seekers Locked Up in the UK*, London, Women for Refugee Women.

Haroon, S. (2008) *The Health Needs of Asylum Seekers* [Online]. Available at http://www.fph.org.uk/uploads/bs_aslym_seeker_health.pdf (Accessed 3 June 2015).

Hynes, P. (2010) 'Understanding the "vulnerabilities", "resilience" and processes of the trafficking of children and young people into, within and out of the UK', *Youth & Policy* (special edition), vol. 104, pp. 97–118.

Joint Committee on Human Rights (JCHR) (2007) *The Treatment of Asylum Seekers* [Online]. Available at www.publications.parliament.uk/pa/jt200607/jtselect/jtrights/81/81i.pdf (Accessed 20 October 2014).

Medical Justice (2010) *Outsourcing Abuse: The Use and Misuse of State-Sanctioned Force During the Detention and Removal of Asylum Seekers* [Online]. Available at www.medicaljustice.org.uk/images/stories/reports/outsourcing%20abuse.pdf (Accessed 14 October 2014).

Montgomery, E. and Foldspang, A. (2008) 'Discrimination, mental problems and social adaptation in young refugees', *European Journal of Public Health*, vol. 18, no. 2, pp. 156–61.

Stonewall (2010) *No Going Back: Lesbian and Gay People in the Asylum System* [Online]. Available at www.stonewall.org.uk/documents/no_going_back_1.pdf (Accessed 20 October 2014).

Stumpf, J. (2006) 'The crimmigration crisis: immigrants, crime and sovereign power', *American University Law Review*, vol. 52, no. 2, pp. 367–419.

Tyler, I. (2006) '"Welcome to Britain": the cultural politics of asylum', *European Journal of Cultural Studies*, vol. 9, pp. 185–202.

Tyler, I. (2013) *Revolting Subjects: Social Abjection and Resistance in Neoliberal Britain*, London, Zed Books.

United Against Racism (2012) *List of 17306 Documented Refugee Deaths Through Fortress Europe* [Online]. Available at www.unitedagainstracism.org/pdfs/listofdeaths.pdf (Accessed 20 October 2014).

United Nations (1948) 'Article 23 of Universal Declaration of Human Rights' [Online]. Available at www.un.org/en/documents/udhr/ (Accessed 7 April 2015).

United Nations High Commissioner for Refugees (1951, 1967) *Convention and Protocol Relating to the Status of Refugees (Geneva Convention)* [Online]. Available at www.unhcr.org/3b66c2aa10.html (Accessed 20 October 2014).

Webber, F. (2012) *Borderline Justice: The Fight for Refugee and Migrant Rights*, London, Pluto Press.

Zedner, L. (2013) 'Is the criminal law only for citizens? A problem at the borders of punishment', in Aas, K.F. and Bosworth, M. (2013) *The Borders of Punishment: Migration, Citizenship and Social Exclusion*, Oxford, Oxford University Press.

Chapter 9
Managing the soundscape

by George Revill

Contents

Introduction

Noise is increasingly recognised as a problem in the media, in social science and environmental studies, and in government legislation. With the din and cacophony of urban traffic, annoying phone conversations in public places, jet fighters screaming low over remote landscapes, and noisy neighbours, unwanted sound seems to permeate life in both urban areas and the countryside in ways that can sometimes feel impossible to escape.

Though it might appear to be a modern problem, the question of unwanted noise is not a new one. In Classical Rome, people complained vociferously about the noise made by 'endless traffic', the sound of the soldiers' hobnail boots on stone cobbles, the shouts of cattle drovers herding animals through the city, the clattering of kitchens and the revels of late-night drunks on the street. In Victorian times, it was the street musicians, the rumble of carts and trams, the calls of itinerant vendors and the sounds of manufacturing that created a disturbance.

The experience of sonic environments changes from generation to generation, along with different capacities to make sound. Today the wider availability of technology results in an unprecedented capacity to make sound both individually and collectively. However, there are other factors in play. First, social life is more complex: more people do more varied things in more places at the same time. In the past in the UK, many, if not most, people got up roughly at the same time, went to work en masse and often socialised together at places of worship, at inns, public houses and in common spaces, sharing both lifestyles and cultural values. Today, life is much more varied and often people have many more choices, and different lifestyles and daily routines. Second, the rights of individuals to do as they please in their own private spaces and to express themselves in public through their lifestyle choices (including music) and the use of potentially noisy technology result in the creation of complex **soundscapes** in which different priorities, needs, wants, tastes and choices co-exist, collide and conflict. Managing the soundscape therefore seems to be centrally concerned with particular spaces and places and how we use them, rather than just more and bigger technology.

Noise
Can be defined as sound out of place (for example, because of its excessive loudness or persistency) following anthropologist Mary Douglas' definition of dirt as 'matter out of place'.

Soundscape
Coined by Raymond Murray Schafer in the 1960s, a soundscape might be defined as the mixture of natural and human-made sounds that can be heard within a particular place, environment or landscape.

This chapter will:

- explore the complex ways in which boundaries are made in sound

- recognise some of the ways social scientists study sound in relation to issues of noise and unwanted sound

- evaluate different ways of managing and controlling unwanted sound.

Tranquillity
A state of being calm, peaceful and worry-free. Research suggests that a predominance of natural sounds and visual landscape features enhance senses of tranquillity.

Zoning
Concerns the spatial separation of different activities, such as industrial, residential and leisure uses, so that sounds produced by noisy industrial machinery or loud music from pubs, bars and public venues do not disturb people in their homes.

Individualisation
Describes the ways certain noise problems, for example, that of neighbour noise, are made the responsibility of the individuals concerned, construed as matters of good neighbourliness or 'civility' rather than legally enforceable set limits.

Section 1, 'Sound signatures', begins by looking at the way people identify with sounds and shows how sounds can define public and private spaces. Think, for example, of how specific sounds might come to be identified with an immigration centre (like those described in the previous chapter), and how this would differ from the sounds you would hear within your living room.

Section 2, 'Unwanted sound', examines how noise or unwanted sound can be understood as matter out of place and how, in turn, sound can be a source of conflict and controversy.

Section 3, 'Mapping tranquillity', turns to the question of **tranquillity** to examine how the issues created by unwanted sound can be sources of inequality.

Section 4, 'Managing unwanted sound', considers the ways in which unwanted sound is managed in terms of the right to peace and quiet. This can be understood in terms of environmental and social justice represented by sound control strategies of **zoning** and **individualisation**.

1 Sound signatures: public and private places

People often identify strongly with particular types of music, specific artists and performers. Music has become an important way for people to differentiate themselves and express their biography, lifestyle and cultural preferences, to show who they are and how they imagine themselves in relation to others.

Activity 1

Think of two ways in which sound can be very useful in helping us to create a boundary around people and separate them either physically or symbolically from others.

Discussion

Your examples may include some of the following:

Sound as a physical boundary

- Listening to music through headphones may physically block out environmental sounds and those made by other people.

- Sometimes environmental sounds such as waterfalls or fountains are used to create zones of calm in gardens by physically blocking out sounds from elsewhere.

- Sonic devices such as the 'Mosquito', which are designed only to be heard by younger people, are used in public spaces to dissuade them from 'loitering'.

Sound as a symbolic boundary

- Favourite music, for example, can provide a symbolic boundary suggesting lifestyle choice as well as expressing differences in age, taste, experience and culture.

- Crowds singing and chanting demarcate themselves symbolically from other groups and individuals; for example, when fans chant at a football match.

- Music is sometimes used by shops both to encourage customers in particular socio-economic groupings and age ranges, and also to dissuade others.

The development of music-playing technologies, such as the MP3 player and before that the 'Walkman'-style portable cassette tape players, has allowed people to carve out a sense of personal space at work, on the street and at home, in an effort to gain control of their daily experience. As one interviewee (Tracy) in sociologist Michael Bull's study of iPod users said:

> Well, I think I've come to the conclusion that overall I feel pretty out of control in my life. Stores play music to get me to buy more. Work tells me what to do and when. Traffic decides how quickly I get from here to there. Even being in public places forces me to endure other people and their habits (the guy slurping his soup, the brat crying for a piece of candy). I didn't realize how much I yearn for control and probably peace and quiet. Strange since I'm blasting music in my ears. I think I'm really tired of living on someone else's schedule. The MP3 digital music revolution has given me some control back.
>
> (Bull, 2005, p. 346)

Listening to music through headphones has been shown to be a useful way to make a barrier between the distracting background noise of the work environment and the work task in hand. In a study of UK office workers, listening to personal music appears to be very common. A study in 2010 showed that 77 per cent of British workers listened to music at work, for a third of their working week on average, and workers in computer-based office environments listened to significantly more music than people in other workplaces. In their study interviewing office workers about listening to music at work, Nicola Dibben and Anneli Haake (2013) found that, though some found music distracting, many workers found it helped them to concentrate. As a manager in one research institute said:

> For me, there's a certain comfort zone that is created by music. And that blocks out people yacking in the next office and people shouting at each other in the corridor, and other people's problems and vehicles arriving outside. It does filter those distractions out, I think. It is giving me total control of my aural environment ... I find myself concentrating, and focus more.
>
> (Patrick, Research and development workshop manager, Research Institute)
> (Dibben and Haake, 2013, p. 156)

Dibben and Haake found that listening to music served other purposes too. For some workers, playing music in their own office marked out this territory as their own private space; for others, wearing headphones symbolised to the rest of the office that they were concentrating and did not want to be disturbed. The researchers also found that there were unwritten rules about who could control the music. In the research institute laboratory they studied, there was a common understanding that whoever was spending the most time there in a day would put their music on. On those occasions when employees found it hard to compromise, they chose to listen to the radio, as it was perceived as 'relatively neutral' because they did not 'have any control over' the content. Other strategies for managing music played over speakers in shared spaces included voluntarily turning music down or off, negotiating with colleagues, or using headphones to block out unwanted music with one's own music (Dibben and Haake, 2013, p. 159). In these ways, Dibben and Haake found that listening to music in offices formed a material barrier to unwanted sound by wearing headphones and physically blocking out the noise. At the same time, sound was part of a complex office culture with powerful unwritten symbolic meanings which told colleagues for example; 'this is my office', 'I'm busy – do not disturb' and 'I am working longest, I can choose the music'.

Activity 2

Name two sounds you associate with specific places. Why do they remind you of those places?

Discussion

You might have thought of something from personal experience: the sound of a clock ticking in a particular room, or the echo of footsteps across hard paving in a town square, or the sound of the sea breaking on a favourite beach. However, you might also have thought of distinctive musical soundtracks to places shared by many people. Such shared sonic signatures include the sound of a carnival, suggesting Rio de Janeiro, Liverpool with the Beatles and other 'Mersey Beat' groups, Tibet with the sound of chanting monks and temple bells, and Paris with the sounds of accordion-playing street musicians, to identify just four well-known examples.

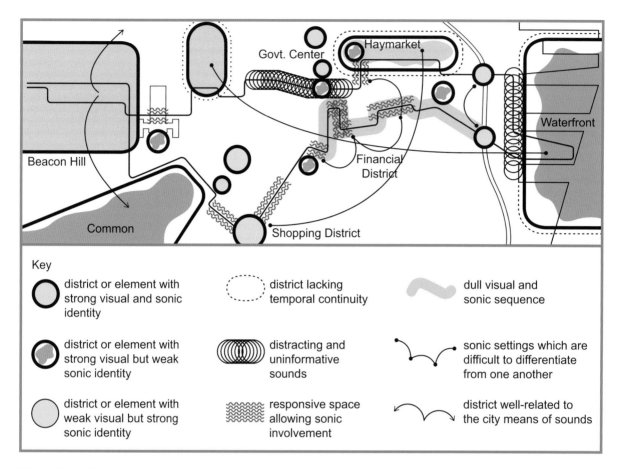

Figure 9.1   Soundscape map of Boston, Massachusetts, by Michael Southworth (1969, p.66)

One important way in which social scientists have begun to engage with the complex sound worlds that characterise places is through the study of 'soundscapes', a term coined by Schafer (1969), and developed by him and those involved in the World Soundscapes Project through the 1970s. Soundscapes might be defined as the mixture of natural and human-made sounds that can be heard within a particular place, environment or landscape. Researchers often make audio recordings of the different sounds that can be heard in a particular place; for example, under a bridge, in an open space, in a city square, or close to large buildings and trees. Sometimes recordings can be made at a particular time in the day – for example, dawn or dusk – to capture the distinctive sounds of animals or birds, or over a period of days or months to capture the ebb and flow of weather and seasons at particular times of the year. Researchers sometimes translate this information into maps. Such maps try to delineate and define areas which have similar sonic characteristics. Figure 9.1 is one attempt to map the soundscapes of the city of Boston, Massachusetts, in the United States.

It is easy to see from this example soundscape map just how complex and difficult it can be to represent sonic environments as a map. Though sounds can be mapped, the nature of sound makes this very difficult; sound is characterised by its ability to echo and resound from place to place, to leak out and infiltrate places and spaces far from its source. Though the map in Figure 9.1 presents many problems of understanding and interpretation, one thing that is noticeable is the number of areas marked either with a squiggly spiral or by a dotted line. These are places in which sound has been recorded as ambiguous, where different soundscapes overlap and mix.

Though the idea of mapping soundscapes is useful, it does not fully take into account the fact that there is no one single soundscape even in places that are dominated by particular sounds. Not only are places often characterised by a range of sound-producing activities undertaken by different groups and individuals with distinctive aims, aspirations and possibly cultural values, but the very soundscape itself is different for particular individuals and groups. What humans hear above the hubbub of background sound is partly governed by what is important to them. Sounds are valued differently depending on who you are and where you come from. Take for example the story told by Andrew J. Eisenberg about researching soundscapes in the Old Town of Mombasa. Eisenberg shows how sound forms a fundamental part of the cultural identity of the Muslim population who live in the old part of the city, among its jumble of narrow streets and historic buildings. He says:

> Mombasa Old Town is every day awash with electrically amplified male voices delivering Islamic devotional and moral texts in Arabic and Swahili. Five times a day a polyphony of cantillated Arabic calls to prayer emanates from the roof top loudspeakers of dozens of neighbourhood mosques, its 'soaring yet mournful, almost languid harmonic webs' (Hirschkind, 2006, p. 124) somewhat harshened by the crackling of overstressed or substandard sound reproduction technologies. The constant rhythm of this key 'soundmark' (Schafer, 1994 [1977]) is further punctuated each week by the polyphony of Arabic and Swahili sermons that emanate from many of these same loudspeakers. Between these periodic sonic events, a random assemblage of

radios and computer speakers in local shops and homes supply the neighbourhood's private and semi-private spaces with layers of Qur'anic recitations, sermons in Arabic, Swahili and sometimes English, and religious songs in Swahili and Arabic (Swa. *kaswida*; Ar. qaṣīda) – producing a continuous (e)merging of vocal performances that I refer to as an Islamic soundscape.

(Eisenberg, 2013, p. 190)

Eisenberg shows how what he calls an Islamic soundscape is an important part of 'Old Town' culture, helping to identify its long-established Muslim community as a self-defined urban civilised elite in distinction to Christian groups and poor rural migrants. This latter group are incomers who have been brought to the city as part of government plans to modernise the city and expand the economy. All these groups are considered 'barbarian' by a long-established 'Old Town' Muslim community who are proud of their heritage and traditions. The sound of the Islamic soundscape resonates out across the city for all to hear. Yet Eisenberg claims that an important attribute of this soundscape is that it is believed to be only for the ears of the Muslim faith community in the Old Town and demands their attention and participation alone. The words broadcast from minarets and loudspeakers are sacred and private to this community. Eisenberg said that he was made acutely aware of this when he recorded some of the Friday prayers from the balcony of the apartment in which he was staying. Some members of the Old Town's Swahilli community called a meeting to discuss possible ways of preventing him from making further recordings. Fortunately he was able to explain his purely academic interest and the problem was defused (Eisenberg, 2013, p. 200).

Eisenberg had overlooked the very different interpretations of the soundscape, which sounds were culturally important and to whom they belonged. Where for him, as an academic researcher from Europe, broadcast sound belonged to no one in particular, for the Muslim residents of Old Town Mombasa, the broadcast of Friday prayers belonged to them alone and was an important marker of their community and culture. To try to 'capture' the sound by recording, or even to admit to listening to, the sound of Friday prayers as an outsider was interpreted by Old Town residents as an invasion of private space.

Summary

- Sound can create both physical and symbolic boundaries.

- It can play a role in making individual, group and place-specific identities.

2   Unwanted sound: in and out of place

Because sounds reflect social and cultural values, and because they carry an awareness of actions and activities to other people situated well beyond the places in which those sounds were made, sound can often be a source of conflict and controversy. Eisenberg's research in Mombasa Old Town is just one example of this. The experience of sound apparently out of place is key to the ways in which you can begin to understand noise and why unwanted sound can raise passions and make people feel angry, desperate and helpless.

Activity 3

Remember an example of when you thought a sound was in the wrong place. Why did you find it inappropriate?

Discussion

Examples might include the rumble of heavy farm machinery or aircraft screaming across the sky when you are trying to enjoy a peaceful moment of contemplation in the countryside; or maybe raucous laughter in a quiet workspace; perhaps even someone reciting poetry in the street. Sounds often seem out of place either because they invade personal space and stop people doing what they want to do, or they represent the actions of people believed to be acting inappropriately in a place defined by particular sorts of behaviour. This might include, for example, talking in a space designated for listening (such as a concert hall or lecture theatre) or being irreverent in a sacred space (a place of worship or commemoration).

In this context, unwanted sound, or what might be called 'noise', can be defined as sound that seems to be in the wrong place. This follows the anthropologist Mary Douglas's (1966) definition of dirt, or pollution, as 'matter out of place'. Douglas shows how people try to find meaning in the world by creating a sense of order that categorises some things as appropriate to some places and not to others. In this way, earth on the carpet is dirt because it is out of place, but in the garden it is soil, the essential medium in which plants are grown. Rather than sound defining a particular place, sound out of place and

considered as noise often contradicts and conflicts with socially and
culturally agreed definitions of place.

By examining how sound demarcates certain behaviour as in place or
out of place, Matless (2005) shows how sound highlights conflict
concerning increasing visitor numbers and leisure use of the Norfolk
Broads landscape. The Broads were designated as a National Park in
1988 but reports that sought protection for the 'natural music' of
wind, reeds and bird song from the playing of loud party music on
boats can be traced back through the 20th century to the beginnings of
mass tourism in the region. Sonic judgements placing bird watching
and walking as appropriate but partying as inappropriate continue into
the 21st century and are evident in debates about rural tranquillity and
the appropriateness of rock, pop and dance music in the countryside.
Examples of such conflicts can be seen in the increasing number of
rural music festivals, such as that at Glastonbury in Somerset, or the
attempts by government and police during the 1990s to stop rural rave
parties (Figure 9.2), or indeed conflicts over traffic noise.

Figure 9.2   A rural rave

A programme instigated by the Conservative Government in the UK
in 1989 produced a series of high-profile road-building schemes.
Combined with growing environmental awareness exemplified by the
1992 Rio Earth Summit, these resulted in increasingly active and
vociferous protest movements. High-profile cases such as the cutting

of the M3 through Twyford Down, near Winchester (1992), and Oxleas Wood in London brought the UK Government into conflict with the European Union and with environmental groups such as Earth First! (formed in 1991). At the same time, UK Government attempts to reduce what they deemed antisocial behaviour in the countryside impacted directly on protestors who were often young people. The Criminal Justice Act of 1994, for example, had a section aimed at curbing rural rave parties and the actions of so-called 'New Age Travellers', sometimes associated with both the rural rave scene and environmental protest. Part V of the Act covered collective trespass, and nuisance on land included sections against raves and against music 'characterised by the emission of a succession of repetitive beats'. The prohibition of music defined by 'repetitive beats' was designed to prohibit the sort of electronic dance music played at rave parties but also enjoyed by many road protestors. The anti-trespass laws worked against road protests and rave parties alike so, to this extent, the Criminal Justice Act has parallels with the example of the Norfolk Broads because both concern the actions of government authorities to limit and circumscribe particular forms of behaviour as appropriate in the countryside by defining it in sonic terms. Both imply that forms of passive quietness characterise the way people should behave in rural environments.

As has been seen, sound out of place can seem like a threat to group senses of belonging and widely held ideas about what behaviours are appropriate in particular places. Unwanted sound can also cause significant problems for an individual's sense of themselves as they try to hold on to and control their own privacy at times when they feel most vulnerable. Sociologist Tom Rice's study of the experience of hospital soundscapes provides some quite disturbing examples of this. Rice shows how hospital wards can be noisy places, crowded with sound. Patients undergoing treatment in close proximity, intense staff activity, machines giving out signals, tones and alarms: these sources can combine to produce what Rice (2013, p. 170) calls 'a cacophony of illness'. He says some medical professionals are rightly concerned that excessive (and largely preventable) noise on wards might negatively affect patient health and recovery times. For the patients participating in his study, sounds certainly played a key role in identifying a loss of privacy in hospital. Many found they were unable to escape the sonic details of suffering by their ward neighbours. Sounds would infiltrate and pervade both patients' immediate physical environment and what they tended to describe as their 'mental' space. At the same time, most patients were acutely conscious that they themselves could be overheard by those nearby. It was difficult for them to control or restrict the spread of intimate sounds.

Sometimes the sounds coming through the curtain could be harrowing for patients. One lady to whom Rice spoke grimaced as she described the whimpering that had come from behind the screen as her neighbour used a bedpan for the first time since undergoing a bowel operation. Another had endured prolonged cries of agony from nearby as a man underwent an unpleasant procedure hidden from view. A man named Gordon, who had recently been discharged, described how during his stay in hospital his ward neighbour had suffered a heart attack late at night. Nursing staff had been quick to help and pulled the privacy curtains around all the beds. A resuscitation team was called and Gordon had been obliged to listen to the dramatic sounds of their attempts to save the man's life. Eventually he heard them agree that their efforts had failed and after the necessary preparations had been made, he heard the body wheeled away. Rice recounts how Gordon confessed that he 'was shattered for days by these horrible noises'. This violent eruption in the hospital soundscape, associated in this case with death, was deeply disturbing for him (Rice, 2013, p. 172).

While the hospital radio, and occasionally televisions, on the wards could sometimes provide an auditory distraction, most of the time there was little else for patients to do but listen to the ward around them or do their best to turn a deaf ear. Rice recalls how one day as he walked down a ward, a patient being attended to behind a curtain could be heard vomiting profusely. The lady in the adjacent bed was sitting up, turning the pages of a magazine. She held a fixed, bland smile as she pretended to be oblivious to the sounds that were loud and plain. Of course, she had little choice but to do exactly this. Unable to escape the sound, she was obliged to tolerate it as best she could. Rice says that he felt her facial expression encapsulated the effort made by many simply to put up with the sounds, however invasive, irritating or distasteful. This attempt to remain unperturbed could be understood as a way of managing the auditory environment (Rice, 2013, p. 174).

Rice concludes that:

> Privacy, then, is partly compromised through patients being constantly within earshot of other people. Of course, being

audible could be reassuring. Patients knew that if they needed help, they could call or cry out and someone would hear and come to assist them. But they resented the fact that they could not remove themselves from being in the presence of their neighbours if desired. Not only did they have little control over what sounds intruded into their immediate private acoustic space, but they were also limited in their ability to restrict how their own bodies projected into the public acoustic space shared by others.

(Rice, 2013, p. 175)

For the hospital patients in Rice's study, sound out of place constituted an important threat to personal dignity and integrity at a time when they felt most vulnerable and defenceless. Unwanted sound, or sound out of place, clearly has important impacts across many areas of life and at a variety of scales, from that of the individual person to specific places, landscapes and regions. In this respect sound can both define and undermine socially agreed ways of drawing boundaries around spaces and places.

Summary

- Noise can be defined as sound out of place following anthropologist Mary Douglas's definition of dirt as 'matter out of place'

- Sound out of place can be perceived as a threat for individuals and groups, which both defines and undermines socially agreed ways of drawing boundaries.

3 Mapping tranquillity: inequality in valuing sound socially

As can be seen from the previous section, sound becomes a problem when people understand it to be in the wrong place or even in the right place but at the wrong time. The idea of noise as sound out of place was recognised early in the 20th century by the British physicist G.W.C. Kaye. Kaye's conception of noise relates closely to Douglas's definition of dirt. Like Douglas, Kaye claimed that sound could be understood as out of place, by its:

> ... excessive loudness, its composition, its persistency or frequency of occurrence (or alternatively, its intermittency), its unexpectedness, its untimeliness or unfamiliarity, its redundancy, inappropriateness, or unreasonableness, its suggestion of intimidation, arrogance, malice, or thoughtlessness.
>
> (Kaye, 1931, pp. 443–5, cited in Bijsterveld, 2008, p. 240)

Activity 4

From Kaye's description, why do you think it might be so difficult for everyone to agree on what constitutes noise?

Discussion

It is clear from Kaye's description that the physical qualities of sound – its loudness, duration and intensity – form only one part of the equation. Equally important for Kaye are issues of inappropriateness, unreasonableness, arrogance and thoughtlessness. These latter components of unwanted noise depend on human judgements and are therefore subject to interpretation, as well as contested and competing claims and counter-claims in relation to what is and is not appropriate and permissible.

In hospitals, as in the countryside, human responses to unwanted sound are heavily dependent on the context in which the sounds are heard and on the ways in which particular sounds acquire social value that marks them as appropriate or inappropriate. Mike Goldsmith (2012) shows how this was probably first demonstrated through social scientific study in the Wilson Report into noise nuisance in the UK, produced in 1963. The report found that people judge noise levels partly from their knowledge of the source. Annoyance from sound depends on who or what is making the noise as well as the loudness and intensity of the sound itself. The study found that people claim the intrusiveness of noise differently depending on whether they are indoors or out and that people are more tolerant of noises outdoors. Attempts were made to compare the findings of the Wilson Report with the results of surveys and studies in other countries, but problems emerged because words such as 'annoyance' do not always have exact equivalents in other languages and cultures.

It is now widely identified that human recognition of noise nuisance reflects place and culture. The research that informed the European Noise Directive (2002) found, for example, that people in Mediterranean towns and cities were more tolerant of neighbour noise than those in Northern Europe. This is thought to be because often in Mediterranean cultures, more time is spent socialising outdoors at home and in local neighbourhoods and because in warmer climates windows and doors remain open for longer periods than in colder northern European cities. In this way, people in southern Europe may become more accustomed to noise spilling over from one place to another and entering their domestic spaces. Goldsmith (2012, p. 208) further suggests that a wide range of social values are involved in human recognition of noise nuisance, including, he says, issues of trust and respect. Surveys of people living near Düsseldorf Airport, for example, have consistently shown higher levels of annoyance than those of people living near other comparable airports. The difference stems from 1992, when the local authority, which had previously owned the airport, sold it to a private company, which then launched an expensive and successful campaign to get permission for a 30 per cent increase in flights. In this case, claims concerning noise nuisance reflect the fact that local residents feel betrayed and ignored by the private company that now runs the airport.

The concept of tranquillity illustrates many of the problems concerning noise nuisance sketched out earlier. It is, for example, very difficult to quantify, while ideas of what constitutes tranquillity change from person to person and from culture to culture. In addition, access to, and experiences of, tranquillity are distributed very unevenly across the world and through societies. Tranquillity is highly valued but can be a rare commodity; it can be expensive to find and, as you saw from the example of patients in hospital, it can be in short supply for some of those who might need it most. One reason why it is difficult to quantify and provokes such a personal and subjective response is that tranquillity is about more than just absence of sound. As Trevor Cox (2014, p. 224) found in his investigation of the 'quietest places in the world', a scientific study of human responses to tranquillity using an MRI (Magnetic Resonance Imaging) brain scanner to study brain activity showed that tranquillity was dependent on a variety of sensual stimuli working together. Respondents were played an ambiguous sound recording through headphones, which could have been either waves crashing on a beach or light road traffic. Researchers found that responses to this sound in terms of tranquillity depended on whether they were shown pictures of coastal landscapes or urban street scenes simultaneously with the sound recording.

In England, the Campaign to Protect Rural England (CPRE), an organisation dedicated to countryside conservation, access and rural communities, has made several attempts to map tranquil areas to show the extent and degree of tranquillity across the country. It reported:

> The word 'tranquillity' appears in a great many policy and planning documents, and also numerous publications which promote places for tourism and inward investment. It is clear that whatever tranquillity is, and wherever it is to be found, it is important and judged to be worth protecting.
>
> Being in tranquil places allows people to relax, to escape from the stresses and strains of everyday life and to 'recharge their batteries'….

(CPRE/Countryside Agency, 2005, p. 3)

Activity 5

What does tranquillity mean to you?

Discussion

Your definition might include:

- atmosphere and mood: words such as peace, quiet and calm
- place and location: rural, garden, The Lake District, the library and my room
- time and activity: dawn, dusk, coffee time and walking the dog
- sounds and experiences: peaceful music and a gentle flowing river.

When tranquillity was first mapped for England in 1995 (see CPRE/ Countryside Agency, 2005), it was defined as 'places which are sufficiently far away from the visual or noise intrusion of development or traffic to be considered unspoilt by urban influences'. These places were identified through specific criteria, with *Tranquil Areas* being found certain distances away from features such as roads, towns, airports and power stations. However, when the exercise was repeated in 2005, the researchers began by asking members of the public what characteristics they thought defined and detracted from tranquillity. The survey of public attitudes to tranquillity found the following important:

What is tranquillity?

- Perceived links to 'nature'
- Positive features in the landscape such as:
  - openness of the landscape
  - perceived naturalness of the landscape
  - rivers in the landscape
  - visibility of the sea

- The importance of wildlife
- Peace, quiet and calm

What is not tranquillity?

- Disruptive behaviour of other people

- Noise, especially from cars but also:

  - road, train and urban area noise
  - aircraft noise
  - military training noise

- Overt signs of human development – perceived negative features in the landscape such as:

  - presence of other people
  - visibility of roads
  - general signs of overt human impact
  - visibility of urban development
  - night-time light pollution.

Look at the following tranquillity maps for the East Midlands region of England produced on behalf of the CPRE in 2007 (CPRE/Countryside Agency, 2007). The first (Figure 9.3) shows calculations made using data available in the early 21st century to show areas susceptible to the intrusion of urban and industrial noise in the early 1960s. The second (Figure 9.4) shows the situation approximately 47 years later in 2007. Comparing the two maps, it is relatively straightforward to see the changes that have taken place:

- The principal change has been the dramatic increase in the area of the map coloured yellow to show areas disturbed by noise and visual intrusion, mostly related to changes in transport.

- The M1 motorway opened through the region between 1965 and 1968, creating a corridor of noise and visual intrusion heading south to north, running between the urban concentrations of Leicester, Derby and Nottingham.

- Major road corridors along the A1 running south to north midway between Nottingham and Leicester, and between the urban centres of Nottingham, Derby, Leicester and Lincoln, also carve swathes of intrusion through formerly less disturbed rural areas.

- On the 2007 map (Figure 9.4), there are road corridors through the Peak District National Park in the top western corner of the map, and through the great expanses of agricultural Lincolnshire and the

Sherwood Forest area of rural Nottinghamshire in the middle and to the east of the map.

- Expansion of East Midlands Airport as a major UK cargo hub has brought many parts of the Nottingham–Derby–Leicester conurbation under its intensive flight paths.

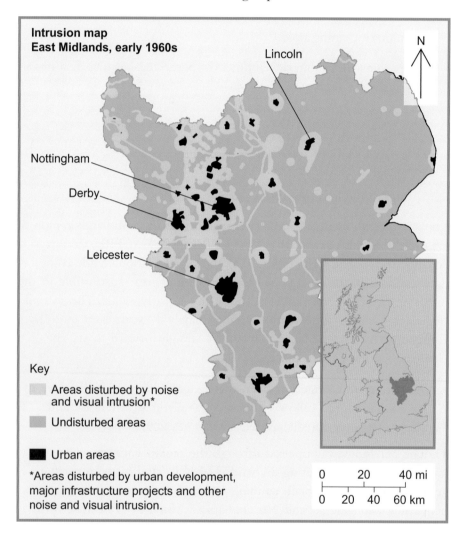

Figure 9.3   CPRE tranquillity map, 1960s (CPRE, 2005)

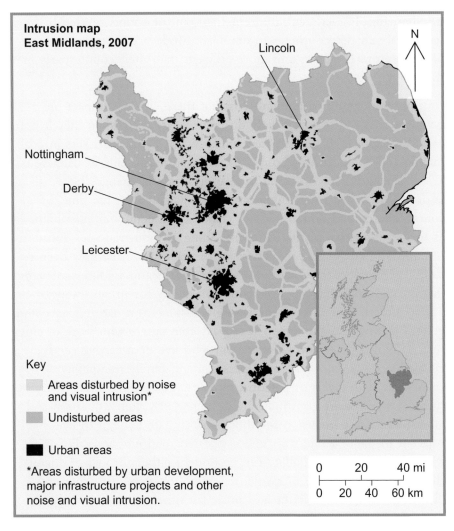

Figure 9.4   CPRE tranquillity map, 2007 (CPRE, 2007)

Though this seems a familiar and plausible story of increased intrusion into a formerly peaceful world by increased levels of mechanically generated noise, maps such as these only tell a part of what is happening and hide as much as they show. Much of the centre of this region was formerly heavily industrial and the landscape was characterised by coalmines, iron and steel works, heavy engineering and textile manufacturing. Even some of the apparently rural parts had significant industrial concentrations in textiles, mining and quarrying activity. As many parts have lost their old Victorian-style industries, they have in some respects actually become quieter as the banging, hammering, clanging and clattering of heavy industry has become a thing of the past. Though traffic on the roads, railways and in the air has dramatically increased, the actual amount of sound emitted by individual vehicles continues to diminish. Modern cars, trains and planes are much quieter and more efficient than their counterparts in the 1960s.

An important point to remember is that these changes impact on people across the region in very different ways, even when they live in areas that appear to be classified similarly. For former workers in coal mining and engineering whose work exposed them daily to dangerous levels of sound likely to result in hearing loss, the changes have improved personal sonic environments. It has at the same time, of course, altered and diminished life chances and economic possibilities as former industrial plants fall silent. Some ex-industrial sites, locations of concentrated sound production in former times, have now been re-landscaped and incorporated into country parks and wildlife sanctuaries that create important new islands of tranquillity for urban dwellers whose lifestyles seem to be increasingly distant from nature, peace and quiet. Elsewhere in the region, well-paid commuters who work in cities such as Nottingham and Leicester but who live in attractive rural village locations enjoy increased personal and family tranquillity enabled by high levels of personal mobility. The higher levels of traffic such lifestyles create contribute to an increased volume, duration and intensity of noise intrusion for those unfortunate enough to live adjacent to major route ways and congested road junctions. For those who can afford it, tranquillity can be bought either through residential choice or by holidaying in exotic or remote locations. In either case, the search for tranquillity creates noise for others, either through commuting traffic or through increases in long- and medium-haul air travel.

Summary

- Tranquillity exemplifies the ways unwanted sound is as much a problem of perceived inappropriate behaviour as actual noise levels.

- Inequality in the experience of, and access to, tranquillity is related to differences in life chances, opportunities and other resources, including ability to pay.

4   Managing unwanted sound: equality and justice

Given that so many people seem to value tranquillity, it is remarkable that it appears so difficult to find and that it is so unequally distributed both geographically and socially. If, as the CPRE claims, tranquillity is vitally important for quality of life and indeed mental and physical health, then it might be quite legitimate to argue that people have some sort of a basic right to peace and quiet. Such a right to be able to sleep without disturbance and enjoy the privacy of home as well as experience nature, parks, gardens and countryside without undue intrusion may seem to many a matter of common sense. Yet, actually defining tranquillity and devising a regulatory framework in which peace and quiet can be enjoyed equally by all provides considerable problems. To this extent, the question of tranquillity highlights some fundamental problems with managing unwanted noise. If peace and quiet is a right that should be available to all, then it is one that is matched by other individual rights relating to sound, which seem to be claimed as both equally important and mutually contradictory. As Karin Bijsterveld (2008) shows, there has long been a widespread acceptance that people have both some kind of right to express themselves and at the same time some kind of right to peace. Add to this the realisation that what bothers one person does not necessarily bother another and the result is that attempts to govern noise have to manage a range of potentially incompatible claims to individual rights and freedoms. This is within the context of what are at best partial and highly subjective assessments of the impact of unwanted noise.

Due to the complexity of noise problems and the apparently contradictory and potentially incompatible principles at stake, the right to make sound while at the same time being free from the consequences of other people's sound-making can be handled in a variety of ways. Karin Bijsterveld (2008) argues that the two major ways of doing this can be summarised under the two headings 'zoning' and 'individualisation'.

Thought of as an environmental problem, the issue of unwanted sound might be considered an issue for what is termed distributive justice. Derived partly from the work of John Rawls (1971) whom you met in Chapter 6, 'Introducing boundaries and justice', distributive justice concerns the fair, just or equitable distribution of benefits and burdens through society. Environmentalists argue that people throughout the world should as a matter of right receive a fair share of the world's resources and, if deemed sufficiently important to human health and happiness, this could include tranquillity, as well as other basic environmental goods such as clean water, food, shelter and warmth. One way of attaining greater distributive justice is through government regulation. This is often thought necessary because legal means provide a way of enforcing a more equal distribution of environmental goods; tranquillity or the 'right to quiet' might be included among these (Caney, 2001).

The primary means of legislating against unwanted noise is through zoning. This concerns the spatial separation of different activities, such as industrial, residential and leisure uses, so that sounds produced by noisy industrial machinery or loud music from pubs, bars and public venues do not disturb people in their homes. As a technique for managing sound, zoning emerged from attempts in the 1920s and 30s to regulate the legacy of Victorian city development in places such as New York and Chicago, where noisy trades and industries such as metalworking had grown up alongside and within residential streets and neighbourhoods. This was taken further during the 1960s when the development of commercial jet airliners and the dramatic rise in civilian air travel provoked public concerns in relation to aircraft noise. In the UK, this ultimately resulted in the banning of night flights from Heathrow Airport and the development of sound maps that use the readings from noise measurement equipment to chart those areas worst affected. In this way, zoning schemes can map out legal limits for sound production in terms of both location and timing. This goes hand in hand with the development of technology and techniques to set objective limits to exposure to sound through the use of sound maps. Some planning regulations, for example, those concerning the location and opening times for leisure activities such as pubs and clubs, combine both place- and time-based zoning.

Activity 6

What do you think are the advantages and disadvantages of zoning as a way of achieving environmental justice in terms of sound?

Discussion

Your answer may include some of the following:

Advantages

- Zoning is based on objective criteria, including measured levels of particular sound output and specifically identified forms of sound-making activity.

- It creates clear boundaries and a legal basis by which particular types and levels of sound and sound-making activities are prohibited.

- It can incorporate both spatially and temporally based noise nuisance by prescribing the times of day for some activities, such as pub opening hours or airport flight times.

Disadvantages

- Zoning creates anomalies that are hard to manage. Sound does not travel across the landscape uniformly and does not diminish in neat steps according to the lines drawn on a map. Residents just outside an exclusion zone or just beyond the zone designated for extra soundproofing may well suffer just as much as those who are included within the zone.

- Zoning is also much less successful when dealing with infrequent and random sound events such as the occasional very noisy motorcar, or shouting and arguing in the street. Studies show that predictability is an important issue enabling residents to manage their experience of a noise problem, and zoning is less successful in managing this aspect of the problem.

Thought of as a social problem, the issue of unwanted sound can be understood as a matter of civility and therefore understandable in terms of the rights and responsibilities that go hand in hand with citizenship. To this extent, the problem of unwanted sound is closer to the conception of social justice you met in Chapter 6, 'Introducing boundaries and justice'. Here issues of justice can be understood in terms of mutual obligations and responsibilities, and the forms of appropriate and inappropriate behaviour that result in noise nuisance and disturbance. Environmentalists sometimes talk about what they call 'environmental' or even 'ecological' citizenship. One characteristic of this is that those who have power and wealth have an obligation to those less fortunate to minimise the harm they might cause through their own actions, and actively work to improve environments for others (Smith and Pangsapa, 2008). Where sound is concerned, this would include individuals acting in a civil manner by consciously seeking to curb the amount of potentially intrusive sound they make themselves – listening to music, mowing the lawn or driving a vehicle. It also encourages people to actively maintain, promote and create environments that preserve the right to quiet for others.

In her history of public noise problems in the 20th century, Bijsterveld (2008) understands such issues of civility and social justice in terms of what she calls 'individualisation'. Individualisation describes the ways in which certain noise problems, for example, that of neighbour noise, are made the responsibility of the individuals concerned. In these circumstances, noise issues are often designated by the authorities as matters of good neighbourliness or civility rather than legally enforceable set limits. In many countries where legislation exists, neighbours are expected to negotiate with each other and arrive at some mutual understanding of each other's experiences, feelings and needs. From this perspective, the role of government is merely to provide public education, outlining acceptable and unacceptable behaviour. Individualisation relates back to the contradiction in social thinking about noise that upholds, on the one hand, the right for free self-expression and, on the other, the right to peace and quiet. In both cases there is an understanding that what bothers one person does not necessarily bother another, and that annoyance is both subjective and dependent on someone's circumstances and the context in which the sound is heard. Claims concerning what constitutes unwanted sound are very subjective and the basis for evaluating claims and counter-claims is hard to fix. What might annoy someone who works nights, or has young children, might not necessarily concern someone who is frequently away from home, enjoys a bustling lively atmosphere, or indeed might be hard of hearing.

For many countries, the role of government in neighbour noise is first and foremost to educate citizens in how to control their own noisy behaviour and to teach them how to be tolerant and accept some incidental noise. In the UK and elsewhere, one cornerstone of this approach is advice concerning how to approach a noisy neighbour about the problem and couch any claims about the problem in a calm and prudent manner. In this way, the government adopts a position that steps back from what might be understood as too much direct intrusion into home and family life.

NEIGHBOUR NOISE
a guide for the public

ENCAMS

Figure 9.5   Neighbour noise information leaflet

Activity 7

What do you think are the advantages and disadvantages of individualisation as a way of achieving social justice in terms of sound?

Discussion

Your answer may include some of the following:

Advantages

*   Individualisation recognises that unwanted sound is often context-dependent rather than a matter of absolute standards.

*   It prevents governments from interfering with what people do in the privacy of their own homes.

- It encourages people to be active environmental citizens by taking responsibility for their own 'noisiness'.

Disadvantages

- Where agreement cannot be reached between neighbours, it is not possible to resort to an absolute standard to resolve competing claims.

- People who feel under threat from noisy neighbours are forced to take the initiative and may feel neglected and abandoned by the authorities in their quest for a solution to the problem.

- Feelings of powerlessness that often accompany the experience of unwanted sound are merely intensified and extended by this process.

Evaluated alongside each other, it is clear that neither zoning nor individualisation provide adequate or complete solutions to the problems of managing unwanted sound in relation to the complex claims, rights and responsibilities raised by issues of environmental and social justice. As Bijsterveld suggests, an inability to choose definitively between these strategies and continued confusion over exactly how issues of justice and equality should be handled in relation to sound are important reasons why noise nuisance and sonic environmental pollution remain unresolved at local, national and international levels.

Rather than making a clear choice, Bijsterveld (2008, pp. 254–5) concludes that strategies adopted to govern sound change, from zoning to individualisation, depend on whether we consider the space in which sound bothers us to be public and the source of the sound collective, or private and the source of the sound individual. Sometimes this changes over time. The case of the mobile phone is a good example of this. With the introduction of the cell phone (or mobile phone) in the 1990s, people started using their phones while travelling by train. The first response by those forced to become 'unwilling eavesdroppers' to private conversations was to claim that this noise unjustly transgressed the boundaries between social classes. This annoyance was partly grounded in the fact that the phones were expensive and acted as a status symbol for highly paid workers in business and the finance sector. The unashamedly public use of such phones was then perceived as a form of boasting derived from the conspicuous display of wealth and position (Agar, 2003, p. 71). Because of this perceived social incivility, mobile phone sounds were considered as socially disrupting sounds, as sounds out of place. Historically, the sense that new sounds are disrupting and therefore out of place has been a common response to their novelty, but one that wears off over time as the sound becomes more familiar. As Bijsterveld says, it is therefore not surprising that the first publicly proposed solutions focused on an individualised solution by calling for civilised mobile-phone behaviour, or mobile etiquette. Yet, in the 21st century, now that mobile phones are significantly cheaper, in common everyday use and owned by a very wide cross-section of society, the problem has ceased to be one that can be handled by individualisation. Now as a public rather than private problem, control of mobile phone use has been delegated to zoning. Today, trains and public spaces have no-phoning zones where they once had no-smoking zones.

Summary

- Zoning and individualisation are important ways of managing conflicting rights to make sound and be protected from unwanted sound.

- Evaluated alongside each other, neither zoning nor individualisation alone provides an adequate solution to the problem of unwanted noise. Both are used depending on whether noise problem is understood to be public or private, and individual or collective.

Conclusion

This chapter has shown how sound can define public and private spaces. Sound can be a very powerful means of creating a boundary around and between individuals and groups both physically and symbolically. After showing how sound can help people to locate themselves in the world, the chapter then turned to examine sound which is 'out of place'. It showed how noise or unwanted sound can be understood as matter out of place and how this in turn can signal what is understood as inappropriate or uncivil behaviour. Because sound reflects social and cultural values, it can often be a source of conflict and controversy due to the competing claims made about the nature and effects of sound. The chapter then went on to look at how tranquillity is very difficult to quantify and how ideas of what constitutes tranquillity depend on human values, preferences and claims concerning what is appropriate and inappropriate in particular locations. Finally, the chapter considered tranquillity in terms of the right to peace and quiet. It evaluated the ways in which zoning and individualisation are only partial responses to the problems of justice and inequality set by unwanted noise. It concluded by showing how management strategies depend on whether a particular noise nuisance is understood as either a public or private problem. Throughout this chapter, you will have realised the difficulty that social scientists, as well as governments and individuals, face when searching for solutions to complex social problems where different people's values and viewpoints collide. The next chapter takes forward this point, encouraging you to consider both the advantages and disadvantages of a very different kind of social intervention.

References

Agar, J. (2003) *Constant Touch: A Global History of the Mobile Phone*, Cambridge, Icon Books.

Bijsterveld, K. (2008) *Mechanical Sound: Technology Culture and Public Problems of Noise in the Twentieth Century*, Cambridge, MA, MIT Press.

Bull, M. (2005) 'No dead air! The iPod and the culture of mobile listening', *Leisure Studies*, vol. 24, no. 4, pp. 343–55.

Caney, S. (2001) 'International distributive justice', *Political Studies*, vol. 49, no. 5, pp. 974–7.

Cox, T. (2014) *Sonic Wonderland: A Scientific Odyssey of Sound*, London, Bodley Head.

CPRE/Countryside Agency (2005) 'Mapping tranquillity: defining and assessing a valuable resource', London: CPRE [Online]. Available at www. cpre.org.uk/resources/countryside/tranquil-places/item/1856- (Accessed 17 April 2015).

CPRE/Countryside Agency (2007) 'Mapping tranquillity: national map with 2001 regional boundaries', London: CPRE [Online]. Available from www.cpre. org.uk/resources/countryside/tranquil-places/item/1839- (Accessed 17 April 2015).

Dibben, N. and Haake, A.B. (2013) 'Music and the construction of space in office-based work settings', in Born, G. (ed.) *Music, Sound and Space: Transformations of Public and Private Experience*, Cambridge, Cambridge University Press.

Douglas, M. (1966) *Purity and Danger*, London, Routledge and Kegan Paul.

Eisenberg, A.J. (2013) 'Islam, sound and space: acoustemology and Muslim citizenship on the Kenyan coast', in Born, G. (ed.) *Music, Sound and Space: Transformations of Public and Private Experience*, Cambridge, Cambridge University Press.

Goldsmith, M. (2012) *Discord: TheStory of Noise*, Oxford, Oxford University Press.

Kaye, G.W.C. (1931) 'The measurement of noise', *Proceedings of the Royal Institution of Great Britain,* vol. 26, pp. 435–48.

Matless, D. (2005) 'Sonic geography in a nature region', *Social & Cultural Geography*, vol. 6, no. 5, pp. 745–66.

Rice, T. (2013) 'Broadcasting the body: the "private" made "public" in hospital soundscapes', in Born, G. (ed.) *Music, Sound and Space: Transformations of Public and Private Experience*, Cambridge, Cambridge University Press.

Schafer, R.M. (1969) *The New Soundscape: A Handbook for the Modern Music Teacher*, Rochester, VT, Destiny Books.

Smith, M.J. and Pangsapa, P. (2008) *Environment and Citizenship: Integrating Justice, Responsibility and Civic Engagement*, Scarborough, Ontario, Berndol Music Limited.

Southworth, M. (1969) 'The sonic environment of cities', *Environment and Behavior* , vol. 1, no. 1 pp 49-70 [Online]. Available at http://eab.sagepub.com.libezproxy.open.ac.uk/content/1/1/49.full.pdf+html (Accessed 3 June 2015).

Chapter 10
Fair trade: bridging boundaries?

by Katy Wheeler

Contents

Introduction

Farmers in **less-developed countries**, producing commodities like coffee, tea and sugar, are in a precarious position. They are subject to fluctuating prices, which makes it difficult to be certain they will receive a price that is high enough to meet their basic costs. They participate in a global trading-system that is weighted in favour of large corporations looking for low prices and countries that can afford to pay their local farmers large subsidies (or payments) to continue growing their crops. On top of this, weather conditions are becoming more unpredictable, making it difficult for some farmers to grow and sustain their crops.

Less-developed countries
A group of countries that have been classified by the UN as 'least developed' in terms of their low gross national income, their weak human assets (such as low levels of education and poor public health) and their high degree of economic vulnerability (because they rely on agriculture, which is often subject to price fluctuations and instability).

Figure 10.1   The Fairtrade logo appears on all its packaging

The plight of farmers in the developing world is the subject of public debate and it provokes suggestions about different ways to help those reliant on agricultural commodities to stabilise their income and improve their standard of living. In this chapter, you will evaluate one such 'suggestion' – fair trade, a market intervention and consumer movement that is attempting to address trade injustices. The fair-trade model was developed to alleviate poverty in developing countries by helping the producers of commodities like coffee to improve their living and working conditions by paying them a fairer price for their crop. Fair trade intervenes in the market and sets a minimum price to protect farmers when prices fall very low. It relies on consumers (usually in the West) choosing products that carry the Fairtrade label (see Figure 10.1), which may or may not be more expensive than non-Fairtrade alternatives. The idea that it is possible to change the world by simply choosing a different brand of coffee or chocolate is seductive. But does it work?

Box 10.1   'Fairtrade or fair-trade?'

There are different meanings attached to the different ways of writing 'fair trade', and you'll see all of the below in this chapter.

fair-trade

When 'fair trade/fair-trade' is written as two words without capital letters, it refers to the wider fair-trade movement. This encompasses the labelled and non-labelled products, as well as the wider movement seeking to secure trade justice for the world's poorest producers.

Fairtrade

When 'Fairtrade' is capitalised and written as one word, it refers to Fairtrade labelled goods and the towns'/cities' movement in the UK and Europe.

Fair Trade

When 'Fair Trade' is capitalised and written as two words, it refers to the labelled Fair Trade products certified in the United States by Fair Trade USA and organisations certified by the Fair Trade Federation, as well as the 'Fair Trade towns' movement in the United States.

Trade justice
Seeing trade as fundamental to the goal of realising fair distribution of wealth and resources between the developing and industrialised worlds.

In this chapter, you will be asked to consider a set of debates that question how effective fair trade is at helping producers and raising awareness amongst consumers. Like most social problems, how to promote **trade justice** and encourage consumers to make alternative choices has no easy solution and different people can have very different ideas about the best way to resolve the same problem. Indeed, in the last chapter, you were introduced to the concepts of zoning and individualisation as ways of managing conflicts around noise. Attempts to regulate or govern this controversial social problem have varying success because of the different values, norms and beliefs of various individuals and groups. Social scientists often have to evaluate a range of opinions and perspectives in order to get a better understanding of a social issue. This chapter will develop the valuable skill of using social science evidence to evaluate claims. Social scientists regularly interrogate the claims of different organisations, drawing on research evidence to inform their position. You will learn that evidence is open to different interpretations and views. Learning to use this evidence critically and to communicate your findings to a wider audience is a vital tool for any social scientist to grasp.

The material presented throughout this chapter utilises the theme of 'justice' – specifically trade justice. You will learn how there are different understandings of the pathways to trade justice, with the boundary between what is fair and unfair contingent on a range of factors and social relations (such as whether you consider the consequences of fair trade for just one community or try widening your analysis to a global context). You will also be asked to think about whether the boundaries between citizens and consumers are bridged when fair-trade consumption opens the possibility of using the sphere of shopping to realise the goal of trade justice. Through the course of this chapter, you will realise that these boundaries are never fixed and are made and re-made through our interventions in the social world.

This chapter will:

- introduce you to the claims of the fair-trade movement and debates about its efficacy

- develop your skills in drawing on social science evidence to interrogate claims and engage in debate

- use the theme of justice to help you evaluate the effectiveness of fair trade for producers and consumers

- question how far the boundaries between the consumer and the citizen have been bridged.

This chapter has two main sections that deal with either side of the fair-trade relationship – production and consumption.

Section 1, 'Fair trade and alternative pathways to trade justice', presents an overview of the fair-trade scheme that claims to help farmers, more commonly referred to as 'producers', in the developing world. It also introduces an opposing position (that fair-trade does not help farmers) and shows how academic social scientific evidence can be used to evaluate both positions.

Section 2, 'Consumer-citizenship' looks at the claims that fair-trade empowers consumers to act as global citizens, and presents an alternative position for you to critique.

1   Fair trade and alternative pathways to trade justice

Many farmers in the developing world grow agricultural products that they can sell on international exchange markets, rather than crops that they consume themselves. These are known as 'cash crops' and include coffee, cocoa and cotton. Some farms may decide to grow these crops because it is a lucrative business model, while others may have grown these crops for centuries as a way of life that has been passed down through the generations. Income from the export of goods is crucial for promoting development within poorer parts of the world. If you look at Figure 10.2 below, which shows the total trade of goods divided by the population size, you should notice that the countries that have the highest trade income are the countries that are the most developed.

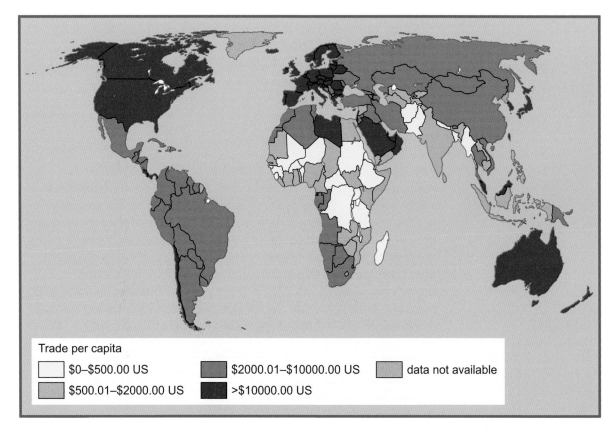

Trade per capita

$0–$500.00 US	$2000.01–$10000.00 US
$500.01–$2000.00 US	>$10000.00 US

data not available

Figure 10.2   World map showing trade income per capita (WTO, 2014)

Giving producers fairer access to international trading markets is a goal of many international development agencies because it can provide a route out of poverty by increasing trade income. However, despite the gains it can bring, achieving this goal has not been easy because of a number of factors, including poor local infrastructure (like roads), lack of awareness of international exchange markets in poorer, remote regions of the world, and the imposition of tariffs on imports, which makes it difficult for foreign producers to compete in a given market. The World Trade Organisation (WTO) has called on its members to end all tariffs and subsidies, except in limited situations. However, this requirement has not been fulfilled because international trade is an incredibly complex arena in which different actors compete in the pursuit of their own interests.

This section explores some of the claims made by the fair-trade movement about its work with producers in the developing world. It then presents some counter-arguments about the fair-trade model made by the Adam Smith Institute. In this debate, you will see how different institutions can have very different perspectives about the best way to achieve trade justice (see Box 10.2). You will also learn how social scientists can participate in this debate, providing evidence in support of these different perspectives.

Millennium Development Goals
Eight goals established by the United Nations with the aim of reducing global poverty and increasing equality.

Box 10.2   Trade justice

The theme of justice – 'what is considered fair or equitable in relation to rights, rewards, resources, punishments and sanctions' within society (O'Leary, 2007) – is highly relevant to the discussions in this chapter. Trade justice sees trade 'as fundamental to the goal of realizing a fair distribution of wealth and resources between the developing and industrialized worlds' (Lowes, 2006). Development agencies, governments and non-governmental organisations around the world recognise the importance of opening up trade and making it fairer for all. At the turn of the century, the United Nations developed eight key **Millennium Development Goals** (MDG), with the aim of reducing poverty and increasing equality. A key platform of the eighth MDG called for the further development of 'an open, rule-based, predictable, non-discriminatory trading and financial system' (United Nations, 2013, p. 54).

1.1 Fair trade: its aims and mechanisms

Figure 10.3   Trade justice sign outside the UK Parliament

Although fair-trade activities can be traced back to the 1940s, the movement really took off in the 1990s. Coffee prices had fallen to their lowest point in over 100 years after an international system to stabilise prices was disbanded in 1989 and following a frost in Brazil, which initially increased the price of coffee. However, a situation of oversupply soon developed. The 'coffee crisis' devastated coffee farmers across the globe, causing poverty, hunger and migration to the cities. Meanwhile, in the Netherlands, the first Fairtrade-labelled coffee – the Max Havelaar label – was introduced into Dutch supermarkets in 1988. This initiative offered a small number of coffee farmers from Mexico the opportunity to access a fairer price for their crop in return for their cooperative meeting certain standards (such as a democratic structure and no discrimination on the basis of sex, 'race' or religion) that were independently certified. Unlike earlier fair-trade initiatives, whose products had mainly been distributed via alternative channels, such as church halls, specialist catalogues or world shops, the Max Havelaar label pioneered the mainstream distribution of Fairtrade products. It was a trend soon replicated across Europe and North America, with coffee being the flagship Fairtrade product in most countries. Guaranteeing coffee farmers a fair price at a time when they were really struggling was a popular intervention that many development agencies and charities supported.

As the movement developed, an overarching organisation was established – the Fairtrade Labelling Organisation (FLO) – to bring together all the national initiatives behind universal Fairtrade standards and to create a single Fairtrade mark. To be certified as Fairtrade, there are certain standards that have to be met (see Box 10.3) and these vary slightly depending upon the type of product and organisation. When Fairtrade certification began, it focused on small-scale coffee farmers organised into **cooperatives**. These standards are evolving over time to incorporate large plantations with hired labourers but just for certain crops, such as bananas and tea, which are grown only on plantations. The decision to allow only these plantations to become Fairtrade-certified has proved controversial and in 2011, Fair Trade USA left the FLO because it wanted to work with both small-scale coffee farmers and coffee plantations.

Cooperative
A farm, business or other organisation that is owned and run jointly by its members, who share the profits or benefits.

Box 10.3   Summary of Fairtrade standards

1   Producers must be guaranteed a minimum price for their product which is able to cover the costs of its sustainable production. If the current market price is higher than this minimum price, the producer should receive the higher of the two prices.

2   Producers are paid an additional social premium which they must invest into community development projects. Producers should democratically decide how the premium will be spent. The types of project it has funded are local schools, healthcare facilities, toilets and water pumps.

3   Importers of Fairtrade goods need to offer producers pre-finance of up to 60 per cent of the purchase value of seasonal crops, which is crucial for paying cooperative members when they deliver their harvest.

> 4   Long-term trading relationships between producers and traders are essential to help producers to plan their development and invest in their farms.
>
> 5   Producers have to demonstrate they meet specific economic, environmental and social requirements, such as:
>
>   ○   being a small-scale producer (in the case of coffee, cocoa and other crops where small-scale production is common)
>
>   ○   establishing a democratic body to make decisions about the use of the Fairtrade premium and to share profits equally
>
>   ○   sound environmental management of crops (including no genetically modified organisms and limited use of pesticides)
>
>   ○   fair labour conditions, such as no forced or child labour.
>
> (Source: adapted from Bowes, 2011; FLO, 2014a)

When consumers buy products labelled with the Fairtrade mark, they are promised that these products have been produced and exchanged according to the standards listed in Box 10.3. Of course, this assurance involves the need for auditing and checks, which are provided by an independent arm of the Fairtrade Labelling Organisation (FLO), called FLOcert. Both producers and importers have to pay fees to be certified by this organisation and to have access to the Fairtrade scheme.

A key element of the fair-trade movement's approach is to empower producers to improve their lives for themselves, rather than relying on handouts from international aid and charitable donations. Around 1.2 million workers and farmers in 58 developing countries benefit from Fairtrade (FLO, 2014b). By giving these producers the tools to participate in the global trading system, FLO maintains that Fairtrade offers:

> an alternative approach to conventional trade […] based on a partnership between producers and consumers. When farmers can sell on Fairtrade terms, it provides them with a better deal and

improved terms of trade. This allows them the opportunity to improve their lives and plan for their future.

(FLO, 2014c)

Activity 1

Before moving on, consider the following two points:

1   How do you think farmers/workers benefit from the fair-trade system?
2   Identify one barrier that might prevent a farmer from becoming Fairtrade-certified.

Discussion

1   Benefits of the fair-trade system include:

   - a minimum price that covers the cost of production
   - long-term trading partnerships that enable producers to plan and develop their businesses
   - access to training and technical assistance
   - access to credit
   - opportunities to invest in local infrastructure and community development projects, which in turn can lead to better health care and education.

2   A barrier to becoming a Fairtrade-certified farmer is the certification fees that must be paid to FLOcert to cover the costs of auditing. This can be prohibitive, especially in light of the many criteria producers must fulfil before they can be considered eligible as Fairtrade producers. Another barrier is that the system is only open to small-scale cooperative producers in crops like coffee and cocoa, meaning that labourers working on these crops on plantations are not eligible for the scheme.

1.2   Free trade is fair trade?

Fair trade has become a well-known and well-supported movement, with retailers, central government, local authorities, schools, faith groups and development charities promoting and championing the label in the UK. However, according to the Adam Smith Institute, fairtrade does little to aid economic development and is not the most effective means of promoting trade justice. Rather, they maintain that free trade 'is the most effective poverty reduction strategy the world has ever seen' (Sidwell, 2008, p. 3). As you will remember from the chapter 'Putting a price on common resources' (Shipman, 2015), the concept of free trade is often attributed to Smith (1723–1790) whose ideas informed the writing of Hayek (1986). Hayek believed that intervening in the market is counter-productive because the greatest good is achieved when individuals are left alone to pursue their own self-interest. In spite of this, governments across the globe do engage in central management of their economies with the aim of protecting their country's interests. The most common way is through the imposition of trade tariffs and barriers, which make it difficult for all countries to realise the benefit from the free movement of goods and services. The Adam Smith Institute is an organisation that is committed to ideas that support the free market and argues that fair trade, with its fixed minimum price and its removal of consumer choice, is a violation of these principles.

Box 10.4 shows a slightly adapted version of the executive summary of a key report written by Marc Sidwell for the Adam Smith Institute, released in February 2008.

Box 10.4   Executive summary from Unfair Trade (Sidwell, 2008, p. 3)

1 Fairtrade Fortnight is a marketing exercise intended to maintain the Fairtrade mark's predominance in an increasingly competitive marketplace for ethically-branded products. The hype is necessary, because there is every reason for the shrewd consumer to make other choices.

2 Fair trade is unfair. It offers only a very small number of farmers a higher, fixed price for their goods. These higher prices come at the expense of the great majority of farmers, who – unable to qualify for Fairtrade certification – are left even worse off. [...]

3 Fair trade does not aid economic development. It operates to keep the poor in their place, sustaining uncompetitive farmers on their land and holding back diversification, mechanization, and moves up the value chain. This denies future generations the chance of a better life.

---

4 Fair trade only helps landowners, not the agricultural labourers who suffer the severest poverty. Indeed, Fairtrade rules deny labourers the opportunity of permanent, full-time employment. [...]

5 The consumer now has a wide variety of ethical alternatives to Fairtrade, many of which represent more effective ways to fight poverty, increase the poor's standard of living and aid economic development.

6 Fairtrade arose from the coffee crisis of the 1990s. This was not a free market failure. Governments tried to rig the market through the International Coffee Agreement and subsidized over-plantation with the encouragement of well-meaning but misguided aid agencies. The crash in prices was the inevitable result of this government intervention, but coffee prices have largely recovered since then.

7 Free trade is the most effective poverty reduction strategy the world has ever seen. If we really want to aid international development we should abolish barriers to trade in the rich world, and persuade the developing world to do the same. The evidence is clear: fair trade is unfair, but free trade makes you rich.

You will notice that the Adam Smith Institute make a number of claims about the fair-trade movement but how can investigative social scientists check whether these are credible? When evaluating claims, it is useful to begin by asking yourself a number of simple questions.

- **What** is being said? Is it clear and understandable, and does the line of reasoning seem possible?

- **Why** is it being said? Is a new piece of evidence being reported? Or is this claim being made in response to a particular event, person or organisation?

- **Who** is saying it? Does the author have an agenda that they want to communicate, and who to? Bear in mind how the position and values of the author can shape the claims made.

Activity 2

Look again at Box 10.4 and take a moment to reflect on the three questions: What? Why? Who? (Don't worry if you can't think of points for each of the questions because discovering the gaps will be the first step of your evaluation.)

Discussion

What: Among other things, the report states that Fairtrade is unfair because the higher prices are only accessible to a small number of landowning farmers. These higher prices come at the expense of farmers that are not Fairtrade certified or that work as casual labourers. The coffee crisis was caused by market intervention and coffee prices have now risen showing that free trade (not intervention) is the best way to help farmers in the developing world. Consumers would be better off looking for more efficient ways of helping farmers' development – these are not named here.

The arguments made seem clear (free from jargon) and the claims may be possible, depending on the evidence for them. This evidence is not visible in the summary and warrants further investigation.

Why: The report was released in February 2008 and was timed to coincide with the yearly event in the Fairtrade Foundation's calendar, Fairtrade Fortnight. It is aimed at the consuming public and those supportive of the fair-trade movement.

Who: The Adam Smith Institute has a commitment to free trade and their arguments are critical with no acknowledgement of any positive benefits of being a fair-trade farmer or consumer.

By asking these simple questions, it is likely that you will have noticed that there is a need for further evidence in order to evaluate the claims made. Indeed, in their response to the report, the Fairtrade Foundation questioned the credibility of the evidence drawn upon by Marc Sidwell, and said that many of their own producers would contest his claims. Yet, again, social scientists may question the anecdotal evidence supplied by successful Fairtrade farmers who could be unlikely to offer a critical account of their own scheme. Fortunately, research conducted by social scientists can offer more balanced insights to help you to evaluate the claims of both organisations; but as you will see, the picture is far from clear.

1.3   Does fair trade help?

Figure 10.4   An agricultural labourer picks tea in Rwanda

In 2007, the Department for International Development (DFID) commissioned a group of academics from the School of African and Oriental Studies (SOAS) to undertake the most comprehensive evaluation of Fairtrade to date. The team of researchers focused on both Fairtrade-certified and non-Fairtrade-certified farms in Ethiopia and Uganda across the coffee, tea and cut-flower industries (FTEPR, 2014).

Activity 3

Why do you think SOAS researchers evaluated both Fairtrade and non-Fairtrade farms and different types of crop?

Discussion

By adopting contrasting cases, it was possible for the researchers to identify key differences between Fairtrade and non-Fairtrade farms, enabling them to say something about the difference that being certified made to farmers. By looking across different crops, they were also able to explore whether Fairtrade makes more difference to coffee farmers than flower growers, for example, given the different ways these two commodities are cultivated and processed.

The researchers decided to focus on what they considered the most vulnerable group of people working on these farms – the casual-wage labourer, with a particular focus on female workers who make up the vast majority of casual labourers. You may remember that one of Sidwell's criticisms of Fairtrade was that it only helped landowners and not the people who worked as casual labourers on these farms. The researchers surveyed over 1700 casual labourers and re-surveyed around 400 of these two years later to take account of any changes over time. 100 of these workers also provided in-depth accounts of their life–work histories, providing rich qualitative insights. The researchers found that Fairtrade certification had 'no positive effect on either wages or working conditions of manual agricultural wage workers' (FTEPR, 2014, p. 70). Waged casual labourers appear to do so badly from Fairtrade because the scheme has consistently overlooked their existence and holds on to a 'romantic ideology of how co-operatives operate in poor rural areas' (FTEPR, 2014, p. 121). For example, certification assumes that farms are family-run and ignore the significant need for outsourced casual-wage labour. With Fairtrade not accounting for their existence, small-scale farmers are unable to provide better working conditions for their labourers than those employed on the larger-scale farms owned by multinational corporations (FTEPR, 2014). The researchers also reported that female workers, especially those who are divorced or widowed, suffer particular disadvantages, including lower wages than their male counterparts and regular sexual harassment. This was the case on both the Fairtrade and non-Fairtrade farms, which suggests that there are wider structural inequalities that must be addressed.

The SOAS report highlights an area where Fairtrade schemes are performing poorly, but that does not necessarily mean that the scheme is not performing better in other areas. In a review of 23 published reports, Nelson and Pound (2009) concluded that Fairtrade provides favourable economic opportunities for smallholder farming families but that this does not always translate into higher incomes than their non-Fairtrade neighbours. Indeed, the sociologist Daniel Jaffee (2007) compared the conditions of two small coffee-farming communities in Mexico (one Fair Trade-certified and one not) and found that although the Fair Trade families were somewhat better off than their non-Fair Trade neighbours – they were less indebted, their children had better education and their homes were better furnished – their incomes were almost equivalent. To sell their coffee as Fair Trade, there are extra labour requirements that include providing high-quality coffee beans (pre-sorted), weed and pest management that limits the use of chemicals (thus requiring more manual labour) and active involvement in an organisation that meets at several points throughout the harvest to manage their Fair Trade status. All of these factors mean that Fair Trade farmers have to hire more labourers to help on their fields. Unlike the SOAS report, Jaffee highlights that these wages provide a vital source of income for rural labourers (many of whom have their own coffee farms), suggesting that the impact of Fair Trade is distributed beyond the families it directly serves.

If Fair Trade farmers and labourers are not always economically better off than their non-Fair Trade counterparts, does this justify Sidwell's assertion that free-trade systems would perform better? On this issue, Jaffee disagrees and instead argues that the market must not be left to its own devices but be regulated further to ensure that certain standards and fair practices are followed. For Jaffee, fair-trade is a non-state/consumer-led regulation of the free market that is important, but insufficient on its own to really ensure social and economic justice. He argues that what is needed is 'concerted action by states and other global institutions – backed by organised civil society and grassroots movements … to counteract the harmful effects of global free trade and economic activity' (Jaffee, 2007, p. 263).

An example of the important role that state regulation can play in reducing poverty through both overseeing and opening up international trading markets is offered by the case of coffee production in Vietnam (Fridell, 2014). The Vietnamese government was the central player in promoting a national coffee economy and invested heavily by offering cheaper land, subsidised inputs, low-cost loans, irrigation infrastructure and transport links to help millions to become coffee farmers. There is no denying how important this strategy has been for lifting from poverty some 2.6 million people (3.5 times the number of certified Fairtrade coffee farmers) whose livelihoods depend on coffee (Fridell, 2014). However, Vietnam is often accused of flooding the market with low-quality coffee, bringing down the global market price and harming those farmers that Fairtrade certification seeks to help. By using mechanised methods of production, Vietnamese farmers are able to harvest more coffee per hectare than small-scale farmers in other parts of the world.

This approach has not been without its critics because of the consequences such intensive farming is having on the natural environment, as well as on other farmers whose methods are less efficient. Indeed, the fair-trade movement often blames Vietnam for the coffee crisis of the early 1990s because its highly productive farms drove down the international price of coffee and led to a situation of oversupply that was detrimental to the small-scale coffee farmer (FLO, 2014d). Free-trade advocates also find problems with this type of state-led intervention and argue that the prices that farmers receive for their coffee are controlled by the state, which inevitably seeks to profit from this powerful position. (Although many of the coffee farms in Vietnam are owned by private firms, the collection, processing and export functions are conducted by a state-led enterprise that sets the prices that farmers receive for their crop.)

1.4   The different pathways to trade justice

So far in this section, you have explored different perspectives on routes to achieving trade justice for farmers in the developing world. Take a moment to reflect on these different models by completing Activity 4.

Activity 4

Who is responsible for delivering trade justice in each of these three models:

- Fairtrade
- free trade
- Vietnam's coffee industry?

Discussion

- Fairtrade believes it is up to both farmers and consumers (often aided by the intermediary institution of FLO) to work towards greater trade justice. Farmers work hard to meet certain standards and consumers then pay more for their products.

- Free trade sees the market as the key engine of trade justice – the market must be free from state intervention that creates unfair advantages and disadvantages to different actors, such as trade subsidies and tariffs.

- Vietnam's coffee industry was made possible by intervention from the state who provided initial subsidies to help these farmers to compete in the market.

While the fair-trade movement calls for consumer-led regulation of the market, another school of thought (shown by the coffee industry in Vietnam) argues that the market ought to be regulated by the state. Free-trade advocates like the Adam Smith Institute would disagree with both positions, believing that the market is best left alone to ensure greater trade justice for all. Much of this debate reveals how there are different understandings of the best way to achieve both trade justice and social justice for farmers in the developing world. There are no simple answers to these questions and different types of intervention are supported by those with different perspectives about the underlying causes of poverty and routes to development. While the fair-trade movement wants farmers to continue farming and earn a better living from this, free-trade advocates believe that larger structural changes are necessary to increase productivity and farmers' incomes. Social scientists can contribute to this debate by questioning, analysing, evaluating and communicating the relative merits of these different interventions, making suggestions for improvements and highlighting what it is about a scheme that makes it work/not work. The boundaries between what is fair and unfair are fluid and cannot be evaluated in isolation from the broader social context – what is fair for one group of farmers and workers may create problems for other farmers and workers or for the environment.

As a social scientist, it is important to interrogate the assumptions and values that lie behind the claims made about the social world. Both the accounts from the fair-trade movement and the Adam Smith Institute represent particular value positions and Section 1.3 may have helped you to formulate an opinion regarding these claims. The evidence is mixed and often unclear but you may have recognised that there are both some benefits and some problems with the fair-trade model – just as there are with free trade and state intervention.

Summary

- Greater trade justice can reduce poverty and inequality in the developing world but achieving this goal is incredibly difficult.

- The fair-trade movement claims to help farmers by providing greater incomes, education and training in farming and trading practices, and access to community development.

- Free-trade advocates, like the Adam Smith Institute, disagree with fair-trade claims and instead argue that it is *un*fair.

- Social science evidence helps us to question and evaluate these claims, highlighting both benefits and problems with fair-trade schemes and other forms of intervention.

2   Consumer-citizenship

Having considered some of the debates around the efficacy of fair trade for *producers*, you will now move on to the other side of the fair-trade relationship: the *consumers*. The UK has the biggest market for Fairtrade goods with shoppers spending £1.7 billion on Fairtrade-labelled goods in 2013 (Fairtrade Foundation, 2014, p. 6). Both advocates of the fair-trade movement and some social scientists have argued that growing Fairtrade sales signal that more and more consumers are using the sphere of consumption to vote for trade justice. However, others have argued that there are limits to the role that consumers can play through their shopping choices. This section will explore both of these claims and, like Section 1, will reveal how social science evidence can contribute to, and inform, this debate.

It is useful to keep in mind that much of this debate rests upon the supposed bridging of the boundary between the consumer and the citizen (Micheletti, 2003). Consumption and citizenship have traditionally been understood to sit at opposite ends of the political spectrum, with the consumer indulging their individual, private wants in the market place while the citizen is an outward-looking figure who embraces the public interest (Clarke, Newman et al., 2007).

Figure 10.5   Are there limits to the role consumers can be expected to play through shopping choices?

Activity 5

What different qualities do you associate with the consumer and the citizen?

Discussion

Below are some of the qualities usually associated with these two identities. However, you may want to consider whether it is really the case that they are so easily separated. For example, think about the last time you went shopping and whether your choices could really be described as individual and selfish, or whether in fact your choices were shaped by your involvement in broader social networks, such as your family or work colleagues, and were in part a response to their wishes/ needs.

Table 10.1   Consumer or citizen?

Consumer	Citizen
Individual	Collective
Selfish	Public-minded
Concerned with their rights	Concerned with their duties
Private	Public
Passive	Active

Social historians have argued that the boundaries between the consumer and citizen have always been blurred and are stitched together in new ways at particular times and places (Cohen, 2003; Trentmann, 2007). Regardless of how new or unusual this bridging is, it has been claimed that there is something about contemporary global society that has created the possibility for consumers to step in and use their shopping choices as a form of individualised political action, or 'vote'. Is shopping the new politics and do consumers really think about their shopping in this way?

2.1   The rise of the fair-trade citizen-consumer

In *Fighting the Banana Wars*, written by the then-Executive Director of the Fairtrade Foundation (now CEO of FLO), Harriet Lamb states that:

> The beauty of Fairtrade is, of course, anyone can support it. We can all spend those extra few seconds in the coffee aisle of our local shop, stick out our hand and suddenly we're part of the solution.

(Lamb, 2008, p. 180)

Fairtrade is an easy action that, she claims, links 'citizens in the rich world with farmers and workers in Peru or Burkina Faso or India' (Lamb, 2008, p. 2). Fairtrade is described as the 'people's movement for change' in which consumers act as citizens by choosing Fairtrade products. In this vision, the typical fair-trade consumer is imagined as an ordinary person who thinks carefully about the purchases that they make and uses their knowledge of the fair-trade movement's aims to vote for this system.

You may have noticed that this account of the fair-trade consumer paints a picture of a powerful figure that has the moral/political responsibility to act. With the **globalisation** of supply chains, the rise of transnational corporations and the weakening power of individual nation states, it is now consumers who are imagined to uniquely have 'the power and duty to safeguard both fair economic distribution and the natural environment' (Sassatelli, 2006, p. 230). Because consumers have to rely on the global marketplace for the provision of goods, most are forced to trust the retailers and corporations they depend upon for their daily existence. However, this does leave customers with little recourse to action when they become aware of the bad practices of global corporations. In the face of the consumer's lack of control over production processes, this approach believes that citizens are prompted to 'take politics in their own hands … creating new arenas for responsibility-taking' (Micheletti, 2003, p. 5).

Globalisation
The process through which economic, political and cultural systems across the globe are integrated into an interdependent whole system.

In an analysis of the promotional material developed to encourage consumers to buy fair-trade and other ethical consumer goods, Clarke et al. (2007) conclude that consumers are indeed being called upon to regulate economic institutions – to become 'citizens of the world by virtue of their status as consumers' (Clarke et al., 2007, p. 243). Consumers are encouraged to reflect upon their position within systems of global exploitation and to use their purchases in this global market to act upon their responsibilities. Ethical consumer organisations, like the Fairtrade Foundation, are turning the discourse of globalisation, which has traditionally highlighted the dominance of companies over individuals, on its head – now the consumer is the one with the power.

Returning to the debates in Section 1, the model that sits behind this line of reasoning is a version of the free-market model in which the consumer uses their free choices to intervene for the greater good. In their response to the Adam Smith report, the Fairtrade Foundation defended their approach by stressing this very point:

> Two billion people work extremely hard to earn a living but still earn less than $2 per day and the FAIRTRADE Mark enables British consumers to choose products that help address this injustice. As no-one is forced to join a fair trade producer organisation, or to buy Fairtrade products, you would think that free market economists like the Adam Smith Institute would be pleased at the way the British public has taken our voluntary label to its heart – and to the supermarket checkout – to the tune of nearly half a billion pounds worth of goods in 2007 alone.
>
> (Fairtrade Foundation, 2008)

But who are these citizen-consumers who are taking this label to heart? Do they really consider their purchase of Fairtrade goods as a vote for the fair-trade movement?

2.2 Shopping for justice?

In their analysis of promotional material produced by ethical-consumer organisations, Clarke et al. (2007) found that the audience for ethical consumption campaigns tends to be rather self-selecting. This audience are already interested and have some sympathy with the fair-trade movement's aims, rather than being generic 'consumers'. This suggests that those who already have an interest in fair trade are more likely to view their consumption choices as votes for the fair-trade movement than those without an interest in fair-trade. My research (Wheeler, 2012) with self-defined fair-trade supporters and people without any real commitment to the movement can provide some insights into this point. I based my research in a **Fairtrade Town** and conducted focus groups and in-depth interviews with both sets of consumers (fair-trade supporters and non-fair-trade supporters). Fair-trade supporters were recruited through Fairtrade Town events, whereas non-fair-trade supporters responded to adverts in local

Fairtrade Town
A community which has made a commitment to supporting Fairtrade-labelled goods and the wider fair-trade movement. There are over 500 Fairtrade Towns in the UK, as well as hundreds of Fairtrade schools, churches and workplaces.

supermarkets to discuss their coffee/chocolate routines. The non-fair-trade supporters were not anti-fair-trade but rather people not actively involved in local fair-trade activities. The two groups of consumers were asked how effective they thought shopping choices were at tackling poverty in developing countries.

The fair-trade supporters gave a number of reasons for buying fair-trade products, from wanting to support small producers to 'doing one's bit', acting like a 'good Christian' and making themselves 'feel better' about their shopping choices. Most had attended events where fair-trade producers had described how fair trade had helped their community and believed that fair trade is an effective way of making a difference in the developing world. Most fair-trade supporters, however, did not imagine themselves as individual consumers but as a member of a group of like-minded people who were doing something together to tackle trade injustices. For Matt (a 67-year old education consultant), fair-trade shopping choices were also viewed as a powerful way of sending a message to transnational corporations:

> It's not only whether all the contributions in buying fair trade goes to fair trade, that's obviously very important, but I mean there is also the benefit that if I buy a pound of bananas, fair-trade bananas, I'm not buying a pound of non-fair trade bananas, so as this balance of trade shifts [uses hands as scales] the Fyffes of this world actually sit up and take notice and say, I mean, this is the optimistic view, 'Hey hang on a minute, there's something going on here which if we don't, if we ignore, you know it might eventually hit our bottom line, our profits'. So, you know, there is that beneficial aspect as well, that it may incline the multinationals to actually themselves review their own practices and in that way improve things for the Third World as well.

> (Wheeler, 2008)

Importantly, shopping choices alone were not considered to be the solution to tackling problems of trade injustice. Peter (a member of the Co-op party) explained that:

> you could never replace government aid and government negotiation on multi-national agreements to support places, I mean we're talking basically places like Africa and South America,

and you could never replace those things with fair trade but it obviously does help individuals and also, we come back to the fact of people doing something personally to help, and handing money over to an organisation that's trying to do something.

(Wheeler, 2008)

The majority of fair-trade supporters did not limit their activities to only buying fair-trade goods but also engaged in a number of additional campaigning activities – such as being a member of Oxfam or the Trade Justice Movement, writing to politicians, or being involved in local campaign events.

On the other hand, non-fair-trade supporters were more sceptical about the fair-trade movement's claims and were less likely to believe that, as a consumer, they could make a difference. In the following exchange from one of the focus groups, notice why Steven thinks that he cannot make a difference as an individual:

Steven: The money doesn't filter down, cos it'll come into the country and the government will say well we'll have some of that, otherwise we'll shut you down and what do they do? That's the problem, you get people like Mugabe obviously who just runs their country, and all the money just rises to him basically.

Jesse: That's right.

Michael: Yes his empire's still going up and up.

Steven: If the government can't make a difference then what difference can we make? That's the way you see it.

(Wheeler, 2008)

As an individual, Steven does not feel empowered as a customer of transnational corporations, nor does he accept that he has the ability to tackle the problem of poverty in the developing world. Non-fair-trade supporters' consumption was often intimately tied to other personal commitments and practices, such as parenthood for example. Rather than taking up their responsibilities as citizen-consumers, as is suggested in Section 2.1, they tended to argue that their consumption could not be expected to bear the level of responsibility that the fair-trade movement placed upon it. In many cases, they called for some organised body, generally either supermarkets or governments, to act in order to improve the conditions for workers:

> **Hazel**: But is it down to us to do fair trade or is it down to governments to insist on fair trade by companies?
>
> **Linda**: Yeah if people don't know about it then obviously no one's been educated enough about buying it, cos considering that not a lot of us knew about it and we're just a handful of us, you know what does everybody else not know about it.
>
> **Hazel**: But why should two different chocolate bars 50–75 per cent exactly the same, one is fair trade and the other one isn't, so is it down to us to decide what's fair trade or shouldn't it just be somebody else deciding it … that we shouldn't do fair trade, it shouldn't be down to the consumer it should be up to the governments to fair trade with other countries, not us buying one kind of chocolate over another.
>
> (Wheeler, 2008)

Interestingly, there is a parallel here between the attitudes of fair-trade and non-fair-trade supporters towards the role of the government in the alleviation of poverty in the developing world. Both call for greater governmental intervention and policy changes but while fair-trade supporters believe that the amalgamated impact of their purchases will send a message that will become a catalyst for this greater political change, non-fair-trade supporters argue that governments and big businesses ought to act regardless of their preference for one type of chocolate over another.

Activity 6

According to Wheeler's study (2012a), do consumers believe they have the power to make a difference to poverty through their shopping choices?

Discussion

The degree to which consumers believe they can make a difference through their shopping varies depending on their values and existing commitments. Those who are very committed to the fair-trade movement do believe their collective shopping choices make a difference – both to fair-trade producers and by sending a message to large corporations and governments that more needs to be done to ensure trade justice. Those who are less committed to the movement are sceptical about the impact of their individual choices and tend to reject the idea of consumer power, instead calling for more action to be taken by corporations and governments.

2.3 The power of the citizen-consumer

Numerous studies of ethical consumption have faced a paradox – on the one hand, consumers profess to care about fair working conditions for producers, but on the other hand, only a small percentage of these consumers regularly buy ethical goods. In their study of ethical consumption in the UK, Malpass et al. (2007) offer a 'scandalous suggestion' (p. 245) to deal with the persistent findings that consumers reject or make excuses for not organising their consumption in a sustainable way. They suggest that rather than hear these rejections as excuses from *consumers*, we should listen to them as statements from *citizens* who are 'asserting finite limits to how much they, as individuals, can be expected to be responsible for' (p. 247). Shopping is a complex practice that is already influenced by a number of socio-economic and cultural constraints, including price, taste, preference and availability. Consumers such as Hazel recognise there are limits to how much they can achieve through their shopping choices and expect some other institutions to intervene to ensure that trade justice is achieved.

Owing to the early successes of the fair-trade movement in the UK, all of the major supermarkets now offer Fairtrade-certified products. In 2006, Sainsbury's switched to selling Fairtrade-only bananas and in 2007 they announced their decision to switch their own-brand coffee and tea to Fairtrade-only lines. In 2009, the nation's favourite chocolate bar, Cadbury's Dairy Milk, became Fairtrade-certified. Sainsbury's sales of Fairtrade goods accounted for one third of all Fairtrade retail sales in the UK in 2008 (Sainsbury's, 2009), and the switch by Cadbury tripled the sales of Fairtrade cocoa (Fairtrade Foundation, 2009). The growth of fair-trade sales has also been influenced by an ever-growing network of Fairtrade Towns (as well as Fairtrade schools, universities, churches and workplaces), whose key aim is to encourage local councils/municipalities, businesses and retail outlets to make the switch to Fairtrade products, often by removing non-Fairtrade alternatives.

Figure 10.6   The UK's favourite chocolate bar, Cadbury's Dairy Milk, became Fairtrade-certified in 2009

Many people in the UK are now buying Fairtrade, not because they actively choose it but because it is all that is available. In my study, many of the non-fair-trade supporters I spoke with had bought Fairtrade products in their most recent shopping visit but were unaware of it. The rise of the 'accidental Fairtrade consumer' raises questions about how Fairtrade consumption acts are understood and represented. So, considering that most Fairtrade goods are sold through supermarkets that have made the decision to stock Fairtrade-only lines, do consumers have a choice/vote at all? You may think that removing the choice of non-Fairtrade goods from the shelves answers Hazel's call for someone else to take the responsibility. However, the fair-trade movement has a broader political agenda beyond encouraging consumers to buy Fairtrade – to count the number of Fairtrade purchases and use this as an indication of the level of support amongst the population for changes to international trading laws. Indeed, the Charter of Fair Trade principles states:

> Demand for Fair Trade products enables Fair Trade Organizations and others who adopt Fair Trade practices to extend the reach and impacts of their work, as well as visibly demonstrating and articulating public support for changes in international trade rules to governments and policy makers.

(WFTO, 2009, p. 6)

The Adam Smith Institute had a problem with this, but what do you think? Given what you have learnt about the fair-trade movement in this section and in Section 1, should the fair-trade movement be counting their growing sales as votes from citizen-consumers supportive of their approach?

Summary

- A boundary has traditionally been seen between consumers and citizens with opposing identities in terms of levels of civic engagement.

- The fair-trade movement claims that growing Fairtrade sales signal that consumers are using the market place to 'vote' for an alternative model of trade relations, bridging that boundary.

- Social science evidence helps us to question and evaluate these claims, highlighting different levels of belief in, and opportunities for, the citizen-consumer to vote in the market place.

Conclusion

This chapter has introduced you to a number of claims made by the fair-trade movement about the effectiveness of its scheme and has encouraged you to interrogate these claims by drawing on social science evidence. The theme of justice was examined in relation to global trade and you learnt that different organisations and institutions have different ideas about the best way to achieve trade justice. It was argued that the role of the social scientist is to investigate these differing claims and communicate their findings in the hopes of informing wider societal debate. In the case of fair-trade producers, you learnt that the fair-trade scheme has had some success but it does not always protect those who are most vulnerable in the global trade relationship – the (usually) female casual worker. You looked at different possibilities for intervening in the social world, from government intervention to free-market doctrines, in your evaluation of the scheme. In the case of the fair-trade consumer, you were encouraged to question whether, given the rising Fairtrade sales figures in the UK, the identities of the consumer and citizen have really been bridged. You learnt that the citizen-consumer identity is only relevant to some individuals but, in spite of this, it is an identity that is mobilised to demonstrate widespread support for the fair-trade movement.

References

Bowes, J. (2011) 'A brilliant idea', in Bowes, J. (ed.) *The Fair Trade Revolution*, pp. 1–18, London, Pluto Press.

Clarke, J., Newman, J., Smith, N., Vidler, E. and Westmarland, L. (2007) *Creating Citizen-Consumers*, London, Sage.

Clarke, N., Barnett, C., Cloke, P. and Malpass, A. (2007) 'Globalising the consumer', *Political Geography*, vol. 26, pp. 231–249.

Cohen, L. (2003) *A Consumers' Republic*, New York, Alfred A. Knopf.

Fairtrade, Employment and Poverty Reduction Research (FTEPR) (2014) *Fairtrade, Employment and Poverty Reduction in Ethiopia and Uganda* [Online]. Available at http://ftepr.org/publications/ (Accessed 31 October 2014).

Fairtrade Foundation (2008) 'Response to Adam Smith Institute Report' [Online]. Available at www.Fairtrade.org.uk/press_office/ press_releases_and_statements/feb_2008/ response_to_adam_smith_insititute_report.aspx (Accessed 25 June 2009).

Fairtrade Foundation (2009) 'Cadbury Dairy Milk commits to going Fairtrade' [Online]. Available at www.Fairtrade.org.uk/press_office/ press_releases_and_statements/march_2009/ cadbury_dairy_milk_commits_to_going_Fairtrade.aspx (Accessed 7 December 2011).

Fairtrade Foundation (2014) 'Unlocking the power together: Annual Impact Report 2013–2014' [Online]. Available at www.fairtrade.org.uk/FTDoc/ Fairtrade-Annual-Impact-Report-2013-14.pdf (Accessed 25 March 2015).

Fairtrade Labelling Organisation (FLO) (2014a) 'Our standards' [Online]. Available at www.Fairtrade.net/our-standards.html(Accessed 31 October 2014).

Fairtrade Labelling Organisation (FLO) (2014b) 'Frequently asked questions' [Online]. Available at www.Fairtrade.net/faqs.html (Accessed 31 October 2014).

Fairtrade Labelling Organisation (FLO) (2014c) 'What is Fairtrade?' [Online]. Available at www.Fairtrade.net/what-is-Fairtrade.html(Accessed 31 October 2014).

Fairtrade Labelling Organisation (FLO) (2014d) 'Coffee' [Online]. Available at www.fairtrade.net/coffee.html(Accessed 30 November 2014).

Fridell, G. (2014) 'Fair trade slippages and Vietnam gaps: the ideological fantasies of fair trade coffee', *Third World Quarterly*, vol. 35, no. 7, pp. 1179–94.

Hayek, F. (1986) 'The moral imperative of the market', in *The Unfinished Agenda: Essays on the Political Economy of Government Policy in Honour of Arthur Seldon,* London, The Institute of Economic Affairs.

Jaffee, D. (2007) *Brewing Justice*, Berkeley, University of California Press.

Lamb, H. (2008) *Fighting the Banana Wars and Other Fairtrade Battles*, London, Rider.

Lowes, D. (2006) 'Justice', in *The Anti-capitalist Dictionary* [Online], London, Zed Books, available at http://libezproxy.open.ac.uk/login?qurl=http%3A%2F%2Fsearch.credoreference.com.libezproxy.open.ac.uk%2Fcontent%2Fentry%2Fzedacd%2Fjustice%2F0 (Accessed 8 May 2015).

Malpass, A., Barnett, C., Clarke, N. and Cloke, P. (2007) 'Problematizing choice', in Bevir, M. and Trentmann, F. (eds) *Governance, Consumers and Citizens*, pp. 231–56. Basingstoke, Palgrave Macmillan.

Micheletti, M. (2003) *Political Virtue and Shopping*, New York and Basingstoke, Palgrave Macmillan.

Nelson, V. and Pound, B. (2009) *The Last Ten Years: A Comprehensive Review of the Literature on the Impact of Fairtrade*, Natural Resources Institute, University of Greenwich.

O'Leary, Z. (2007) 'Justice', in *The Social Science Jargon-Buster* [Online], London: Sage UK, Available at http://libezproxy.open.ac.uk/login?qurl=http%3A%2F%2Fsearch.credoreference.com.libezproxy.open.ac.uk%2Fcontent%2Fentry%2Fsageukssjb%2Fjustice%2F0 (Accessed 8 May 2015).

Sainsbury's (2009) 'Corporate responsibility: sourcing with integrity' [Online]. Available at www.j-sainsbury.co.uk/cr/index.asp?pageid=36(Accessed 19 November 2009).

Sassatelli, R. (2006) 'Virtue, responsibility and consumer choice', in Brewer, J. and Trentmann, F. (eds) *Consuming Cultures, Global Perspectives*, pp 219–50. Oxford, Berg.

Shipman, A. (2015) 'Putting a price on common resources', in Drake, D., Morris, A., Shipman, A. and Wheeler, K. (eds) *Investigating the Social World 2*, Milton Keynes, The Open University.

Sidwell, M. (2008) *Unfair Trade*, London, The Adam Smith Institute.

Trentmann, F. (2007) 'Before "fair trade": empire, free trade, and the moral economies of food in the modern world', in *Environment and Planning*, vol. 25, pp. 1079–1102.

United Nations (2013) *The Millennium Development Goals Report*, UN: New York [Online]. Available at www.undp.org/content/dam/undp/library/MDG/english/mdg-report-2013-english.pdf (Accessed 30 June 2014).

Wheeler, K. (2008) Unpublished interviews with focus group

Wheeler, K. (2012) *Fair-trade and the Citizen-Consumer: Shopping for Justice?* Basingstoke, Palgrave MacMillan.

World Fair Trade Organisation (WFTO) (2009) 'A charter of fair trade principle' [Online]. Available at www.wfto.com/index.php?

option=com_content&task=view&id=1082&Itemid=334 (Accessed 31 October 2014).

WTO (2014) 'Tariff and trade indicators' [Online]. Available at www.wto.org/english/res_e/statis_e/statis_maps_e.htm (Accessed 30 November 2014).

Acknowledgements

Every effort has been made to contact copyright holders. If any have been inadvertently overlooked the publishers will be pleased to make the necessary arrangements at the first opportunity.

Grateful acknowledgement is made to the following sources:

Chapter 1: *Figure 1.1 left*: © Toter Alter Mann. This file is licensed under the Creative Commons Attribution-ShareAlike Licence http://creativecommons.org/licenses/by-sa/2.0/; *Figure 1.1 right*: © iStockphoto.com/tacojim; *Figure 1.2*: © Paul Kennedy/Alamy; *Figure 1.3*: © Forestry Commission, www.forestry.gov.uk; *Figure 1.4*: © The Boy That Time Forgot. This file is licensed under the Creative Commons Attribution-ShareAlike Licence http://creativecommons.org/licenses/by-sa/3.0/; *Figure 1.5*: © Allan Cash Picture Library/ Alamy; *Figure 1.6*: Adapted from ChartsBin statistics collector team 2009, Historical Population of United Kingdom, 43 AD to present, ChartsBin.com, viewed 3 March 2015, http://chartsbin.com/view/28k. This file is licensed under the Creative Commons Attribution-Noncommercial-ShareAlike Licence http://creativecommons.org/licenses/by-nc-sa/3.0/; *Figure 1.7*: © Jesus College, Cambridge; *Figure 1.9 left*: © Niday Picture Library/Alamy; *Figure 1.9 right*: © Mary Evans Picture Library/Alamy; *Figure 1.10 left*: © GL Archive/ Alamy; *Figure 1.10 right*: © David Gordon/Alamy.

Chapter 2: *Figure 2.1*: © Bettmann/CORBIS; *Figure 2.2*: © King's College London, Foyle Special Collections Library, www.kingscollections.org/exhibitions/specialcollections/to-scrutinize-nature/silviculture/john-evelyns-sylva; *Figure 2.3*: © William Morris Archive; *Figure 2.4*: © WildernessCommittee.org; *Figure 2.5*: © Alexander Pope. This file is licensed under the Creative Commons Attribution-Noncommercial-NoDerivatives Licence http://creativecommons.org/licenses/by-nc-nd/2.0/; *Figure 2.6*: © Fourpeaks; *Figure 2.7*: © Wendy, wenzday01. This file is licensed under the Creative Commons Attribution-Noncommercial-NoDerivatives Licence http://creativecommons.org/licenses/by-nc-nd/2.0/; *Figure 2.8*: © PA/Press Association Images; *Figure 2.9*: © Copyright Guardian News & Media Ltd 1952; *Figure 2.10*: Met Office, © Crown Copyright. Contains public sector information licensed under the Open Government Licence v1.0; *Figure 2.11*: © NASA Ozone Watch; *Figure 2.12*: © Intergovernmental Panel on Climate Change (IPCC); *Figure 2.13*: ©

Intergovernmental Panel on Climate Change (IPCC); *Figure 2.14*: © Dr Mark Brandon; *Figure 2.15*: © BURRELL DURRANT HIFLE; *Figure 2.16*: © AP/Press Association Images.

Chapter 3: *Figure 3.1*: © Pablo Blazquez Dominguea/Stringer/Getty Images; *Figure 3.2*: © iStockphoto.com/Wirepec; *Figure 3.3*: Adapted © BGR Hannover; *Figure 3.4*: © US Federal Government image; *Figure 3.5*: Original source unknown; *Figure 3.6*: GlobalSecurity.org, US Government public domain; *Figure 3.8*: Graphic Author: Sam Pepple, Sample Cartography. Foreign Affairs, Council on Foreign Relations, 2012.

Chapter 4: *Figure 4.1*: © Photography by Steve Allen/Alamy; *Figure 4.2*: © John Sturrock/Alamy; *Figure 4.3*: © iStockphoto.com/ Kevin Miller; *Figure 4.4*: Courtesy of the Ronald Coase Institute. Photographer: David Joel; *Figure 4.5*: © Oliver Gill; *Figure 4.6*: © Scanpix/Press Association Images.

Chapter 5: *Figure 5.2*: Courtesy of Ashoka Trust for Research in Ecology and the Environment; *Figure 5.4*: © Photo by Robert Alexander/Getty Images; *Figure 5.5*: © Natural Justice.

Chapter 6: *Figure 6.1*: © David R. Frazier Photolibrary, Inc./Alamy; *Figure 6.2*: © Jim West/Alamy; *Figure 6.3*: © riddypix/Alamy; *Figure 6.4*: © Jenova20. This file is licensed under the Creative Commons Attribution-ShareAlike Licence http://creativecommons. org/licenses/by-sa/3.0/; *Figure 6.5*: © Matt Green. This file is licensed under the Creative Commons Attribution-Noncommercial-ShareAlike Licence http://creativecommons.org/licenses/by-nc-sa/2.0/; *Figure 6.6*: Adapted from North West London Eruv Organisation; *Figure 6.7*: Used by kind permission of Nancy Fraser.

Chapter 7: *Figure 7.1*: © Tullio M. Puglia/Stringer/Getty Images; *Figure 7.4*: © The Photolibrary Wales/Alamy; *Figure 7.5*: © Matthew Clarke/Alamy; *Figure 7.6*: © Chris Radburn/PA Archive/Press Association Images.

Chapter 8: *Figure 8.1*: Adapted from BBC using information source via ONS; *Figure 8.2*: Adapted from The Migration Observatory, Source: ONS, Long-Term International Migration (LTIM), Home Office; *Figure 8.3*: Adapted from The Migration Observatory. Source: Home Office, 2011; *Figure 8.4*: © Faculty of Public Health.

Chapter 9: *Figure 9.1*: Southworth, M., 'The sonic environment of cities', *Environment and Behavior*, vol. 1, no. 1, pp. 49–70, Copyright ©

1969 SAGE. Reproduced by permission of SAGE Publications; *Figure 9.2*: © David White/Alamy; *Figure 9.3*: Adapted from Campaign to Protect Rural England; *Figure 9.4*: Adapted from Campaign to Protect Rural England; *Figure 9.5*: Reproduced by kind permission of Keep Britain Tidy, www.keepbritaintidy.org.

Chapter 10: *Figure 10.2*: Adapted from World Trade Organization map; *Figure 10.3*: © Mark Boulton/Alamy; *Figure 10.4*: © iStockphoto. com/Guenter Guni; *Figure 10.5*: © Alex Hallatt/www.CartoonStock. com; *Figure 10.6*: © iStockphoto.com/ProjectB.

DD103 Module team

Academic team

Fiona Barnes, Associate Lecturer

Shonil Bhagwat, Lecturer in Geography

Jonathan Blundell, Associate Lecturer

Melissa Butcher, Senior Lecturer in Geography

Victoria Canning, Lecturer in Criminology

Daniel Conway, Lecturer in Politics and International Studies

Sue Cowley, Associate Lecturer

Deborah Drake, Senior Lecturer in Criminology (Deputy Module Team Chair)

Umut Erel, Lecturer in Sociology

Jessica Evans, Senior Lecturer in Cultural and Media Studies

Steve Garner, Senior Lecturer in Social Policy

Kim Hammond, Research Associate

Martin Holborn, Associate Lecturer

Janet Hunter, Associate Lecturer

Vicky Johnson, Associate Lecturer

Nikoleta Jones, Lecturer in Human Geography

Giles Mohan, Professor of International Development

Andy Morris, Staff Tutor (Deputy Module Team Chair)

Karim Murji, Senior Lecturer in Sociology (Module Team Chair)

Mel Nettle, Associate Lecturer

Stuart Parris, Senior Lecturer in Economics

Rob Parsons, Associate Lecturer

Rajiv Prabakhar, Lecturer in Personal Finance

George Revill, Senior Lecturer in Geography

Alan Shipman, Lecturer in Economics

Elizabeth Silva, Professor of Sociology

Roberto Simonetti, Head of Economics Department

Bradon Smith, Research Associate

Joe Smith, Senior Lecturer in Environment

Matt Staples, Staff Tutor

Andrew Trigg, Senior Lecturer in Economics

Dave Turner, Associate Lecturer

Edward Wastnidge, Lecturer in Politics and International Studies

Sophie Watson, Professor of Sociology

Katy Wheeler, Lecturer in Sociology

Teresa Willis, Associate Lecturer

External assessor

Professor Fran Tonkiss, London School of Economicsr

Production team

David Adamson, Curriculum Assistant

Roshni Amin, Sound and Vision Producer

Melanie Bayley, Media Project Manager

Wendy Chalmers, Learning and Teaching Librarian

Sian Contell, Sound and Vision Assistant

Nicholas Dragffy, Production Editor

Jane Fransella, Commissioner

Ryan Hayle, Interactive Media Developer

Paul Hillery, Graphics Media Developer

Matthew Holley, Sound and Vision Media Developer

Diane Hopwood, Licensing and Acquisitions Assistant

Gareth Hudson, Senior Project Manager

Jason Jarratt, Interactive Media Developer

Alex Keable-Crouch, Online Services Media Developer

Joanna Mack, Senior Sound and Vision Producer

Adam Nightingale, Digital Development Editor

Neil Paterson, Media Assistant

Eileen Potterton, Curriculum Manager

Lauren Robinson, Licensing and Acquisitions Assistant

Lindsey Smith, Digital Development Editor

Eddie Tunnah, Senior Careers and Employability Adviser

Howie Twiner, Graphics Media Developer

Laura Underwood, Digital Development Editor

Amanda Vaughan, Curriculum Assistant

Liz Vidler, Curriculum Manager

The module team would also like to thank the following freelance staff: Mandy Anton (cover design), Clare Butler (proofreader), Isobel McLean (indexer) and Nina Randall (book editor).

Video production

Jane Diblin, Series Producer, Angel Eye Media

Rosa Rodger and Morgan Phillips, Camera/ Director, Angel Eye Media

Sam Piranty, Researcher, Angel Eye Media

Index